Praise for *The Mask of Motherhood*

"A gust of fresh air and an antidote to romantic notions of motherhood. Susan Maushart writes with terrific verve and style."
—Sheila Kitzinger

"A lively, illuminating, and eminently intelligent look at mothering today."
—Harriet Lerner, Ph.D., author of *The Mother Dance: How Children Change Your Life*

"A wonderful contribution to the growing body of literature that forever breaks down the walls of the Mommy and Mommy Track ghettos. Maushart incisively captures motherhood in the millennium."
—Elizabeth Perle McKenna, author of *When Work Doesn't Work Anymore: Women, Work and Indentity*

D1010146

ABOUT THE AUTHOR

Susan Maushart, the mother of three young children, was born and raised on Long Island, New York, and holds a Ph.D. from New York University. She migrated to Australia in 1986 and is now a Senior Research Associate in the School of Social Sciences at Curtin University. She is also a featured columnist in the weekend magazine of the national newspaper, *The Australian*, and for Australian *Parents* magazine. Maushart is also the author of *Sort of a Place Like Home*, which won the Festival Prize for Literature at the Adelaide Writers' Festival.

THE MASK OF MOTHERHOOD

How Becoming a Mother Changes Everything
and Why We Pretend It Doesn't

SUSAN MAUSHART

PENGUIN BOOKS

PENGUIN BOOKS
Published by the Penguin Group
Penguin Putnam Inc., 375 Hudson Street,
New York, New York 10014, U.S.A.
Penguin Books Ltd, 27 Wrights Lane, London W8 5TZ, England
Penguin Books Australia Ltd, Ringwood, Victoria, Australia
Penguin Books Canada Ltd, 10 Alcorn Avenue,
Toronto, Ontario, Canada M4V 3B2
Penguin Books (N.Z.) Ltd, 182–190 Wairau Road,
Auckland 10, New Zealand

Penguin Books Ltd, Registered Offices:
Harmondsworth, Middlesex, England

First published in the United States of America by The New Press, 1999
Published in Penguin Books 2000

9   10   8

Copyright © Susan Maushart, 1999
All rights reserved

(CIP data available)

ISBN 0 14 02.9178 4

Printed in the United States of America
Set in Walbaum MT

Except in the United States of America, this book is sold subject to
the condition that it shall not, by way of trade or otherwise, be lent, re-sold,
hired out, or otherwise circulated without the publisher's prior consent in
any form of binding or cover other than that in which it is published and
without a similar condition including this condition being
imposed on the subsequent purchaser.

For my mother,
Patricia Sappé Maushart

For my children,
Anna, William, and Susannah

Contents

Acknowledgments

Grateful acknowledgment is made to Family and Children's Services, Western Australia, administrators of the Year of the Family (WA) Family Research Project, for funding the study "Mother Knows Best? Four Australian women learn to mother."

Introduction

I N   T H E   D E B A T E S about education, employment, and equity that have dominated the feminist agenda ever since Betty Friedan, motherhood is the one issue that seems to have been left behind. "Omigod!" shrieks the woman in the feminist cartoon. "I left the baby on the bus!" Indeed, and so have we all.

In the introduction to *The Feminine Mystique*, Friedan writes that she was motivated to begin her research when she realized that "there was a strange discrepancy between the reality of our lives as women and the image to which we were trying to conform . . ."[1] In some senses, the problem remains precisely the same today. The content of women's daily realities has changed enormously, as has the nature of the images to which we seek to conform. But the identity crisis—the mismatch between expectation and experience, between what we ought to be feeling and how we do feel, between how we ought to be managing and how we do manage—remains as painful and as intractable as ever.

The housewife of the 1950s and 1960s was told she had it all, and was left to wonder guiltily, "Is that all there is?" Today's woman is also told she has it all—and there are times when she would give almost anything for a refund. Whereas our mothers' generation suffered a sense of emptiness, we are more likely to be feeling distinctly overfull. And the impoverished expectations and life choices of women a generation ago have given way to an embarrassment of riches.

Professionally, financially, socially, and spiritually we are primed for achievement. The more we can do, the more we should do. But the more we do, the worse we feel. And the sillier we look. It is surely worthy of note that the word contemporary women use more than any other to describe the management of their lives is the verb "to juggle." The women Friedan described felt as if their lives had been tranquilized (and in many cases they quite literally were). For women in the 1990s, by contrast, life is hyper-caffeinated; it's going so fast we can't assimilate it, let alone enjoy it. Yet when things slow down, we go into withdrawal, panicking that we must be somehow missing out. We are indeed the generation of "women who do too much."

Motherhood is, of course, one of the balls we are trying to keep in the air. Yet mothering is not simply one of the things we do and suspect we are doing badly. The role of mother is different, in degree and in kind, from any other role a woman fulfills. Although it is considered politically incorrect to speak in such terms, bearing and caring for children has an indisputably biological base. The vexed question of "instincts" aside, mothering is *ipso facto* something to which women are compelled to bring their entire beings: their bodies as well as their hearts and minds.

Women can choose not to mother of course. And some women despair because they cannot choose—because they are infertile or because they lack a partner or at least a willing accomplice. But for women who do become mothers—and in our society as in every other in the world, that means most women—the responsibility and the commitment on every level are enormous and unprecedented. They are the non-negotiable terms of a biosocial contract into which one does not so much enter as tumble headlong. There is no opportunity to study the fine print. And it is binding for life.

Yet hasn't it ever been thus? I suspect that men and women have always experienced parenthood as rather more than they bargained for—even in the most traditional small-scale society, where childbearing and child rearing are as much a part of the community's everyday experience as eating and sleeping, growing up and growing old. Conveying the realities of parenthood to non-parents is a bit like telling a complicated anecdote that never quite gets off the ground: the kind for which you end up apologizing, "I guess you just had to be there."

No matter what the cultural setting, a woman's preparation for parenthood will inevitably prove partial and imperfect. Yet in our own society, the evidence suggests, we increasingly bring to the experience expectations that are not simply inaccurate, or ill-informed, but downright disabling. Maybe even delusional. American women today— for all our educational attainments, professional savvy, and unprecedented economic power—remain as disadvantaged for success in motherhood as our third world sisters are for success on Wall Street.

The messages we receive about mothering promise an Easymix lifestyle: having kids will prove not only fun and good for us, but will blend effortlessly with the other ingredients that go to make up "the good life" (work, leisure, relationships, sex, to name just a few). The reality hits when the ideal baby in our minds is abruptly displaced by the real baby in our lives. It is then we realize there are no "easy steps" to follow. Sooner or later we realize we're going to have to make the whole thing up from scratch.

Is it any wonder that the transition to motherhood among American women is increasingly associated with the onset of a full-scale identity crisis? As Friedan noted, the degree of correspondence between expectation and experience, between image and actuality, is a kind of algorithm of adjustment. In other words, the smaller the gap between what we foresee and what we get, the better we will cope. For women approaching motherhood right now, that gap yawns wider than perhaps ever before in human history.

It has been observed that a little bit of knowledge is a dangerous thing—that "where ignorance is bliss, 'tis folly to be wise." Yet it strikes me these principles are accepted as axiomatic only among the "information rich," a fact that makes me instantly suspicious. I find it hard to accept that because we cannot know everything about X or Y, we would be better off knowing nothing about X or Y. Sure, our little bit of knowledge may prove dangerous—but to whom or to what? More often than not, I would argue, the only real threat is to the imbalance of power itself, to the monopoly created by the unequal distribution of knowledge in the first place, and upheld by those with a stake in keeping it that way. In the case of knowledge about motherhood, one of the most important (and jealous) keepers of the flame has been the medical professional itself—especially with respect to childbirth.

Yet here is one case where women have succeeded in breaking down the knowledge monopoly. And where our transition to "information haves" from "information have-nots" has had a clear and dramatic impact on the quality of our experiences. Overwhelmingly (although not, admittedly, exclusively) that impact has been positive.

The physiological realities of moving a baby from womb to world have not changed one iota since the introduction some thirty years ago of intensive childbirth education for pregnant women. But women's knowledge and expectations

about that process have altered dramatically in that time—
to the point, indeed, where childbirth is regarded as an opportunity for personal development rather than a trial by
ordeal. As a result, women's experiences of childbirth have
undergone profound changes as well.

A friend in her late fifties, now a grandmother, told me
recently of her terror when she entered a delivery room for
the first time, thirty-five years ago, in virtually total ignorance of the physiology of childbirth, let alone any of the
subtler psychological nuances. "But had you never asked
your mother what it was like, what to expect?" I asked.
"Yes," she replied. "She told me to ask my doctor. And when
I did, he answered, " 'You'll soon find out, dear.' "

Such callous, or embarrassed, dismissal seems almost medieval to today's superbly schooled primigravidas (women
expecting their first child). Most can bandy terms like
"Braxton Hicks contractions," "cervical dilation," and "pos-
terior presentation" and actually know what they are talking about. They can make informed decisions about
epidural anesthesia, episiotomies, and vacuum extraction.
Heaven knows, they've mastered a bewildering repertoire of
breathing techniques. They can even clench their pelvic
floors. If only motherhood ended with the cutting of the umbilical chord, we'd be cruising.

The problem, of course, is that this is where it all
begins—precisely at the point where, for most of us, our
formal knowledge and our informal experience end. When
it comes to the business of parenting, our society is still giving the same collective answer as my friend's arrogant doctor gave: "You'll soon find out, dear." Indeed, in the most
important respects, the present generation is faring even
worse.

Our mothers' generation began the journey to parenthood with a grasp of the rudiments of childcare. They knew how to fold a diaper, how to rock a crying baby. They knew what thrush looked like. They had observed breast feeding in action, even if they were a little fuzzy on the psychobiology of lactation. They didn't have Penelope Leach or Sheila Kitzinger, let alone private obstetricians. But what they did have was a working understanding of the challenges ahead.

Perhaps equally important, they were thoroughly at home with being at home. In an age where most girls passed from their father's house straight into their husband's, the demands of domesticity were no less arduous than they are today (indeed they were a great deal more arduous, in terms of sheer physical exertion). At the same time, a social structure that valued and supported the role of "housewife" gave meaning to the drudgery. For good or for ill, the value of "women's work" was beyond question, and it was a source of deep pride and satisfaction for many, many women.

By our own standards, the horizons of our mothers and grandmothers were claustrophobically contained. But they were also clearly visible, and the small space in which they were allowed to move was at least coherently defined. The "career path" they trod was narrow indeed, but the progression was steady and often satisfying. It was mothering that set the pace for this journey, and the growth and development of children that marked the way.

For new mothers of the present generation—the beneficiaries of three decades of feminist-led social change—an explosion of gender-appropriate career and lifestyle options has all but obliterated the ideal of home-based "women's work." But with the multiplication of choice for women has come, no doubt inevitably, the fracturing of coherence. We have lost the dreadful claustrophobia of living life in a box. But in the process we have also lost a sense of place. We are a generation in transit: we know exactly where we've been (and good riddance!), but we're not at all certain where we ought to be going. It's no wonder that, like Stephen Leacock's famous rider, we jump on the horse and ride off furiously in all directions. And motherhood is, of course, one of them.

The desire to bear and raise children is as strong among today's young women as in any previous generation. The vast majority envisage a life in which motherhood is (to use the preferred figure of speech) "combined" with a career. The role of mothering is seen as an option among many others, another potential string to one's bow, another avenue of achievement, another opportunity for personal growth and development. On the face of it, such expectations seem reasonable, even laudable.

So why do women start off with the expectation of "combining" motherhood with (for want of a better term) the rest of life, and end up with the reality of "juggling"? The disjuncture between these two revealing little verbs—the one suggesting blend and balance, the other precariousness and trickery—typifies the gap between expectation and reality.

It is my belief that our thinking about motherhood as a role and as an institution has become hopelessly muddled over the course of the last two or three generations. In certain key respects, we remain mired in the models and metaphors of previous generations despite their painful lack of fit with present realities. Hence, for example, our continuing ambivalence on the subject of day care ("every child deserves a full-time mother at home"); the guilt we suffer over convenience foods ("a good mother cooks meals from scratch"), disposable diapers ("a row of clean laundry on the line shows you care") and even the size and composition of our families ("children need brothers and sisters"; "A child needs a father at home").

It's not that we refuse to use day care and disposables, or that we resolutely ban Happy Meals or "only children" or—heaven knows—the possibility of separation and divorce. It's just that we feel guilty about these things. We feel, in our heart of hearts, that the life we're offering our kids is really not quite good enough. It's not what we remember of childhood. And that feels sad and wrong. As one working mom poignantly put it, "I consider myself a good mother. But my kids aren't having a good childhood."[2]

Apart from how we "do" motherhood, there are the multitudinous and equally ambivalent ways in which we "feel" it. With our minds we know that we're not supposed to experience motherhood as the all-fulfilling apex of human achievement. But our hearts, our treacherous, truth-telling hearts, again whisper against us. For there are those (in plenty, the evidence suggests) for whom motherhood *is* experienced as all-fulfilling—those who, after the birth of a child, find their professional and social ambitions dwindling into disorienting indifference. They were led to anticipate motherhood as simply another of life's interesting options, and what they got instead was a full-scale transformation in values, identity, and lifestyle. Somewhere along the line, the smooth jet flight of adulthood got hijacked. When they become mothers, these women end up in a foreign country that nevertheless feels peculiarly like home. It's no wonder they're in culture shock.

On the other side, of course, are the growing numbers of young women who find the experience of motherhood—as much feminist rhetoric has led them to expect—a distinct anticlimax. They abhor the isolation and drudgery of the domestic sphere and—as much as they love their small children—find the incessant demands of parenting both physically and emotionally exhausting. Of course, they never expected that motherhood would confer instant fulfillment or answer all of life's questions. And yet somehow, somewhere, they are deeply disappointed. These women tend to return with relief to their careers and other adult pursuits. Yet they can't help feeling a nasty, residual guilt, coupled with a sneaking suspicion that they have been cheated of something terribly important.

Most women who become mothers experience something in between—or, to be more accurate, little sharp stabs of each extreme with a lot of gray space and tedium in the middle. Almost inevitably, the bearing and rearing of children precipitates an identity crisis for women. After the initial trauma of transition comes the painful process of re-evaluating life choices, of bringing to consciousness our most deeply embedded assumptions about the way things ought to be. In this sense there is no doubt that for today's young women motherhood presents unsurpassed opportunities for personal growth and development.

In traditional societies, the birth of a woman's first child marks her acceptance into full adulthood. It is the initiation rite par excellence: the portal through which, once having passed, one can never return. The momentousness of this transit sits uneasily with us, as does the closely related notion that, in some enduring sense, biology really *is* destiny. While the capacity for reproduction no longer absolutely determines our destiny as women, it persists in playing a much more profound role in shaping it than we have been prepared to admit. Yes, technology has made it possible for women to be sexually active and childless. Yet the reality is that 94 percent of married women will "choose" to mother anyway. From this point of view, motherhood seems about as much of a "lifestyle option" as walking upright.

Motherhood can be, and almost always is, performed alongside other forms of work. Indeed, the practice of something called "full-time motherhood"—in which a woman's sole responsibilities in communal life revolve exclusively around home and child—is an historical aberration of twentieth-century industrialized life. No other human society that we know has experienced the luxury (or the folly?) of this particular form of social organization. But although motherhood is almost always one form of work among many that women perform, it is not the equivalent of any one of them. Motherhood is not simply one job among many, whether one chooses to interpret that uniqueness positively or negatively.

My contention is that our deeply confused notions about motherhood are engendering a tidal wave of guilt, resentment, and anxiety among today's women. Yet it is not the confusion per se that worries me. Indeed, I am convinced that a period of healthy disorder is a necessary stage of development on the way to a new and more workable set of assumptions about what we're doing and why we're doing it. What really worries me is our reluctance to confront the chaos. Whether we hide behind traditional motherhood mythologies, seek refuge in the new and equally unworkable mythology of "having it all," or desperately cobble together a crazy quilt from bits and pieces of each, we are implicated in a dangerous process of denial.

As we shall see, there are many masks of motherhood. But this one—the mask of silence—is the most treacherous one of all. Deciding how and to what end we mother our young is the most serious of all women's business. It is no exaggeration to say that we owe it not only to our own mental health but to the very future of the species to take motherhood seriously, to strip off the masks we have been wearing, and to see with clear eyes and speak with open voices about the realities we experience.

In my research as a social scientist, and in my experience as the mother of three young children, I have been struck again and again by two observations: that women without children seem disturbingly unprepared for the challenges of motherhood, and that women with children seem disturbingly unprepared to discuss those challenges. (And I have no doubt that the two are closely related.) By writing this book, I hope to make some inroads in both directions.

For expectant mothers (whether that expectation is imminent or still distant), I hope to be able to offer a "backstage" look at the realities of contemporary mothering in the kind of uncompromising detail that is either overlooked, underplayed, or downright denied in the standard mothering discourse. I am interested both in documenting the silences with which this discourse is hedged about and in doing my part to disrupt them.

For women on the other side of the "great divide" of parenting, especially those involved in mothering young children as they read this book, I wish to offer the comfort that comes from learning that one is not alone; that the fears, frustrations, and confusions they are experiencing are not evidence of personal incompetence but the legacy of unworkable social structures and contradictory cultural demands.

Faking Motherhood
The Mask Revealed

---

*Oh Mother, was it tender to tell me nothing of what was to come
and what it meant: about marriage, motherhood, death? Tender
not to whisper to me even once about resistance or escape, about
honor and freedom?*

—Phyllis Chesler

ALL MASKS ARE PROPS for pretending. They
can be tragic or comic, serenely composed or agape
with horror. Yet every mask, regardless of the content of its expression, projects uniformity, predictability, stasis. Which is why, of all the many kinds of masks in the
world, there is no mask of ambivalence or of metamorphosis.
Masks portray emotion inert and unmixed in a trade off of
range for impact.

At the same time—and for the very same reasons—we
need our masks. Or at least we need some of them, some of
the time. For all human beings, but perhaps especially so for
those inhabiting complex urban environments, social masks
are an indispensable accessory in our emotional wardrobe.
Indeed, a person incapable of masking her "true" feelings is
often (and quite rightly) regarded as immature, sick, or
both. To a very considerable degree, what we call self-
control depends on our ability to "mask," to deny and re-

press what we experience, to misrepresent it, even to ourselves.

Although he is deeply misunderstood on this point, it was Freud who pointed out the multiple dividends such repression can pay. Our facility with masks, he argued, has made possible the very infrastructure of our collective lives, which he called "civilization." It is difficult to dispute the point. The capacity for emotional make-believe, for pretense, for the construction of situationally appropriate masks, is perhaps our most enduring evolutionary advantage. It is also our greatest curse. The critical distance, it seems to me, lies between self-control and self-delusion.

The mask of motherhood refers to a repertoire of socially constructed representations that have crossed that line. What I am calling the mask of motherhood is in fact an assemblage of fronts—mostly brave, serene, and all-knowing—that we use to disguise the chaos and complexity of our lived experience. Like all social masks, the mask of motherhood is an invaluable means for organizing and domesticating the more rapacious aspects of the realities we confront. Yet the personal and political price we pay for this control has far exceeded the value of its social dividends.

The mask of motherhood is what keeps women silent about what they feel and suspicious of what they know. It divides mother from daughter, sister from sister, friend from friend. It creates an abrupt and tragic chasm between adults who have children and adults who don't. It distorts the distance between childhood and adulthood, cutting ever deeper gaps between the generations. It pits male parents against female, amplifying the disjuncture between the verbs "to mother" and "to father." Above all, the mask of motherhood, by minimizing the enormity of women's work in the world, nourishes and sustains the profound ignorance that confuses humanity with mankind.

We see the mask of motherhood in

- the values of a culture that glorifies the ideal of motherhood but takes for granted the work of motherhood, and ignores the experience of motherhood
- media images of Supermom, complete with briefcase, "serious" hair, and a pair of designer-clad preschoolers scampering happily to help with the dishes
- the secret worry of the new mother that "I just wasn't cut out for this"—and the gnawing fear that it shows
- books that describe labor contractions as "forceful urges"
- the apologetic tones of the embarrassed mother who murmurs over the screams of her toddler's tantrum, "She's not normally like this . . ."
- breast-feeding propaganda that portrays bottle feeding as a form of child abuse
- women's magazines that promise "Great Sex after Baby!"
- child-care manuals that imply that "easy" babies are made, not born, and that an infant's digestive tract is somehow linked by fiber-optic cable to its mother's state of mind
- the grim one-upmanship of play-group moms comparing relative rates of vegetable consumption and verbal development
- the tolerance of women for the selective deafness of fathers at 3:00 A.M., especially in the belief that "a man needs his sleep" so he can "go to work in the morning"
- debates about child care that pass judgment on "what's best for the child" as if a child's needs were separable from those of its mother, father, and siblings
- the smugness of the mother at-home who looks with disdain on her sisters in the workforce
- the smugness of the mother in the workforce who looks with disdain on her sisters at-home.

I was recently asked to speak to a group of undergraduate sociology students about my research into the meaning of contemporary motherhood. I started by dividing the group into two teams: parents and non-parents. I asked them to sit on opposite sides of the lecture hall, leaving a gap of empty seats in the middle. "Do you believe there is a 'great divide' separating parents from non-parents in our society?" I asked. "That people who have children are fundamentally different from people who don't have children?"

I asked the non-parents to comment first. "Of course not," explained one young woman. "Having a child doesn't change who you are as a person." Her fellow teammates nodded in agreement, despite the stifled groans and giggles from the other side of the room. I called for a vote and found the vast majority of non-parents rejected the notion of a great divide.

I addressed the same question to the parent group. Or I should say, I tried to. Before the words were out of my mouth, people were fairly shouting their responses: "Absolutely!" "You better believe it!" "YES!" Most of the people on this team happened to be women, and they proved by far the most vocal contingent. "Let me tell you something," one fortyish woman began, "Not only is there a great divide between those who have kids and those who don't, but there's a conspiracy about keeping the whole thing a secret." Another added, "Yeah, and by the time you figure it out, it's too late!" With this, the parenting team exploded in laughter.

The non-parents were slightly nonplussed. And who could blame them? What the parent group had to say sounded positively sinister, yet there they were, cackling away gleefully and starting to trade wisecracks. Within a few more moments, they were beginning to sound like a group of old army buddies reminiscing about life in the trenches. I didn't even bother taking a vote. The consensus was clear, and it was total.

To me, this scene was forceful illustration of two truths

about contemporary parenting. The first is that yes, Virginia, there does seem to be a great divide between parents and nonparents in our society: becoming a parent does change you in significant and irreversible ways into a different person. And the second is that admitting as much publicly means breaking one of our society's most enduring taboos. To tell the truth (or some of the truths) about motherhood to non-mothers, we seem to feel, would be a bit like debunking Santa Claus on the front page of the *New York Times*. There's no disputing the facts, but you'd have to be a pretty bad sport to go around advertising them, wouldn't you? What's more, the odds are good that the naive audience for whom such revelations would be "news" might never believe them anyway.

For the uninitiated, the realities of parenthood and especially motherhood are kept carefully shrouded in silence, disinformation, and outright lies. The conspiracy of silence is real, and it's documentable. That much is clear. What is much less clear is what purpose the conspiracy serves, and why the vast majority of women participate in it.

What I am calling the mask of motherhood is the outward and visible sign of this silent conspiracy—the public face of motherhood that conceals from the world and from ourselves the momentousness of our common undertaking. The mask of motherhood is what mutes our rage into murmurs and softens our sorrow into resignation. The mask of motherhood is the semblance of serenity and control that enables women's work to pass unnoticed in the larger drama of human life. Above all, the mask keeps us quiet about what we know, to the point that we forget that we know anything at all . . . or anything worth the telling.

At the same time, the mask of motherhood is a useful coping mechanism. Yet the danger—and it is one to which women are particularly prone—is that the make-believe can become so convincing that we fool even ourselves. When the coping mechanism becomes a way of life, we divest ourselves of authenticity and integrity. We diminish our knowledge, our power, our spirit as women. Ultimately, we no longer *make* a life—we *fake* a life.

Psychologist Harriet Goldhor Lerner believes that "pretending is so closely associated with femininity that it is, quite simply, what the culture teaches women to do."[2] Yet women themselves are clearly co-conspirators in perpetuating the grand illusions of femininity, and the mask of motherhood is no exception. The mask is a disguise of our own choosing, a form of personal armor that, as Lerner points out, ensures the viability of the self as well as our relationships. Pretending, in other words, is a form of self-protection. From this point of view, the mask of motherhood is like a camouflage, rendering our experience safely indistinguishable in a hostile environment. As Lerner writes, "Pretending reflects deep prohibitions, real and imagined, against a more direct and forthright assertion of self."[3]

For the present generation of women, the mask of motherhood is among the most deeply repressed and destructive of all female deceptions. Today, women confess guiltily—or gleefully—to faking orgasms. Yet how many of us will admit, or are even aware, that we are faking motherhood? As Lerner points out, when we fake orgasm, we deceive another. But when we fake motherhood, we betray our deepest selves.

The mask of motherhood not only mutes our voices. It also muffles our ears. Journalist Nina Barrett relates the experience of a young mother whose marriage is coming adrift in the wild wake of early parenthood. "In some of the mother's groups I've joined, I've brought this up in a roundabout sort of way," she confesses. "But people don't seem to want to talk about it. I've heard other women make references to similar problems. It seems like they're almost bursting to talk about it, but they're embarrassed. Like it's somehow their fault. Or maybe they shouldn't be feeling these things . . ."[4]

The mask of motherhood keeps women from speaking clearly what they know, and from hearing truths too threatening to face. That for every woman who "blooms" in pregnancy there's another who develops root rot. That childbirth—however transcendent or relevatory it may or may not be—still hurts like hell. That the persistent cry of a newborn can make your husband's snoring sound like a sonata. That your child's physical demands will diminish at only a fraction of the rate at which her emotional ones will multiply and intensify. That getting the knack of combining motherhood with career is like getting the knack of brain surgery: nice work if you can get it, but 99.99 percent of us never will. That having a "joint project" called a baby drives most couples farther apart, reducing intimacy as it reinforces gender-role stereotypes.

It's not as if we enjoy the dishonesty. It's more that we seem to need it. It is scary enough to face the fact that you yourself are faking it. But the possibility that everyone else may be faking it too is downright terrifying.

The gap between image and reality, between what we show and what we feel, has resulted in a peculiar cultural schizophrenia about motherhood. Canadian sociologist Amy Rossiter argues that our public discourse on the subject of motherhood tells us simultaneously "everything" and "nothing" that we need to know.[5] On the one hand, today's mothers are virtually flooded with "information." On subjects ranging from pregnancy and childbirth to toilet training and preparation for preschool—in virtually every mass medium from books, magazines, and pamphlets to hotlines, videos and web sites—we have an unprecedented number of facts at our fingertips. Yet getting a grip on them seems to get harder and harder. It was Cervantes who remarked that "facts are the enemy of truth." For all the information we have amassed on "how to do it," we remain more clueless and insecure about what we are doing and why we are doing it than perhaps any previous generation.

Anthropologist Sheila Kitzinger has pointed out that the media bombard mothers with advice on health care, self-care, and the maintenance of relationships: how to look good, feel good, and be assertive; how to "keep the romance in her relationship with her man, cook gourmet food and produce candlelit dinners, and at the same time be a perfect mother."[6] Women's magazines, child-care manuals, and parenting classes dispense "tips" on every aspect of mothering from toilet training to postnatal depression. "But the image of motherhood that is presented is a false one," Kitzinger concludes. "A woman who catches sight of herself in the mirror"—as it were, unmasked—"sees a very different picture. And the message is clear: she is a failure."[7]

Quite simply, what we see of motherhood is not what we get. As a result, the conviction that we are not measuring up becomes almost inevitable. Women's magazines, with their relentless emphasis on "personal development," "success," and "achievement," depict a version of motherhood as glossy as any pin-up—and about as representative.

A generation ago, Betty Friedan described what happened when one such magazine invited readers to respond to the topic "Why Young Mothers at Home Feel Trapped." When the editors had finished digging their way out from under the twenty thousand responses, they wondered if they

8

might have touched a nerve.[8] Twenty-five years later, there is a new generation of young mothers, and many of them are not "at home" at all, at least not exclusively. Yet for many women the perception of entrapment remains, along with the sense that life is somehow living them instead of vice versa. The fit between our images of motherhood and the realities we confront is more uncomfortable than ever.

Basically, we have swapped our old set of stereotypes for a new and improved set. In traversing the distance between June Cleaver and Murphy Brown, we've come a long way, baby, without making any appreciable progress at all. Today's media no longer glorify the housewife. Instead, the spotlight has shifted to the celebrity Supermom, She-who-has-it-all. The headlines tell us "Celebrities' Lives Change Completely After They Give Birth." Kathleen Turner volunteers for library duty at her child's school. Meg Ryan takes her kids along on shoots. Julie Walters's newly delivered daughter smelled so "divine" that she "wanted to lick her all over."[9] With such tales of metamorphosis to sustain us, it's no wonder we're starving to death. Such images are the maternal equivalents of Playboy bunnies, nicely proportioned lives with soft curves in all the right places. Trouble is, they bear about as much relation to reality as a backlit, airbrushed cleavage does to a set of lactating glands with cracked nipples.

Meanwhile, as Susan Sarandon breast-feeds her daughter during an important interview, researchers in the United Kingdom are working on a slightly different angle. They find that fully half of all mothers with kids under five years old experience symptoms of intense emotional distress on a regular or continual basis; that women are five times more likely to be diagnosed as mentally ill in the year after their first child's birth than at any other time in their lives.[10] As one mom who has never starred in anything told researcher and parenthood educator Margaret Gibson, "Every mother does not cope. It is a myth that she does. It is a big lie. Not every mother copes, but few are brave enough to admit it."[11]

Research suggests that in our society motherhood can be and often is dangerous to our mental health. If fully half the population of young mothers is having trouble "coping," but almost no one will say so publicly, whose lie is it anyway?

"The most common question I am asked by women with young children is, 'why didn't someone tell me that it was going to be like this?' " writes the editor of one recent study of contemporary mothering.[12] In another study[13], new mothers were asked "Is looking after the baby anything like you thought it would be?" Only 9 percent said "yes." One among the remaining 91 percent commented, "It's really like living in a different world." Amy Rossiter, who conducted an intensive study into the transition to motherhood, found the major categories to emerge from her interview data were "Shock," "Being unprepared," "Panic," "Anxiety," "Not knowing," and "Feeling out of control."[14]

Yet we are unprepared for mothering in less obvious ways too. It's not just that we don't anticipate the horrors and the hard work. Perhaps more than anything, we fail to anticipate the depth and breadth of the mothering experience, its sheer transformative power in a woman's life. In her classic reflection on the myths and meanings of motherhood, *Of Woman Born*, Adrienne Rich evokes this sense of the emotional complexity and richness of new motherhood that no one mentions:

> That calm, sure, unambivalent woman who moved through the pages of the manuals I read seemed as unlike me as an astronaut.

No one mentions the psychic crisis of bearing a first child, the excitation of long-buried feelings about one's own mother, the sense of confused power and powerlessness, of being taken over on the one hand and of touching new physical and psychic potentialities on the other.[15] Child-care specialist Penelope Leach writes, "Bringing up children is probably the most difficult life task people undertake, yet society offers less preparation for it than for any other . . . Who would embark on breeding horses or rearing dogs in such ignorance?"[16]

While reading this research, I found myself thinking back to a conversation I'd had with my older sister some thirteen years ago. It was a few weeks after the birth of her first child. In hindsight I realize that Gregory was a classic "high needs" baby: irritable, alert, and colicky. At the time I was aware only that he was cute and cried a lot. I could see that Karen was spending what seemed to me an inordinate amount of time in her darkened bedroom. She was trying to concentrate on breast feeding, she explained. (What was there to concentrate on, I wondered? Could putting a nipple into a little mouth really take so much time and thought?)

I recalled asking later, in a playful sort of way, "Well, tell me about motherhood. What's it really like, anyway?" I was taken aback by the intensity of her response. She looked away from the baby (and that in itself was a rare occurrence), and stared straight into my eyes. "I'm going to tell you this now, and I want you to remember it," she began. "Everyone lies. Do you hear me? Everyone lies about what it's like to have a baby. Don't listen to them. Just watch me, and remember."

I had no idea what a gift she was giving me. I was in graduate school then, just embarking on a career. I didn't even have a boyfriend, let alone an agenda for family planning. But because she was my big sister, I took it on trust. I did watch her closely in those years. In fact, I had very little choice. Because, after Gregory's birth, I found it almost impossible to have a conversation with her. Her body was there, of course, but her mind? Her attention? Her ability to focus? to empathize? to get "outside herself"? These seemed to have vanished. And with each of two succeeding children things only got worse.

"Maybe she should go back to work," I used to think. "Her mind has gone completely to dust." I was aware that she was intensely (and, to my mind, ridiculously) focused on her children. But it was only after my own mind had gone to dust, several years later, that I was able to fathom why and to give some structure to those observations she had forced on me during her years of exile in Motherland.

"Hang in there," she says to me now—now that I am the one juggling three small children and the vestiges of my former self. "The end is almost in sight. And by the time you get there, you'll wonder how on earth you ever coped at all. Instead of berating yourself for the times you've snapped, you'll stand in awe that whole days went by when you didn't snap. And by the time that happens, none of it will really matter any more." Other women who have traveled even further down the road of parenthood assure me (somewhat sadly) that "It all goes so fast. And before you know it, they're gone." Just when you've finally figured out what you're doing, in other words, it's all over.

The thought of each of us laboriously reinventing the wheel of motherhood is disturbing enough. But the prospect of having nowhere to travel with it is even worse. Feminist critic Phyllis Chesler believes that in our society "pregnancy and childbirth are savage tests of your ability to survive the wilderness alone. And to keep quiet about what you've seen.

Whether you're accepted back depends on your ability to learn without any confirmation that you've undergone a rite of passage . . . You must keep quiet and pretend to return to life as usual."[17]

In her book *Motherself*, Kathryn Rabuzzi describes motherhood as a "heroic quest" for women, a journey into selfhood and ultimate meaning that cries out to be chronicled, celebrated, and, above all, shared. She writes, "If a society existed in which the way of the mother were the norm, tales of mothers would predominate the way tales of heroes do in cultures throughout the world."[18] Yet the way of the mother *is* the norm, and that's the infuriating part. This heroic journey, this steepest of learning curves, this drama of birth and rebirth—whatever fine metaphors we choose to dress it up in, the processes entailed in mothering children lie at the very core of what it is to be human. The fact that it needs saying at all is quite remarkable. And enormously revealing. Like a superior athlete or (to use a more appropriate metaphor) a gifted actor, we make it all look so easy. So that instead of being seen as something we do, the work of mothering is something we are: the dancer become the dance. Yet with every pirouette we execute, we feel heavier, clumsier, more contorted. The effort it takes to appear effortless is enormous.

The urgent task of reconciling the realities of motherhood with the ideals of feminism attracted little enthusiasm among the movement's "first wave" thinkers, possibly because most were still too close to the mask to see it. One who wasn't was the young Shulamith Firestone, whose radical manifesto *The Dialectic of Sex* advocated the complete abolition of motherhood in social terms and, ultimately (for Firestone had high hopes for cloning technology), in the biological sense. It was a particularly bad case of throwing the baby out with the bath water. Understandably, few were willing to go quite this far. At the same time, Firestone grasped a nettle that few others could even discern through the thicket: that the issues surrounding the "unequal distribution" of responsibilities for reproduction and care of the young lie at the center of human sexual politics, that without redressing this particular imbalance in the division of human labor, feminism could provide only stopgap solutions—which is precisely what it has done.

Until very, very recently, this fatal flaw in the feminist vision remained successfully concealed—or perhaps "masked" is a better word—in our public discourse. Increasingly, thanks to the work of contemporary researchers such as Arlie Hochschild (*The Second Shift, The Time Bind*), Sharon Hays (*The Cultural Contradictions of Motherhood*), Martha Fineman (*The Neutered Mother, The Sexual Family and other Twentieth Century Tragedies*), Maureen Freely (*What About Us? The Mothers Feminism Forgot*) and others, our mothering consciousness is rising almost as fast as our expectations. Almost, but not quite.

It remains extraordinary to me that so many of us continue to experience motherhood as so much more, yet so much less, than we were led to expect. During the last trimester of my first pregnancy, I found myself staring in wonderment at total strangers. At crowds passing in the street. "All of these people were born!" I marveled, as if I had never before quite grasped the facts of life. "All of these people had mothers!" I would repeat it to myself slowly and with deliberation, as if translating from code.

For reasons that should be obvious, it was not an epiphany I chose to broadcast. I could picture myself trying to convey my "insight": "Listen everybody! You all were carried in a woman's body! A woman gave birth to each and every one of you! Isn't that incredible?!" It was a revelation that was self-evident to the point of utter banality. At the same time, I was dimly aware then (and am acutely aware now) that the implications of these basic biological facts are profoundly, unutterably significant.

So why are they so fiendishly difficult to discern? How can a woman with a working brain advance to the third decade of her life before the thought occurs to her? When I first began to think seriously and in depth about the implications of motherhood as a central human concern rather than as a peripheral life option, the silences became quite deafening. I began to be aware not so much of barking up the wrong tree but of barking up a tree that the other dogs kept insisting was a broomstick.

As author Sarah Dowse has suggested, the task of unmasking motherhood requires nothing less than a "new imagination—a knitting together of body and mind." She confesses, "When I was younger I imagined that childbirth was incidental, almost irrelevant to the achievements of the intellect, to industry, commerce, or politics." Now a grandmother, Dowse insists that mothering, as the ultimate act of human achievement, needs to be seen as the foreground for such endeavors: "a central, revelatory event."[19]

Other recent writers on the subject of motherhood agree. Yet the suspicion remains that the "new imagination" that dares to move motherhood from the periphery to the center may be sheer self-indulgence—a form of gender parochialism or a peculiarly feminine hubris. The temptation of self-censorship remains almost irresistible. Debra Adelaide has observed how often the urge to speak publicly about motherhood ("the most compelling experience of one's life") is suppressed. "The messages one receives say: Don't write about this. It's self-indulgent. Boring. Of limited interest"—even to mothers themselves.[20] I know exactly what Adelaide means. One prospective publisher of this book, herself a mother, claimed to be personally interested in the topic but had severe doubts about whether anyone else would. "Mothers want to read about their babies, not themselves," she explained apologetically.

This sense that a discussion of motherhood is either immodest or somehow peripheral and irrelevant reflects the feelings of deep unworthiness that women ascribe to their work, a belief that what we do or fail to do doesn't really matter that much anyway. "My mother nearly died during each of her pregnancies," writes author Fiona Place. "But this, like so many details, I only found out by accident. I was dumbfounded. 'Why haven't you told me?' I asked her. 'I never considered it that important,' she replied."[21]

Women's experiences as mothers, writes Sarah Dowse, "continue to be locked out of history."[22] At one level, it is easy to see why. So few ever remark on the centrality of motherhood to the project of being human, because they simply cannot "see" it. It is a precondition of human existence, like air, water, food. For all human beings, motherhood begins as the invisible environment in which we grow and, to greater or lesser degrees, develop. "We don't know who discovered water," the critic Marshall McLuhan used to say, "but it wasn't a fish." It is no wonder we have not yet fully "discovered" motherhood. More than any other field of human endeavor, motherhood is the water in which all of us swim.

Yet this truth is not the whole truth. If it were, the notion of a "conspiracy of silence" would be easy to discount. Fish do not, after all, conspire to keep themselves in ignorance. But human beings do so conspire—both male human beings and female human beings, though for quite different reasons. Let's examine some of these reasons.

One of my favorite nuggets of wisdom is scrawled in a dank, dark subterranean passageway in the bowels of New York's prestigious Union Theological Seminary. It reads, "If men could get pregnant, abortion would be a sacrament." And so, too, using precisely the same logic, would childbirth and the rearing of children. One hugely important reason that scholarship, philosophy, and virtually every other form of public discourse have been so astonishingly silent on the subject of motherhood is simply that men do not experience it. And what we call public discourse is a forum for what men know.

Discounting the last millisecond of human history, human beings have dwelt almost exclusively in what feminists call "the patriarchy," what our grandmothers called "a man's world." Leaving aside for a moment the fascinating theories, both evolutionary and otherwise, that attempt to account for this state of affairs—and leaving aside also the indignation we might feel about it all—the fact remains that, on the "to do" list for advancing human knowledge, the experience of women has yet to rate an entry.

Instead (and quite naturally, given its authorship) the list concentrates on things that men do. This is why "history" is about wars and battles; why literature is so singularly concerned with love and death (and the variety of means by which they may be "conquered"); why philosophy is dominated by abstraction and deduction; and why science has produced atomic energy but struggles with biodegradable diapers. I'm being simplistic, of course. But then again, it's a simple notion.

Where motherhood has been the subject of serious, sustained inquiry, it has been seen almost invariably as a cause, not an effect. This tendency is particularly marked in the field of psychology, where researchers have historically been more interested in apprehending mothers than in comprehending them.

As psychologist Paula Caplan and many others have pointed out, "mother-blaming" is the bread and butter of traditional psychotherapy.[23] Another piece of inspired graffiti illustrates the point: "My mother made me a homosexual." (Response: "If I give her the yarn, will she make me one too?"). The idea that, whatever we become—particularly if it's something socially unacceptable— "mother made us" is deeply ingrained in our collective cultural unconscious. It is no wonder that, as psychiatrist Ann Dally has observed, motherhood is so often approached as a minefield of psychological risk. "It is difficult," Dally writes, "because mothers know that they will have to devote most of themselves, and their time and energy, to it for many years, and that however diligently they do this they will be blamed for whatever goes wrong."[24] We are fascinated with criminal mothers and criminals' mothers, and the mother of the serial killer invariably rates a page-one interview. The mother of the Nobel laureate, on the other hand, remains (like everyone else's mother) discreetly offstage.

Psychological investigation into motherhood, until the past two decades, has concentrated almost exclusively on the impact (usually negative) of mothers on children. To the extent that it has been studied at all, motherhood has been cast in a supporting role in the higher drama of child development. The revolutionary notion that the effect of children on women might be equally worthy of study was identified as a "paradigm shift" as late as 1990.[25]

Again, from one point of view, it is easy to see why. Male researchers have not perceived motherhood as a "primary experience" for the simple reason that men do not mother. Men get mothered. Consequently, motherhood has usually been examined as something that happens to people, and almost never as something that people do.

It's a bit like the way my six-year-old feels about her teacher—and the way, I venture to say, nearly all six-year-olds feel about their teachers. We saw Mrs. Cunningham get into her car one day, and Anna was astounded. "That's Mrs. Cunningham!" she shouted. "Getting into a . . . car! Where is she going?"

It is not that children see their teachers as unimportant, or disempowered. Far from it. They see them as enormously powerful. But at the same time, the notion that a first grade teacher might have a life outside the classroom, or—even more shocking—might have emotions, needs, or desires within it, is almost literally unthinkable.

Does Mrs. Cunningham have an interior life? For that matter, does she have an exterior one? (Or does she, in fact, sleep right there in the classroom, under her desk?) Is she, in short, any more than the sum of her impressive individual effects on 26 semi-literate six-year-olds? These questions are easy to answer from a grown-up's perspective. But for a child they are not only unanswerable; they are inconceivable.

Male investigators have tended to regard mothers in much the same way as children regard their teachers. Those to whom mothering is done will inevitably frame the experience in the passive, rather than the active, voice (for example, "He was raised by his mother"). So that, in the psychological literature, motherhood is interesting to the extent that it is a "cause" of something beyond itself (of deviance, for example, or adjustment). But the imaginative leap required to see it as an "effect" in its own right, has been rarely, if ever, taken. Studies examining the impact of children on mothers are about as common as research into the effect of lung cancer on smoking.

There is no doubt that we see the world not as it is, but as we are, whether we are six or sixty, male or female. When we couple this brute fact with the equally brute fact that most of the world's recorded "observers" have been male, we can explain a great deal about how the mask of motherhood has been created. But the problem of perception, enormous as it is, is only the first obstacle to understanding. The limits of one's perceptual field might be described as a kind of "structural ignorance." Thus, men are necessarily structurally ignorant of women's experience, just as women are structurally ignorant of men's. The second great barrier to understanding, after ignorance, is fear.

Motherhood is fearsome because it is so intensely powerful, entailing acts of creation before which all other human endeavor withers into shadow. In the creation stakes, motherhood is the big league, and everything else—art, science, technology—is a farm team. Is it really any wonder that (as the evidence suggests) at some subconscious level all men are terrified, awestruck, and deeply envious of the gender-specific miracle of creation? This "womb envy" is apparent in the male initiation rites of traditional societies, which typically center on a symbolic mimicking of the childbirth experience. Our society has found its own ways, equally dramatic, to even up the score between the reproductive haves and have-nots.

Some observers have argued that the social contract called patriarchy rests on a trade-off in which the control by men of the "means of production" (of social and economic power) compensates for female control of the "means of reproduction." While impossible to verify or refute empirically, for me the theory makes intuitive sense. It is this trade-off that ensures that the hand that rocks the cradle does not rule the world, or at least not absolutely or for long. From this point of view, the familiar formulations of gender-specific spheres of endeavor—the domestic versus the economic; the heart versus the head; nature versus culture—reflect more than a division of labor. They reflect a primary division of power.

The second factor in our culture's intense fear of motherhood concerns our perceptions of maternal omnipotence: the sense that babies and young children have that mother is the source of all life and (as the flip side of the coin) that her absence, or the withdrawal of her love, threatens them with annihilation and death. This fear is experienced by males and females alike; indeed, it may be a key reason why women have so willingly aided and abetted the conspiracy of silence.

It was Freud who opened up the Pandora's box called motherlove. But the man who brought us the concept of penis envy was ill-equipped to understand the precise dynamics of such love. (We're talking about a person who seriously believed that, given a choice between the capacity to wee with precision into a milk bottle and the ability to conceive and bear new life, most of us would opt instantly for the former.) He did perceive that the terror of maternal power affected males and females quite differently. But it was left to psychoanalyst Nancy Chodorow to grasp the psychological imperatives underlying the creation of gender.

Chodorow argued that for males, who are structurally prohibited from competing with maternal power on its own terms, normal psychological development involves making a decisive flight from all things feminine, and seeking incorporation in an alternative power structure that specifically excludes female participation.[26] Women, on the other hand, are able to resolve the problem more directly. We do not need to flee from mother in order to escape her power. We need only become her—to "reproduce" maternal power through identification and re-enactment of the mothering role.

We are not necessarily comfortable about this; indeed, in our own society, matraphobia—the fear of turning into one's mother—is rampant. The residue of contempt and distrust of female power felt by women themselves remains palpable. Nevertheless, we tend to become what in our mothers we beheld, and sooner or later most of us succeed to the throne of motherhood. Our brothers meanwhile—like second sons sent forcibly to the colonies—must establish alternative dominions.

Analyses of the power of motherlove end up in the same place as analyses of the power of reproduction: with the conclusion that our entire social organization is a highly elaborated attempt to "get even" by culture for the biases of nature. It's exactly the same division of spoils as in the traditional divorce settlement, as a lawyer friend recently explained it to me: "The wife gets the kids, and the husband gets everything else." What we have learned to call the patriarchy is the same notion writ large—a trade-off between biological power and social control.

And therein lies the first of many strange paradoxes of human motherhood: that mothering is the most powerful of all biological capacities, and among the most disempowering of all social experiences.

It's been a nasty piece of work, this business of redressing the biological power imbalance. At the same time as men have labored to develop separate but parallel competencies, they have transformed their subliminal rage against "maternal ominipotence" into contempt for women. Instead of avowing their awe (and thereby acknowledging their dependence), men resist engulfment by belittling what women know and deriding what women do.

It doesn't take much imagination to see why males would feel they have something to fear in relation to female reproductive power. It seems somehow natural (if perverse) for men to minimize motherhood, whether as a creative act or as a form of dignified human labor. But why would women themselves do so? And make no mistake—women *do* do so. If the mask of motherhood is a conspiracy of silence, women are card-carrying co-conspirators. Why?

The multiple reasons why women betray women, and thereby themselves, are complex. One thing is clear: their intricate tangles are woven into the very warp and weft of our social fabric. Among other things, this means that there is no simple cause and effect relationship that will explain the puzzling tenacity with which women cling to the mask of motherhood. An examination of patriarchy as a social structure is indispensable to analysis of this. At the same time, it is important to avoid the intellectual passive-aggression that piously proclaims "the patriarchy made me do it."

An irony that is all too easy to forget is that the majority of this patriarchy is female. Consequently, whenever we assign blame to patriarchy, we implicitly hold ourselves responsible too. Although it is true to say that the mask of motherhood has been forged on the anvil of patriarchy, it is no man-made delusion. Women have made the mask of motherhood, and women have worn it. And so, too, must we wear the responsibility, along with the conviction that what we have made, we can unmake.

As feminist theorist Dorothy Dinnerstein argues, feelings of misogyny are as strongly embedded in the female psyche as in the male because of our common experience of helpless dependency on a mother perceived as infinitely powerful.[27] Only by empowering fathers to assume the real work of "mothering," she contends, will the hateful hegemony of female power be mitigated.

In the meantime, we can't quite bring ourselves to trash our entire sex. At the same time, there is a distinct sense in which we feel about being female the same way Groucho Marx felt about high society: that we don't want to belong to any club that would have us as a member. Consequently, we enact our ambivalence stealthily and through silence, in our deep distrust and disrespect towards other women.

Critic Phyllis Chesler agrees that, in this sense, women are their own worst enemies. As she puts it, we have "learned at a very early age to dismiss the words of our mothers and to listen to our fathers."[28] I thought of this during a recent interview, as I listened to a self-possessed young mother confide, "Most of Mom's ideas about childcare are old wives' tales. If I have a question, I'd rather ask my doctor." There is no doubt that, under patriarchy, what Chesler calls "the power and wisdom of old women" has been debased into what most of the rest of the population calls "old wives' tales." What has less often been remarked upon is the frequency with which the old wives themselves—and the young ones bringing up the rear—have proved willing accomplices in this treachery.

As we have observed already, the mutual fear and distrust that women feel for one another is a key element in the retention of the mask of motherhood, and in the disempowering of women generally. Another possible reason why, according to Paula Caplan, is that "competition is forbidden to women, at least in straightforward terms."[29] Our natural, even instinctual, drives for achievement and success have been diverted into uncomfortably narrow channels. Until quite recently, most of these channels centered on home and family—making motherhood a woman's central "career path," her primary means of self-expression, and her deepest source of self-worth. It's no wonder women have hedged it about with secrecy and silence, with disinformation and downright lies.

As Caplan puts it, "Because of the limitations on what women can do, the mother's success or failure accomplishing this task takes on immense importance . . . she and others measure her personal worth by how well she has accomplished it."[30] Even worse, a woman's sense of personal worth as a successful mother is often enhanced by the perceived failures of others. This can culminate in the pathetic "one-upwomanship" all too frequently encountered among mothers—a phenomenon which seems as prevalent among today's high-achieving Supermoms as it was in the stay-at-home generation that spawned them.

Personally, I have known women with multiple higher degrees who took direct, personal credit for their child's early teething (or walking or reading or whatever), and who obviously derived a deep sense of gratification from the process of drawing odious comparisons with those whose children developed at a different rate. ("No teeth yet? Oh, what a pity! But don't worry, they're sure to come sooner or later.") The implicit assumption that precocity in relation to teeth, or sitting up, or verbal development is somehow an index of a child's intellectual or moral superiority is bad enough. But that these "accomplishments" should be read as signs of the mother's superiority is downright perverse. Yet, wittingly or no, it is a trap into which most new mothers continue to tumble headlong. So that, instead of an honest sharing of the experiences of mothering, women indulge in a fearsome kind of maternal grandstanding which has less to do with sharing their concerns than with showcasing their triumphs.

As one participant in a recent study explained, "I find a lot of my girlfriends and the girls I listen to at playgroup and so on, talk about how their kids go to bed at seven and they eat broccoli."[31] It's no wonder so many women are turned off the notion of a mother's group. An informant from Australia, a biologist in her early thirties and the mother of a much-cherished baby girl, was so repulsed by the prospect of playing Comparative Babies that she refused to visit her local child health clinic (a free screening and advice service). "The first time we went, I saw a knot of mothers and babies in the playground next to the clinic," Caroline explained. "I made sure I crossed the road quickly so I wouldn't have to pass them."

Although Caroline's reaction was an extreme one, the expectation that other women constitute potential rivals, rather than prospective pals, is probably more widespread among mothers than most of us would like to admit. For all our skill and experience as nurturers, we seem constitutionally unable—or unwilling—to provide effective nurturance to one another. Not at all coincidentally, we are equally inept when it comes to nurturing ourselves.

Paula Caplan argues that, as little girls in our society grow into the role of nurturer, they internalize the lesson that, for them, the wish to be nurtured is "inappropriate."[32] By extension, the needs of other females for nurture will come to be regarded with suspicion also.

Caplan's observation is that these dynamics come into play in all female-female relationships, creating structural barriers between women on all kinds of levels. Perhaps this is why, as Kathryn Rabuzzi says, "the feelings of most women for each other in contemporary Western cultures are remote . . . Rather than learning to love other women, we more typically learn to fear and distrust each other. Instead of mirroring ourselves positively, other women therefore more often reflect what is least desirable in ourselves."[33] When it comes to relationships between women in the active phase of their mothering lives, these barriers seem to loom particularly large, creating even more than the usual distance of doubt and distrust.

The reason, I suspect, has much to do with the "nurture shock" most women experience (and almost no woman anticipates) in the transition to new motherhood. There is no doubt that, whatever other changes new motherhood may entail, the neediness of the helpless newborn presents a woman with the ultimate test of her fitness to nurture. Even for the "best," most settled baby, the new mother must confront the realities of being on 24-hour-a-day call; of long periods without proper rest; of the physically gruelling routines of frequent feedings, diaper changes, bathing and washing; of worry over wind, constipation, and other digestive woes; of pain and frustration in the establishment of a breastfeeding routine.

In this virtual frenzy of caring, many women have reported feeling as if they have ceased to function, or even to exist, as people in their own right. To this extent, coping with nurture shock is perhaps the ultimate expression of selflessness. At the same time, to exist without a clear sense of self—however temporarily—means living dangerously. Nurture shock renders women emotionally vulnerable, as their lives become quite literally unbalanced. The sense that the demands of nurture shock are outrageously unfair (by one's former standards of reckoning) is probably widely felt, but rarely expressed. But even more unsettling is the dawning awareness that one's old sense of "justice" has suddenly become a relic, a quaint, vestigial notion rendered abruptly irrelevant by the cutting of a cord. For me, this first epiphany of new motherhood came within a few hours of my first child's birth. I was fortunate in having a "good" birth: drug-free, without complications or interventions. Perhaps partly because of this, I experienced an instant bonding with my daughter, a great, euphoric gush of maternal love of an intensity that I had never imagined possible. In addition to all this was the sheer relief of finding myself gloriously un-pregnant. (Within minutes after the birth, I danced into the shower, laughing gleefully at the flaccid, floppy remains of my tummy.)

Nevertheless, even the "easiest" birth is the end product of the hardest work of which a human body is capable — in this case, a period of active labor lasting about eight hours. Anna had been born at a civilized 7:30 pm. By midnight, I was not only ready for sleep; I desperately needed it. I glanced adoringly at my baby sleeping peacefully in her little plexiglass crib, and closed my eyes. And opened them. Anna was crying.

Ah! She must be hungry again, I thought. I offered the breast, which she accepted greedily. A few minutes later, her eyes closed (just as the La Leche League book said they would), and I gently placed her back in the crib. She opened her eyes wide in what looked to me a lot like terror. And then she screamed. Of course, I picked her up straight away. I tried feeding her again, burping her, rocking her. All the while, she was quiet and happy (just as Penelope Leach had promised). And every time I tried putting her in that damned plexiglass cell, she screamed as if scalded.

By the time an hour had passed in this fashion, and then two hours, my weariness had turned to exhaustion. I found myself wondering guiltily whether a midwife might not want to "pop in" (their favorite phrase) and take Anna to the nursery. But surely this would defeat the whole point of rooming in, I reminded myself sternly. And yet . . . I was so tired. So tired. I had never been more tired in my life. I had never needed sleep more than I did at that moment—not in my whole life. Even more to the point, I had never deserved sleep as much as I felt I deserved it that night.

Yet, against all this familiar assertion of needs and rights, of history and justice and entitlement, there was counter-posed a strange and stubborn reality: a baby who continued to cry heedlessly, and piteously, in spite of it all. My guilty and barely conscious acknowledgment that this was truly unfair was followed swiftly by the shock of acceptance that justice would simply have to be jettisoned, perhaps indefinitely.

"Of course," I think now (and so will any other mother with a child older than about eight hours). Of course. And how naive ever to have thought otherwise. That first night was the merest of trial runs for the unprecedented selfless-ness—the emptying of self—that new motherhood demands. Seven years and three children later, I have come to see the "injustice" with far greater clarity. On the one hand, there is the unmaskable truth that the price of parenthood is almost incalculably high, when reckoned against the adult autonomy once taken for granted. On the other, there is the gift of growth and discovery that comes from breaking those old boundaries of selfhood. The glimpses of the biblical truth that, in order to find life, you must lose it. That in "forgetting" herself, a woman may begin to discover at last who she is.

I know all this now. But at the same time, I wonder about the necessity of the "shock" part of nurture shock in the initiation to first motherhood. So many women have suggested that it is impossible to prepare anyone for this first, full-on plunge into parenthood, and that it is therefore useless even to try. Although I agree to an extent with the first part, I find myself more and more suspicious about the second. It all sounds too much like the old arguments given for keeping women in the dark about childbirth—that you can't know what it's like until you experience it, that no preparation is possible, that it is an experience to be endured, then, mercifully, forgotten. In the case of childbirth preparation, it's easy to see how such attitudes were self-perpetuating, keeping a woman's hard-won knowledge a churlishly guarded secret even from her own daughters, her own sisters.

Of course, no preparation for childbirth will actually equip a woman completely for her time of trial. The intensity, the texture, the timing of the experience—even if it were not so highly variable and individual—could never be simulated. In my own prenatal classes, our partners were asked to pinch our arms to "symbolize" contractions while we dutifully puffed and panted through the pain. It was ridiculous, of course. A labor contraction is about as much like a pinch in the arm as a baby is like a Barbie doll. Yet the experience was still infinitely worth having, if only for the repeated message that something extraordinary was going to happen, something for which one would need to muster all the support and all the strength she could find.

In the same way, I remember being told by a friend that contractions would feel like waves of very painful menstrual cramps. While many would argue that this is putting it extremely mildly, I found the analogy helpful. Of course, it did not adequately prepare me for the sheer force of labor. Nothing but the experience of childbirth itself will tell you exactly what to expect. Everything else is mere metaphor. But there's a lot to be said for mere metaphor. It's a fundamental way in which human beings make meaning, in which we advance stealthily on the unknown by means of the known.

I think of the metaphor of "wilderness," used by Phyllis Chesler, to describe the early days of motherhood. What I am calling nurture shock, Chesler describes as a savage test of a woman's ability to survive the wilderness alone.[34] She believes it is patriarchy that is to blame. Yet I am not so certain. I wonder now why I didn't simply call the midwife and ask for help, why I felt so strongly the need to "take it like a woman," alone and in silence.

Heaven knows we can't blame the patriarchy for the vagaries of infant sleep patterns, for the sheer biological helplessness of the newborn. Yet we do need to think about what our society contributes, or fails to contribute, in the way of preparing us to handle that helplessness. We can't change the wilderness, but do we really need to explore it solo, and under test conditions? And if we do not—and if this looming, amorphous enemy called "the patriarchy" is not to blame—then what exactly is stopping us?

If it is true, as Caplan suggests, that most women's sense of self-worth remains largely bound up with their identification as nurturers, the impact of nurture shock may prove profoundly unsettling, with after-effects ranging from a temporary loss of confidence and feelings of disorientation to depression or even full-blown psychosis.

Although we might prefer to think otherwise, I suspect that the self-esteem of today's young mothers is at least as vulnerable as that of our mothers. We are at least as afflicted by a peculiarly maternal performance anxiety (and probably more so, given the new pressures to achieve under which most of us labor). And, when all is said and done, we secretly believe as fervently as any previous generation that our children reflect to the world our own competence, "goodness" and "success" as people. The anxiety among mothers to get it right has never been higher. Ironically, the odds of doing so have probably never been lower.

This performance anxiety about mothering, which entails a straining for effect in order to mask the underlying insecurity, is what Harriet Goldhor Lerner calls "faking motherhood"—a form of social pretending she sees as endemic among today's young women. The less certain we are of what we're doing, and why we're doing it, Lerner suggests, the more liable we are to resort to bluff and bluster. In the end, we are afflicted with a kind of maternal machisma: we put on the mask of motherhood and make it all look so easy.

When writer and new mother Melissa West attempted to research the experience of motherhood behind the mask, she unearthed the same eerie silence. For, although she located plenty of material on the joys of mothering, West could find "none to tell me as well how truly difficult mothering can be. No one writing about being awake in the middle of the night, in between visits to a sick child's room, no sleep for days, crying from weariness and frustration and helplessness. Nothing. Silence."[35]

But more revealing than West's first reaction on discovering so puny a literature was her second reaction: an almost reflexive guilt about her own maternal shortcomings. "It can't be that I'm the only mother to have felt as if 'me' was disappearing, suffocating under the giant midden of daily tasks. I can't be the only one. Why is nothing written? Why? . . . I KNOW WHY. Because I'm never supposed to feel these feelings, ask these questions . . ."[36]

The machisma of the mask of motherhood conceals a

multitude of expressions: some of them indescribably joyous, others piercingly sad or thunderous with anger. Yet of all the faces of motherhood unmasked, perhaps the commonest—and certainly the most crippling—is the face of maternal guilt. Without doubt, guilt lies at the crux of the crisis of mothering affecting young women today. To an extent unprecedented in previous generations, we suffer guilt over the things we do as mothers and the things we leave undone. In the explosion of options available to our generation, something has apparently been blown up. That something, I would argue, is nothing less than a secure sense of our bearings as women: of the unique and inalienable roles that belong to us, and—equally important—of the awesome responsibilities that may be peculiarly ours to bear.

The gains for women in the past three decades or so of social change, since we ourselves were mothered, have been enormous. Yet it is fitting—indeed it is imperative—that we begin to reckon our losses as well. In relation to motherhood, what we have lost is, in a sense, our innocence. For most of us, there is no going back to a view of mothering as an instinctual, unproblematic, "natural" sequence of events. Mothering is something we are no longer capable of pursuing mindlessly, in the sense of being unmindful of the import of our choices and their potential consequences. Perhaps this helps in part to explain our malaise. We are a bit like the centipede who managed to get along just fine until someone pointed out how hard it must be to coordinate a hundred different limbs. He never walked again.

Indeed, the more we learn about motherhood, the less able we are to mother, it seems. And the more likely we are to fake it instead—adopting techniques and strategies to fill the void of our depleted confidence, placing our trust in medical and/or psychological experts, and spurning the wisdom of the experienced practitioners all around us—ourselves, our mothers, our sisters, our friends. The great sociologist of mothering, Ann Oakley, points out that, in our society, "it is not women . . . who know about motherhood, but health professionals."[37] The result, psychiatrist and mother of four Ann Dally argues, is a generation of mothers whose diligence masks a tragic insecurity. Such women, she writes, "are frequent attenders of general practitioners, pediatricians, clinics and social workers. They buy baby books and magazines galore, thrive on the whole idea of techniques of baby and child care and are always searching for advice from outside rather than for their own feelings and intuition . . . "[38] Yet this "solution" only drives women still further into isolation and uncertainty, leading ultimately to an increased "anxiety about whether one is doing the right thing and to guilt when things go wrong."[39]

Dally and others contend that the present generation is locked into a vicious cycle in which our escalating expectations of performance as mothers leads inevitably to perceptions of inadequacy and guilt. Sociologist Jesse Bernard notes that "our way of institutionalizing motherhood breeds guilt into the very fabric of a woman's character. She blames herself for every deviation from the model . . . And the only way some can assuage their guilt is by constant dedication to the child."[40]

In such cases, as Terri Apter observed in *Why Women Don't Have Wives*, "the boredom of the mother infects the child, and makes the child ask for more and more of the mother's attention, because the child does not understand what is lacking."[41] The result, says Dally, is a "rigid permissiveness" that saps the vitality of the mother even as it thwarts the spirit of the child.[42] Like the full-time working mother whose parenting style degenerates into a round of tricks and treats and cajolery (mirroring that of the full-time working father), we feel too damned guilty to say "no" and say it plainly.

Others, who attempt to find a way out of the motherhood morass by concentrating their energies on professional achievement, tend to fare little better. Their guilt is different in kind perhaps, but rarely in degree, from that of the professional mother at home whose strenuous efforts to stimulate her children leave everyone unfulfilled.

Nature endows women with the capacity to reproduce, but it is culture that has tended to confine women to that capacity . . . nature that has given woman a "golden touch"; culture that has rendered the blessing an infirmity. Yet even beyond the constraints of culture, females pay a price for their biological superiority. Sarah Hrdy has pointed out that sexual asymmetry in the form of male dominance is "nearly universal" among our closest relatives, the primates.[43] The relationship between this social fact and the reproductive responsibilities of females is obvious and incontestable.

Yet what distinguishes the sexual politics of homo sapiens from those of our fellow primates is the meanings we have have made of the distribution of reproductive power. The life of all creatures revolves around the work of conceiving, bearing, and rearing young. What is uniquely human is our choice either to celebrate that power or to fear it—and, out of fear, to deny, subvert, and distort it.

Above all, the mask of motherhood conceals the almost unbearable tension between our power as creators and the dependencies that this power engenders—in our children, in our men, and in ourselves. Yet it is crucial to understand that it is not the tension itself that is the result of "false consciousness," but the attempt to deny that the tension exists, or that it matters. The issues that swirl around motherhood appear problematic because they are problematic—and not because the patriarchy says so. On the contrary, the forces that constrain women today are the ones that minimize the difficulties we face, insisting that motherhood is no big deal after all. Assuring us that once we muddle through, "the real world" will be waiting to receive us on the other side.

Unmasking motherhood means facing the sobering fact that real life is not temporarily elsewhere (back at the office, say, or at the gym, or on the evening news) but right here (on the couch, in the kitchen, curled up in the crib). Unmasking motherhood means accepting that we are all of us making it up as we go along, and wishing we knew better. And when we get that far, we may be able to begin sharing what we really experience, and pooling what we really know, about life on the other side of the great divide of parenthood. We might even have a chance to produce a generation of daughters who will rise to the challenge of motherhood fearlessly, and without apology or pretence. The struggle to unmask motherhood is the first step in reconciling reproductive power with social rights and responsibilities—a peculiarly female challenge with repercussions for all humanity.

"Falling"

The Experience of Pregnancy

Probably more is done by wicked women with their malicious lying tongues to harm the confidence and happiness of pregnant women than by any other factor.

—Dr. Gordon Bourne

IF PARENTHOOD IS INDEED a great divide, then pregnancy is a kind of no-woman's land, in which one is not quite mother, but no longer other. Humorist Robert Benchley once remarked that you can divide the world into two kinds of people: those who divide the world into two kinds of people and those who don't. The irony as well as the poignancy of this observation is, of course, that "either/or" thinking seems to be something the human mind is stuck with. However we struggle to expand our horizons, delinearize our options, or multiply our variables, we are normally in extreme intellectual discomfort when called upon to juggle more categories than we have hands (or, perhaps more to the point, brain hemispheres).

It is perhaps for this reason that human beings find transitions so difficult. We like to be in one place or another, here or there. Which is perhaps why most of us hate "moving days" so much. Combined with the obvious stress of packing and unpacking and the total disruption to one's routine, the experience of temporary homelessness (generally lasting about four hours)—of briefly belonging neither to one place nor the other—can be existentially excruciating.

Being pregnant is a lot like moving to a new house, only instead of lasting four hours, moving day lasts 6,480 hours. You spend most of that time packing, but at the end you are no more prepared than you felt you were at the beginning. This is hardly surprising, because you have no idea what your new address is, let alone how to get there.

My sister says that pregnancy is like being in an airplane: a little bit boring but not unpleasant, and at least you get to sit down a lot. But if you stopped to think about what was actually happening just under the bland surface of the ride ("I'm really 30,000 feet off the ground, hurtling through the atmosphere at a frightening velocity, with my fate in the hands of a stranger who is probably in the grip of a mid-life crisis"), sheer terror would immobilize you.

There is something both miraculous and scary about being pregnant. Maybe all miracles (technological or otherwise) are that way. I remember seeing *Bernadette of Lourdes* on television when I was seven or eight and having nightmares about it. What if the Virgin Mary was tempted to select me next? For a time it got so bad I was afraid to look up on a cloudy day for fear that the Blessed Mother might be lying in wait, scanning our neighborhood for an upward glance. There is an old French proverb to the effect that "miracles happen only to those who believe in them." Yet even those who do believe in miracles are far more comfortable with the idea that they should happen to somebody else. The more abstract our spirituality has become, the more uneasy we grow with the concept of mystery, whatever its provenance. And there is something deeply, darkly mysterious about being pregnant and knowing that you are. It would be hilarious, if it weren't so revealing, that so many women respond to the news of a confirmed pregnancy with an almost reflexive disbelief. "How is it possible?!" we demand to know. When, of course, we know perfectly well how, and in all manner of scientific detail besides. Whether in ecstasy or distress, there is a voice within that demands to know, "How on earth could this have happened? and to me?" In this, we surely echo in some small measure the primordial awe with which humans must first have greeted the signs of new life. In some profound sense we remain aware that pregnancy is a kind of possession in which one is rendered temporarily not herself—or not simply herself, but herself and then some.

Paradoxically, pregnancy is also experienced as a form of dispossession for many women. Strangers feel free to pat our bellies, to call us "Mom," to make casual assessments of how we're carrying (or "what" we're carrying—boy or girl). Women formerly dogged by wolf whistles, catcalls, and assorted public obscenities find (whether to their relief or regret) that pregnancy is a kind of sexual armor, the ultimate weapon in the struggle for safe sex. There is something totemic and forbidding about a pregnant silhouette, before which even modern men totter and flail. I remember a group of teenage boys boisterously remarking on my receding back view as I lumbered to the corner shop one day late in my first pregnancy. On impulse, I turned slowly and revealed my true identity, all eight, swollen months of it. My fan club stopped in its tracks. I thought one boy was going to cry. Then they began to laugh, in the nervous way you must when you realize the joke's on you. "And all this time we thought you were a woman!" What a riot, eh?

The first step in the dispossession proceedings comes well before any visible signs of transformation. Indeed, most of us punctuate our pregnancies—both how they begin and where they end—on the say-so of some external, objective authority. A pregnancy becomes "real" when a chemical test, preferably administered by a medical practitioner, says it is real. So that what we feel, or what we feel we know, has no chance to grow (like our babies, like our bodies) in certainty or stature. Few women allow pregnancy to dawn on them: to watch and wait and wonder seems obstinately old-fashioned. We want to know now, thanks very much, and we want to know for certain.

Yet the woods are full of pregnancy dipsticks wrongly interpreted, wrongly filed, or sometimes just wrongly dipped. Our faith in the infallibility of the pregnancy test would be touching if it weren't so obviously indicative of our lack of faith in ourselves. The advent of the home pregnancy test has theoretically given women back a little of what they'd lost: a redistribution of the power to detect, the credit for discovering what their own bodies have been up to. Yet there is something incongruous, if not downright debased, about a woman staring intently and prayerfully into a plastic cup of urine, therein to discern a future. If we attended as minutely to our bodies' signals we might learn so much more. Yet because pregnancy is such a well-kept secret, who among us would know where to look? Every primagravida is like a new Eve, making it up as she goes along. The depth of our collective ignorance is impossible to underestimate. And when our fleshly experience fails to fit the bare bones of the stories we read in books, we secretly assume the aberration is our own.

Pregnancy is never an unmixed blessing. Indeed, by its very nature pregnancy is ambivalence made flesh. It's the classic instance of "to have and have not," "to be and not to be." This blurring of the boundaries of selfhood, of where

"I" leaves off and "You" begins, is a primary biological fact of pregnancy. Later, it will become the primary emotional reality of parenthood. The delicate yet strenuous agenda of symbiosis—to exist at once separately and in seamless, self-less merger with another—is the central paradox of moth-erhood. In pregnancy the struggle is a frankly physical one. The pregnant body becomes frenzied in its quest to accom-modate the other self, that invader from within. It is no wonder that what the textbooks describe as the "physical symptoms" of pregnancy can be so varied and violent. They catch us off guard and leave us breathless and panting, often quite literally.

These physical enormities with which pregnancy begins are, for many women, the first inkling that the mask of (ex-pectant) motherhood might be concealing more than it re-veals. The experience of "morning sickness" is a perfect case in point. Morning sickness is something most women are socialized to expect as Act One of the approved pregnancy script. Like craving pickles and ice cream and falling in love with your obstetrician, morning sickness is regarded as a normal aberration of pregnancy—and something that some of us secretly rather look forward to. One imagines the luxury of feeling a little unwell, with just enough sympathy, tea, and biscuits to make it all right. Indeed, it is really only in pregnancy that many women confront the notion of ill-ness as a component, or even as a sign, of well-being. It is strangely attractive, this notion that one has received per-mission or even earned the right to be sick.

Perhaps this helps explain why the 50 percent of preg-nant women who never experience morning sickness often feel obscurely cheated. They may also be worried, on the mistaken assumption that sickness signals a healthy em-bryo. "I don't feel pregnant at all!" they complain, as if there is a right and a wrong way of "feeling pregnant." There is almost a social obligation to experience some level of illness if the pregnancy is to achieve legitimacy. I know one woman who was referred by her GP to a specialist because, four weeks after a positive pregnancy test, she showed no "symptoms" of pregnancy. She didn't feel sick or tired, bloated or irrational. She felt great—so great that both she and her doctor began to worry. Pregnant women are supposed to feel pregnant—and, in the first trimester at least, "feeling pregnant" is supposed to equate with feeling unwell.

There are many cultures throughout the world in which morning sickness is apparently unknown or at least unacknowledged. As one woman in an impoverished village in Northern India explained to anthropologist Patricia Jeffery, "illness in pregnancy is an affectation of the rich."[2] But in our own affluent society, it is virtually obligatory. Precisely why we have chosen to frame pregnancy as a form of illness whose "symptoms" require medical "management" is a good question, and a disturbing one. If the cross-cultural research is to be believed, one woman's nausea may be another woman's nirvana.

In our society being female is, in the language of our private health industry, a pre-existing condition. A twenty-weeks-pregnant friend, herself a health-care professional, was denied travel insurance recently. "I have a disease," she explained to me. "I'm pregnant."

The language we use to describe the physical experience of pregnancy reveals a determination to deny and demystify its weird drama. The euphemism "morning sickness" is a perfect example. The term is a neat diagnostic category, with a touch of poetry thrown in for good measure. But, as a reflection of what women actually experience, it is about as accurate as a fun-house mirror.

My own experience of morning sickness, for example, bore about the same relation to textbook accounts as Godzilla does to Bambi. Like the women in the books, I pictured myself wanly nibbling water crackers in bed. What I got instead was an insane urge for fries and Coke, buckets of them. I expected "mild nausea" that "vomiting would instantly relieve." What I got was a sickness so intense that it disordered my senses. I would not have believed (had I not experienced it) that music, for example, could be experienced as an acute physical irritation. There are still some rhapsodies of Rachmaninoff that affect me like the aftertaste of tainted seafood. At the time, even my ears wanted to throw up.

Freud spoke of a condition called polymorphous perversity, a stage of infantile sexuality in which physical pleasure is diffused throughout the body, rendering every millimeter of it a potential erogenous zone. My experience of pregnancy sickness was the precise inverse of this. It was as if my body had become a divining rod for distress. The texture of sand, the mottled pattern of a dress, the reverberation of a rich minor chord: all of these could inspire a full-body nausea profound enough to paralyze.

I expected to experience what the books referred to as "smell aversions," in which the pregnant woman finds herself repulsed by certain everyday, hitherto neutral odors. I had read that the most common smell aversions were to chemical substances and that the reaction was believed to be a kind of primitive warning system, alerting the mother-to-be of potential dangers to the unborn child. It sounded reasonable, and when I found I was repulsed by the smell of my deodorant and the laundry soap I'd been using, I dutifully changed brands. Formerly an enthusiastic smoker, I found my aversion to tobacco became so intense that even a picture of a cigarette made me dizzy with disgust.

Gradually, however, my repertoire of aversions began diversifying far beyond the bounds of reason. Soon, it was not just the chemical whiff of gasoline that made me gag, but the innocuous scent of the sea breeze. (Could fresh air be dangerous for the unborn child, I wondered?) Later still, I had the Kafkaesque experience of developing a smell aversion to my own body and its increasingly copious secretions. (Could it be that my vagina, too, was dangerous to the unborn child?) The smell of dirty laundry was sickening, though understandably. But when the smell of clean laundry sent me reeling too, I started trying to remember what I had read about psychosis in pregnancy.

Admittedly, mine was an extreme case. But, as I would learn from talking to other women over a period of years, the kind of all-encompassing nausea I experienced was well within the bounds of "normal," even if it exceeded the "norm" rather spectacularly. Extreme pregnancy sickness is not an aberration but a fairly common variation on a theme. Perhaps it is not so surprising after all, the belief that pregnancy properly begins with "sickness." And yet in what proportion of cases, I wonder, is that sickness actually associated closely with "morning"? Among the hundreds of women with whom I have discussed morning sickness, no more than a handful were sick in the morning. So whose term is it, anyway?

The "morning" part of morning sickness is clearly another of the great mysteries of our oddly impoverished vocabulary for maternity. There is no doubt that most women who experience nausea in pregnancy do so at any or all hours of the day. For every woman who feels particularly unwell upon rising, there is another who vomits with enviable regularity at suppertime. And there is a third who never vomits at all, but who spends most of her waking hours wishing fervently that she would. Yet all of these women continue to describe their experience in the same hopelessly inexact terms, learned from their doctors, their pregnancy books, and even their own mothers. To call the range of these experiences "morning sickness" is akin to calling all abdominal pain — from a gas bubble to a second-stage contraction — a "tummy ache."

My own obstetrician was, like most I'm sure, aware of the inaccuracy of the term "morning sickness," though he and I continued to use it whenever the topic arose. He listened sympathetically to my plight and recommended sucking on jelly beans. "The glucose might help," he explained, pointing out that some pregnancy nausea seems to have a basis in low blood sugar. He was right: it did help, as did eating vast quantities of potatoes (preferably deep-fried), drinking gallons of sugary soft drinks, and nibbling nonstop on vanilla wafers.

Onlookers were just as puzzled as I was that someone who complained of feeling so violently sick could be so hungry. I tried to explain that what I felt wasn't so much hunger (in fact, I almost never felt hungry in the old sense of the word) as emptiness. Hunger is a matter of one's whole body, and usually one's mind as well, desiring sustenance. But what I experienced was a command that seemed to come directly, and solely, from my stomach — or from the black hole that used to be my stomach.

The sensation began even before my pregnancy was confirmed at around five weeks. I found my tummy feeling "empty" when I knew it had to be full, even minutes after I'd finished a meal. I started eating alarming numbers of bananas before it occurred to me that what I was responding to was not hunger per se, but the signal that I was hungry, a signal in the form of an acidy (empty) feeling in my stomach. The tricky part was that eating actually did address the symptom; so that in the act of consuming I felt the "emptiness" fill up. The problem was the timing: a meal or snack that would previously have satisfied me for hours now seemed to evaporate almost as soon as it was swallowed.

When I arrived for my second prenatal appointment, I found my doctor's patience seemed to have evaporated as well. The man who had charitably proffered jelly beans five weeks ago regarded me now—fourteen pounds of additional assorted carbohydrates later—with disapproval verging on disgust. I was informed that those fourteen pounds amounted to half of my target weight gain for the entire pregnancy. ("My target?" I wondered. The target was news to me.) "It can't keep up like this," he concluded. "Women who gain excess weight in pregnancy have tremendous difficulty losing it afterwards. Some never do," he added ominously.

I hadn't been so humiliated since elementary school, on that dreaded day each year when all the kids were publicly weighed and measured by a local GP. I suffered the joint ignominy of being both the tallest and the heaviest (and in my mind, there wasn't the slightest correlation between the two: my height and my weight were two utterly separate and equally horrific facts of life). Now at age thirty-two I felt just as cornered—and as disgraced—as I had that seeming lifetime ago. Glancing in dismay at my bulge (was it really just so much butterfat?), I stammered out something about feeling sick and hungry a lot. I sounded like an idiot—a fat idiot. I apologized. And I promised it would never happen again.

It did, of course. I continued to gain weight at an "unacceptable" velocity throughout that pregnancy. While it would be an overstatement to say that I began to dread my appointments (in fact, I looked forward to them—as do most pregnant women—as oases of affirmation in the long desert of pregnancy), I came to regard the obligatory weighing in as a kind of penance for my sins of overindulgence. Once or twice, the scales revealed a pleasant surprise, and I would be duly praised for my "restraint." I accepted this praise graciously and with modesty befitting the occasion, for deep down I was convinced that I was no more responsible for the "good" results than I was for the "naughty" ones. Whenever I felt an overpowering urge to eat, I simply did so; and when I didn't, I didn't. Secretly I decided that anyone who had never been nauseated by fresh air was not qualified to pass judgment one way or the other.

Research indicates that women in our society tend to feel guilty and wrong no matter how much, or how little, weight they gain in pregnancy. In a study of body image experiences among sixty-three pregnant women, researcher Peggy Richardson found that while actual weight gain was highly variable, anxiety about weight gain remained a constant. Even women who had "gained a small amount of weight were likely to have indicated that 'it wasn't enough' or 'it wasn't right.' "[3] Clearly, we are deeply invested with the notion that there is a "correct" way for our bodies to perform pregnancy and that everyone else is achieving the standard except ourselves. That we should be conforming to someone else's standard is bad enough. But that we should be struggling so hard to conform to a standard no one else is meeting is truly remarkable.

In my own case, guilt about weight gain was intensified by the constant reminders that, by following what seemed to be the implacable (and inscrutable) dictates of my flesh, I

47

was setting myself up for a lifetime of obesity. With hind-sight, I realize that my obstetrician—a kind but over-stressed man with weight problems of his own—was partly projecting his own anxieties. Yet I have heard the same story from so many women with so many different obstetricians that I am growing increasingly skeptical. They can't all be paunchy.

I accept that there may be some statistical correlation be-tween excessive weight gain during pregnancy and chronic overweight afterwards. But if there is, I'll wager that "diet-ing" has precious little to do with prevention. I still wonder about rigid definitions regarding "excess" (as in "not needed") and "excessive" (as in "over the top"). During my first pregnancy, I gained upwards of forty-five pounds. I was uncomfortable and bloated, and I looked it. Yet within a week after the birth, I shed a third of that weight, and within three months virtually all of it. I made no attempt to diet or count calories. In fact, I seemed to eat twice as much as I had before becoming pregnant, although the quality of my hunger (if that's the word) had reverted to its familiar, pre-pregnancy parameters. Not at all coincidentally, I was also breast-feeding.

I am indulging myself in such detail because I believe the minutiae of what we experience in pregnancy—however outlandish it may seem, or however incapable of solution it may prove—should be articulated, shared, and pondered. To date, when our society has discussed pregnancy at all, it has done so as if it were something that happened to other people, like diabetes or bi-polar disorder. In fact, given that the experience of pregnancy is one of the rare universals of the human condition, to discuss it adequately, we need a lan-guage more nuanced than the pitiable pidgin we currently have at our disposal. It's a bit like doing *Hamlet* with semaphore: just about everything that's worth communicating gets lost in the translation.

For women who value control, pregnancy can be a disorientingly difficult time. Physically, it's like taking the backseat in what used to be your own car. Someone—or is it something?—else is doing the driving. And, what's more, the route, at times stunningly beautiful, at times terrifying and precipitous, is at all times unfamiliar—or perhaps just familiar enough to be recognizable and just strange enough to unsettle. Some women make marvelous passengers in the journey of pregnancy: they sit back and wonder and delight at the passing strangeness. For others, the anxiety of having surrendered the wheel makes joy-riding impossible. Like illness, pregnancy is a kind of hijacking—an invasion from within, which can render a body strange to a mind. It is for this reason that we are accustomed to say, when ill, "I'm not quite myself today." Like the creepy feeling one sometimes gets with a high fever, as if by some oversight one has put on the wrong skin. From this point of view, pregnancy is a crash course in empathy. Physically at least, it forces a woman to perceive the world from a perspective that is radically—and often suddenly—other.

Perhaps this explains why so many women feel a shock of recognition on first beholding their newborn. The living of another life from the inside out is a physiological fact that frequently takes on psychological substance at the moment of childbirth. So that we gaze on our newborns as if they were old, old friends. "Why of course," we exclaim. "It's you!" The miracle of pregnancy is coiled in that wild leap from parasite to personhood.

I know all this now, but I wish I'd known it then. I wish it had been possible to find a more useful frame than illness to describe the experience of that first pregnancy. If it had, I suspect I would have spent much less time in revulsion and revolt, and a good deal more in surrender and silence. The English sociologist of mothering Ann Oakley called her autobiography *Taking It Like a Woman*. It strikes me now that most of us persist in taking pregnancy like a man: we grit our teeth and tough it out. We fight off our symptoms with a grim determination to eat a couple of jelly beans and get on with it, to show the world—especially our partners, especially our watchful colleagues at work—that pregnancy is no big deal, really.

In the weeks in which my nausea paralyzed me for minutes at a time, when I drove to work with my head stuck out the window (my nose covered with a hankie) to avoid smelling both the musty interior of my old car and the pine deodorizer I'd bought to eradicate it, when the scent of a colleague's "Poison" perfume made the name seem distinctly literal, I took it "like a man" because it hadn't occurred to me there was any alternative. I would not have dreamed of revealing my distresss—not publicly anyway—and on the rare occasion when someone asked me whether I'd yet felt any morning sickness, I replied as succinctly as I could. Even to my closest friends, I wouldn't have dreamed of disclosing the details. To have morning sickness was every pregnant woman's right, maybe even her duty. To be turned inside out with nausea to the point where the sickness transcended not only the morning but the very boundaries of my flesh—so that the whole world not only smelled fetid but sounded and felt that way, too—went way beyond a "symptom." This, I felt, must be a form of somatic schizophrenia. And I'd be about as likely to publicize it as I would a bout of bed-wetting.

I did what any pregnant man would do: I tried hard to pretend it wasn't happening. I reported to my office every morning and conscientiously pretended to work. By lunch-time, when the apocalypse within threatened to obliterate even the semblance of civility, I would steal to the pub and order a gigantic take-out meal loaded with fats and carbo-hydrates (maybe the chef would think I was catering a meeting). Returning to my office, I would lock the door, hunch over my desk, and feed until there was nothing left. ("Feed" was the only word for it.) This part of the procedure usually took about three minutes. That left me plenty of time for the next sequence of subterfuge: to disconnect the phone and lower myself with elaborate care onto the little strip of carpet between the bookshelves and the printer (there was just enough room to lie flat there). My mother-in-law was the first person I ever heard use the expression "I died" to describe the experience of a midday nap. Then, I thought it an arresting figure of speech. But I never really understood it until I became pregnant. Those fathomless naps of early pregnancy, from which I would awake be-numbed from the back of my skull to the bones in my heel, were each a delectable little death. Of course, as in all resur-rections, it's the rising again that gets to you.

A popular bumper sticker reminds us that "All Mothers Are Working Women." So, too, it needs to be said, are all expectant mothers. For in pregnancy, particularly the first trimester of pregnancy, a woman's body is performing the internal equivalent of high-impact aerobics. The pregnancy manuals tell us, for example, about "increased blood circu-lation." But what of the means required to achieve this end? What kind of energy must it take to manufacture and pump a third again as much blood as a body is accustomed to con-taining (the kind that leads to a near-death experience whenever one is lucky enough to lay down one's head)? My friend Mary was a strict vegetarian before falling pregnant with her second child, when her cravings for burgers outstripped her scruples. "What on earth are you doing?" asked her husband, genuinely alarmed at the sight of Mary devouring a Big Mac. Mary paused briefly between bites. "I'm knitting a placenta," she explained.

By my second pregnancy, I too had some perspective on the enormity of the physical exertions demanded by placenta knitting. So that when my husband would ask, "What did you do today?" I was satisfied to answer (if somewhat quietly): "I constructed some fingernails" or "I hooked up the small intestines . . . And what did *you* do?" For me such graphic reminders of what my body was up to made bearable the exhaustion, the nausea, the bloating, the soreness. It was still painful, of course. But it was a constructive sort of pain—pain as a means to an end.

Somehow, this notion of significant suffering is easier to grasp in relation to childbirth than in any other context. Here the painful period is acute and finite and its culmination—the newly birthed baby—spectacularly vivid and apparent. Pregnancy is different because the effort is so wholly inner and invisible. And for those who do suffer under its weight (for we need to remember that there are many women who do not), the experience is diffuse and open-ended. Most women feel worst during their first trimester, so that when the onslaught abates, the "reward" remains many months beyond reach. One is left stranded in the no-woman's-land of the twelfth or fourteenth week of pregnancy, often without even the consolation of a signficant lump to show for oneself.

Childbirth, at least, has witnesses. Whether a woman's birth attendants can or will do anything to ease her pain is perhaps less important than the certainty that they will bear witness to it. By contrast, in early pregnancy—a labor of at least equal magnitude—there can be no audience. The drama is entirely offstage, the main player a deaf-mute with gills and a tail.

By the time I was expecting my third child, I felt I had taught myself how to be pregnant, how to deal with the blows it dealt me creatively and, yes, even constructively. I started taking it like a woman—slowly, gently, and with an almost fierce deliberation. Yet still I wonder why the learning curve needed to be so steep. Why is pregnancy left to each woman to thrash out for herself? How is it possible to come to the experience so full of expectation (in every sense of the word) yet so empty of the necessary frames of reference?

At least part of the problem is that our society propagates a ridiculously positive myth of pregnancy. I think of the covers of the books that were my pregnancy bibles, both of them bestsellers. The first, Dr. Gordon Bourne's *Pregnancy*, was recommended by my obstetrician. It is a thick English reference work written for the express purpose of preventing women from sharing their pregnancy experiences.

Today's pregnant woman, Bourne writes in the preface, "is extremely vulnerable to the many old wives' tales, horror stories and unfounded advice which continues to surround motherhood, and there is no comprehensive work to which she can turn to relieve her anxiety and answer her questions. This book is a genuine attempt to fulfil this need."[4] The book's cover is an equally genuine attempt at damage control. In soft focus, it depicts "today's pregnant woman" wearing an empire-waisted gown with puffed sleeves, knitting.

The second book, the breezy *What To Expect When You're Expecting*, written by a mother and her two daughters, in many ways presents a refreshing contrast to Bourne's ponderous paternalism. Yet the expectations to which the title refers are the same familiar territory of physical signs and symptoms, only rather longer on "tips" and "advice" and mercifully shorter on medically defined morbidities. The cover of my edition featured an athletic-looking woman in a vibrant jumpsuit, smiling broadly and dancing.

To an extent, these two images present the entire spectrum of approved role models: a pregnant Barbie (for traditionalists), or a pregnant Barbie's little sister (for trendsetters). If I ever write a book about pregnancy, it will feature an ungainly thirty-something academic in a crumpled jacket, lying prone on a stretch of industrial broadloom. Or possibly a skinny woman with a potbelly wearing stretch pants and devouring junk food. One thing's for certain, if anybody's knitting anything, it's going to be a placenta.

At some primal level, pregnancy is the definitive incarnation of "womanliness." And for many women, pregnancy genuinely does represent femininity in its fullest and most majestic flower. These women experience their pregnant bodies as powerful, seductive, eminently worthy of worship. They carry their young as a steamship carries its cargo, gracious and invincible. My friend Diana was one. She shunned the dowdiness and drapery of traditional maternity clothes. (It's hard to feel like an Amazon in a Peter Pan collar and shirring.) Instead, she opted for jewel-like colors in clingy fabrics. One of her favorite outfits was a fuzzy green sweater that hugged her lump like the skin on a new peach. Under it, she wore a pair of extraordinary aquamarine tights. In the presence of Diana, the force of gravity itself seemed humbled. The way she floated through even her last trimester, one began to wonder whether she was carrying a baby or a bag of helium.

Women like Diana do indeed "bloom" during pregnancy. Their skin glows (the increased blood supply again, say the books), their hair shines. They acquire the requisite layers of subcutaneous fat in just the right places. Yet for every woman who revels, goddess-like, in her pregnant body, there is another who feels downright grotesque. The prevailing mask of expectant motherhood suggests that there is something aberrant about such women, as if the failure to bloom hints at some intrinsic perversity of spirit.

The view that a rotten pregnancy is a form of psychosomatic maladjustment should not really surprise us. In our mother's generation, doctors were still telling women that menstrual cramping was "all psychological," and the cataclysm of pre-menstrual events we know now as PMS was not acknowledged by the medical profession until the 1960s.

The sad and strange fact of the matter is that women continue to ignore or deny the sanctity of their experience and to reject the omniscience of their own flesh. We would rather learn women's business from a schoolmaster or a shaman—anything but a witch, anything but a woman. Deep down we are just like Dr. Gordon Bourne, and we have the same horror of "old wives' tales." Unlike him, however, we have met the old wives. And they are us.

Yet the conspiracy of silence about the physical discomforts of pregnancy persists even into the information age, and even among ourselves. My friend Shari, twenty-nine and pregnant with her second child, was hoping it would be different the second time around—that she'd gain less weight, want more sex, feel and look less like an armored truck. Well, she didn't. "What is it with these women who claim they 'love' being pregnant?" she asked me recently. "Do they 'love' feeling bloated, or not fitting into their clothes? Do they 'love' trying to roll around in bed like a beached whale? Do they 'love' not being able to tie their shoes or clip their toenails?" Like most of us, Shari would have loved to "love" her pregnancy. And the fact that she didn't made her feel wrong and guilty. Clearly, she wasn't doing it right.

A few nights before the conversation quoted above, while Shari and I were at a restaurant with other friends, she excused herself from the table during the entree and was gone a long time. I found her in the ladies' room, bent over the sink. "It's no big deal," she called out brightly. "I'm not sick or anything." She explained that she'd been having attacks of dizziness off and on over the past few weeks.

During the course of the meal, the same thing happened three or four times, to Shari's intense annoyance. Each time she returned to the table, she assured everyone she was fine now. On our last expedition to the ladies' room, a young girl in a black beaded miniskirt paused to observe. (At this point Shari was seated on the toilet, her sarong-style skirt most unceremoniously in disarray, her head between her knees.) The girl glanced around, as if to make certain there were no spies listening, tilted her head towards mine and whispered "Pregnancy sucks!" She pointed conspiratorially to an ever-so-slight bulge beneath her beads. And vanished.

A few weeks later, when blood tests failed to locate a cause for the dizziness, Shari's doctor diagnosed the difficulty as "anxiety attacks." He told her she should try to relax. Well, maybe he was right. I mean, of course he was right. After all, we should all try to relax. Yet the explanation of the girl in the miniskirt seems more real. All kinds of weird things happen in pregnancy which no one can really explain, and it helps to be reminded of that, to be assured that the condition itself confers its own special brand of physical and emotional lunacy. Confronted with the chaos, Shari's doctor decided

that there must be something wrong with her. What the social critic in the ladies' lounge decreed was that there was
something wrong with the mask. Her statement was pure
sedition. No wonder she whispered it and fled.

Would pregnancy "suck" less in a different social and cultural environment? In one, just for starters, that acknowledged and celebrated the centrality of motherhood to all
human endeavor? One that valued the unique labor of
women who mother as the highest form of professional
achievement? One that had the courage to assess the toll of
motherhood on an individual's resources, and the honesty to
mourn the sacrifice? One that regarded the carrying, bearing, and nurturing of children as both an awesome privilege
and a fearsome burden? Yes, I suspect that, under such conditions, the experience of pregnancy might be vastly different. Obviously it wouldn't feel any better, but the meanings
we would collectively (and therefore personally) make of
those feelings would be infinitely more complex and gratifying.

Nothing is so painful as the pain that cannot be acknowledged, the pain of which we are (for whatever reasons)
ashamed or that we construe as weakness or aberration. Or
even worse, as something to which we are somehow not entitled. I am continually amazed at how often I hear women
apologize for their pain, as if the admission of suffering were
somehow unseemly or unwomanly. This bizarre machisma
takes many forms. One of the most typical is the appeal to a
personal lowest common denominator: "I have a friend who
had to spend her entire pregnancy confined to bed/bent
over the toilet/in continual agony from backpain/on the
run from her abusive husband, so I consider myself lucky."
It's reached the point where, whenever I hear women talk-

ing about "luck," I get an uneasy feeling in the pit of my stomach.

Aileen Allen, a participant in a study conducted on the transition to motherhood, was a perfect case in point. She told me she considered herself "lucky" in her pregnancy because she experienced no morning sickness. "I was sick in the afternoon and at night," she explained, "but I was lucky—never in the morning." Another informant, Vanessa Williams, initially described her pregnancy as "perfect—I was really lucky." Later she confided details of two weeks of breakthrough bleeding, back problems severe enough to require physiotherapy and ultrasound, and a gastric reaction that saw her lose weight into her seventh month. Was this really Vanessa's idea of perfection? Or anybody else's, for that matter? Sure, it could have been worse—much worse. She might have miscarried, she might have developed carpal tunnel syndrome, she might have delivered in her twenty-fifth week. In the same way, most people would much prefer a bad bout of gastroenteritis to a bad bout of cancer, but one would hardly characterize diarrhea and vomiting as "good luck."

The fact is, the question "What did I do to deserve this pregnancy?" cuts in two directions at once. On the one hand, there is the sense in which every pregnancy is a bona fide miracle, for which the only appropriate response is abject gratitude. From this point of view, women's obsession with luck—their reluctance to be seen as whining or nit-picking—is quite comprehensible. Every woman who manages to carry a healthy baby to term *is* lucky. And when one weighs the means against the end, there is no question how the scales will tip. Nine months of discomfort, even nine months of acute suffering, are a small price to pay for an entire human being.

In ultimate terms, pregnancy is truly a state of grace. Yet the fact remains that, as human beings who are women, we live our lives both "ultimately," with our minds and spirits, and "existentially," with our blood and bones. It is possible to recognize and celebrate pregnancy as miracle at the same time that we acknowledge and honor it as a time of trial, an hour of intense need. The mask of expectant motherhood shows us the transcendence without the terror; it keeps us from telling what we know, because some of that knowledge is unpleasant and messy and scary.

During my own first pregnancy, I was eager to be a "good patient," careful to avoid troubling my obstetrician with too many questions. Every month he asked me, "And how are you feeling?" And every month I replied with a smile, "Oh, I'm fine thanks. Really good." And he would beam. And I would beam back. Leaving us both in a state of pristine ignorance. I have heard the same story from countless women. "Oh, I wouldn't want to bother him with that," they say. "He's a busy man—look at the size of that waiting room!"

And there is no doubt that the protocol of the typical prenatal visit discourages confidences. In fact, it discourages any interaction at all beyond the kind of small talk normally associated with cocktail parties. My own doctor had a manner of asking "Any worries?" with the same briskness with which people call to their neighbors "How's it going?" Both questions have deep ritual significance. They are each ways of saying "I know you are there," and this is a message pregnant women and neighbors alike genuinely need to hear. But as a means to draw forth information, such questions are absurdly ineffective. Indeed, the subtext to both might reasonably be translated as, "I know you are there, but please, spare me the details!"

In the middle of my last pregnancy, my husband and I

separated. I had two preschool children and no job, and (owing to the complexities of my husband's finances) was declared ineligible for social security benefits. When my doctor queried my change of address, I explained only that the children and I were now living alone. "Do you have support?" he asked. "Oh yes," I replied confidently. "Any worries?" "No, no, I don't think so." I said it slowly, as if miming a mental process.

In my last trimester, my husband and I had an eleventh-hour reconciliation—or perhaps "ninth month" is more like it. At around the same time, and not at all coincidentally, I developed high blood pressure. "Any worries at home?" asked my doctor. "Oh no," I replied. And within seconds I was weeping helplessly. And soundlessly.

I am rather ashamed to admit that he was wonderful. He listened. He asked questions. He may even have put an arm around me—I don't remember exactly. And then he did something: he called my husband at work and explained that, owing to my high blood pressure, I would need an entire weekend of bed rest, with no child-care or domestic responsibilities. If this was not possible, he would admit me to the hospital immediately. I was astonished. (My husband was furious. But, a doctor himself, he was incapable of disregarding a specialist's orders. He did as he was told.) I was mute with gratitude. The "neighbor" had metamorphosed into a friend. It had taken nearly twenty-seven combined months of pregnancy, but it happened.

The mask of expectant motherhood cracked wide open for me that day. The grin that had stretched so tightly from ear to ear finally fractured into a thousand useless fragments. And behind it, in the hot rush of tears so long dammed up, I felt little elation, even less liberation. I was relieved; but more than anything, I was ashamed. I remember walking back through that waiting room—even more crowded now that I had selfishly consumed someone else's time slot—thinking that I had failed. Or worse, that I had been seen to have failed. It had mattered to me, my status as the "perfect patient," much more than I had realized and much, much more than I was able to admit.

I guess the point of this parable of the pregnancy Good Samaritan is that it takes two to make a meaningless relationship, but it may take only one to make it otherwise. Or, to put it a different way: it takes two to keep a mask in place, but only one to let it fall.

In our mothers' generation, it was marriage that marked the dividing line between girlhood and womanhood. For today's women, for whom the boundaries of wedded life are a good deal more permeable, it is motherhood—which may or may not include marriage—that now separates the women from the girls. In the wake of this monumental shift, pregnancy has emerged as the major transitional event in most women's lives. This phenomenon was noted by sociologist Alice Rossi nearly twenty years ago, yet we remain a long way from assimilating (let alone assessing) its implications.

While the popularity of marriage shows no decline whatever, its position as the pre-eminent "tie that binds" has undergone a series of drastic demotions. As a society, we still profess to "believe in" marriage (putting it somewhat in the realm of the tooth fairy). Yet, individually, we are about as likely to remain coupled till-death-us-do-part as we are to remain with the same employer until retirement. It happens, sure. But the odds are increasingly against its happening to you, and even more against its happening to your children and grandchildren. Like a videotape or a good vasectomy, marriage has become conveniently reversible. To this extent, it has ceased to function as a significant rite of passage. By definition, such a rite entails the passage through a door from which there is no return (or at least precious little hope of it). For our mothers and grandmothers, marriage was like that. Wedlock, as the name implies, was a life sentence—whether for better or for worse. But today the economic and social chains that wedlocked women to their husbands are, if not exactly shattered, at least corroded beyond repair.

As a culture, we now set great store by what we call "options," and we are generally loath to limit them. Marriage remains a big step for many couples because it is a huge excluder of options (most of them social). That other serious commitment, joint home ownership, is seen—quite correctly, I believe—as an even bigger step because it excludes even more options (most of them financial). Yet in both of these transactions, the options one suspends are ultimately fully redeemable. So that if things "don't work out," for whatever reason, one can cash in one's chips and go home. (Home is the place where recovered options can be reshuffled and contemplated anew.)

The multiplication of our options for lifestyles, relationships, education, and professional attainment marks a cataclysmic break with our parents' generation. Even more significant than the actual number of choices available to any given individual is our expectation that we are entitled to choice (and lots of it) and the value we place on that entitlement. Keeping our options open is not simply a survival tactic in times of crisis; our generation, like no other before, views options as an inalienable right of adulthood.

And then comes a baby.

Writer Nora Ephron once observed that a baby is a hand grenade tossed into a marriage. I suspect that, for the present generation of parents, a baby is, in fact, a hand grenade tossed into the very center of our improvised lives, blasting our most cherished expectations of entitlement to pursue and undo our choices until we get it right. For anyone to whom the only good option is an open option, parenthood is about as scary as it gets.

For women, there is a small, bleak window of opportunity for "reversing" a pregnancy. There is none whatever for reversing a baby (apart from the unspeakable). By contrast, men—although they cannot reverse paternity—can, with astonishingly little effort, elude parenthood. Reflecting common usage, to "father" a child is a matter of biological circumstance. To "mother" a child is a matter of behavorial consequence. While fatherhood remains one option among many, motherhood revokes the whole concept of free will. It is with motherhood that the myths of equal opportunity and shared autonomy bite the behavioral dust. All men [sic] are not created equal, because some of us have babies. And when we do, you can see those options slam shut faster than a teen-ager's bedroom door.

Thus, motherhood acts as a great divide along two separate dimensions. At one stroke, it separates females in some irreducible, mammalian sense from males. At another, it separates the women from the girls. Which is not to suggest for a moment that motherhood is the sole—or, heaven forbid—the best, means of achieving adult female status in the human community; only that it is the most commonly experienced and most universally recognized way to do so. From this point of view, a pregnancy carried to term is the most powerful and transcendent rite of passage a human being can experience.

It's no wonder the English speak of women as "falling" pregnant. A sheer drop is more like it.

Laboring Under Delusions

As a woman lives, so shall she give birth.

—Gayle Peterson

Why didn't any woman tell me? Why didn't they tell me it would be like a fuckin' bomb exploding? Why didn't anyone tell me the truth?

—Fiona Place

WHEN IT COMES TO CHILDBIRTH, American women today are among the best prepared in the world. More than half of all pregnant women attend Lamaze classes, for example—the most popular but by no means the only form of childbirth education available in the United States.[1] This figure suggests a truly astounding overall participation rate. Our knowledge of the physiology and anatomy of childbirth is prodigious, our grasp of the theory and techniques of pain management superb. We are among the first women in the history of human civilization to approach childbirth fearlessly and with positive anticipation.

Yet most of us emerge from the experience battle scarred, bewildered, and betrayed. The most common postnatal reaction remains (after sheer relief) sheer disbelief. Disbelief at the extent of our ignorance. Disbelief at the extent of our arrogance. Disbelief that we could ever have imagined we could control and direct our responses, that we could "man-age" the pain. In short, most of us emerge from the experi-ence of childbirth in a state of shock, aghast with the discovery that everyone "prepared" us, but no one told us the truth.

In the course of a mere generation or two, we have come a long way in our thinking about childbirth. Yet the real gains for women have remained disconcertingly few. Our expectations about childbirth have skyrocketed along with our access to information. But the fact remains that the vast majority of these expectations will ultimately crash to earth anyway. And when they do, we will experience the drop as even more precipitous, the moment of impact even crueler. In a profound (and profoundly disconcerting) sense, the more women are "taught" about childbirth, the less we seem to know. And, in far more cases than we are comfort-able admitting, our little bit of knowledge is a downright dangerous thing.

At the same time, it would be a mistake to underestimate the positive gains that have been made in our understanding of childbirth. Whatever else our society may have gotten wrong about motherhood, we have at least acknowledged that the quality of a woman's birthing experience matters. And that it matters not only on a personal level, to individu-als, but publicly and to the culture at large.

The shift in childbirth consciousness over the last genera-tion or so has been enormous. The experience of my own mother-in-law, now in her seventies, was not at all unusual among her contemporaries. The eldest daughter in a family of nine, she reported having "no idea" what to expect in labor and delivery at the time of her first child's birth in Australia. She was so shocked by the pain of childbirth that she vowed she would never go through it again. (Somewhere along the line, her resolution weakened. She went on to bear nine more children.)

My own mother, who gave birth to her first child a decade later in the United States, had a drastically different experience, yet her level of "preparation" was precisely the same. She knew nothing of the physiology or the experience of childbirth and, in keeping with the prevailing cultural norms, preferred to keep it that way. She was instructed to trust her doctor and leave the rest to the miracle of modern medicine. She did so—to the extent of surrendering consciousness altogether—and my sister was duly delivered under a general anesthetic. My mother later described as "wonderful" the experience of waking up to find a freshly bathed and swaddled baby whom the nurses assured her was her own. She couldn't wait to do it again!

For their times and places, neither experience was unusual. A mere generation ago, the experience of childbirth remained firmly "in the closet" of the culture at large. It had no place at all in public discourse, any more than did other aspects of the female life cycle. Like menstruation, lactation, and menopause, childbirth for most people—women and men alike—was shrouded in a persistent cloud of unknowing and disavowal. They were "women's business," shameful business, wrapped in euphemism and embarrassment. We perhaps underestimate the extent to which this remains the case today. A mere fifteen years ago, my fiancé—an educated and well-traveled man in his mid-thirties—was horrified to discover a box of my tampons left unconcealed on the bathroom counter. When I stopped laughing (I sincerely believed he was joking), I was forced to consider the tenacity of taboo, and the possibility that the notion of "the curse" was no mere anthropological artifact.

While social policy can change fast, cultural consciousness evolves slowly, as individuals and families grapple painfully with imposed norms that often feel wrong even when they sound right. This seems especially true in matters related to sexuality. In my own case, for example, while my mind is fully committed to a joyous acceptance of my children's sexuality, my gut remains wary. I find the sight of a masturbating child almost unspeakably difficult to accommodate. While I do not condemn, I do the next best thing: I deny.

I've noticed the same tendencies operating in the way our family speaks about its genitals. We haven't even given names to most of the interesting bits: the clitoris, the labia, the scrotum and testicles. They're there, of course, but to listen to us speak about our bodies, you'd never know it. The few times I've resolved to redress this bizarre lexical imbalance, to speak the unspeakable, I've ended up tongue-tied and indecisive. When my oldest daughter was three, I tried a casual lesson in female anatomy and came away quite pleased with myself. Later, when I heard Anna singing "I'm a great big uterus, creeping through the jungle," I had second thoughts (understandably, I think).

Our lingering discomfort with what our generation euphemistically learned to call "the facts of life" reveals many eloquent and uncomfortable truths. A friend in her fifties tells a familiar story of a conscious vow to instruct her prepubescent daughter fearlessly and with love. She spent days rehearsing her account to ensure that it contained, as she so memorably put it, "just the right blend of anatomy and poetry." When she finished, she made sure to ask whether her daughter had any questions. "Just one," the girl replied, a little hesitantly. "How does the baby get out of your mouth?"

The maxim "knowledge is power" is among the first

principles of our assumptive world. Observers since McLuhan have noted that, whereas previous generations clung to the belief that truth would set them free, our own generation believes that information will do the job. And for us, that "freedom" is no Zen-like letting go, no relinquishment of will. In fact, we see it in terms that are precisely the reverse. To us, freedom is not a negative quality—the absence of coercion—but positive, pro-active. Within the context of our individual destinies, we have come to see freedom as the capacity to coerce or, to put it in more neutral terms, the ability to exert control. In this sense, we are members of a profoundly cybernetic culture dedicated to the entwined values of communication and control.

There is no doubt that seismic shifts in childbirth consciousness over the past generation or two reflect a genuine "information explosion." And empowerment for women, at least in relative terms, has been a direct and gratifying consequence. The days when women entered the delivery room literally bound (and sometimes gagged), when complete ignorance was considered a mark of modesty and good breeding, are well and truly over—and good riddance. As we have dedicated ourselves to communicating about childbirth—about its physiology as well as its psychology—our control over its processes has increased exponentially. Indeed, the velocity of this particular shift of the pendulum has been astonishing. From childbirth as punishment to childbirth as privilege is a quantum leap in our social consciousness, an example of "reframing the situation" for which any motivational guru would give her mantra. The transforming power of this shift in the lives of individual women has been profound, to the extent that it is not uncommon to hear expectant mothers express eager anticipation for childbirth, in much the same spirit as athletes training for a big event.

In a 1956 article entitled "Conditioning for Childbirth," C. Tupper wrote, "What might we not achieve if we could persuade women to prepare for labor with the care that we train our young men for war, or even with the care that a prize fighter gives to preparing for a fight."[2] Today, Tupper's vision has more or less become reality. We too have our coaches, our drills, our cheers and affirmations. Clothed in tracksuits and sneakers, we study our musculature, acquire and hone our techniques, put ourselves and our partners through our respective paces. Our vocabulary includes terms such as "endurance," "going the distance," "breaking through." We discuss posture and positioning, movement and massage. We learn to isolate and exercise muscle groups that our mothers never even knew they had. And, like champion runners and swimmers, we develop an almost obsessive concern for breath control.

Childbirth has become not only an athletic event but also an aesthetic one, an arena for personal expression, an opportunity to sculpt transcendence from a fleshly medium of blood and bone and muscle. "As a woman lives," wrote psychotherapist Gayle Peterson, "so shall she give birth."[3] At one level, the idea is inspirational. At another, it is a throwing down of the gauntlet: a dare. In childbirth, we have come to believe, we show what it is we are made of—and we hope like hell it'll turn out to be the right stuff.

In all of this, it is perhaps easy to overlook the greatest shift of all in our social construction of childbirth: that the "object" of the enterprise is no longer seen to be the end product (the baby) but the process itself. Which is not to suggest that we have lost sight of the fact that birth is about babies nor to suggest that the well-being of the neonate is sacrificed to the existential moment of the mother. On the contrary, it is because we can now be so confident about a successful outcome in the form of a healthy baby that we can afford the luxury of examining birth as a process imbued with meaning in its own right. Ironically, our intense interest in "natural childbirth" is in this sense a direct consequence of the triumph of medical technologies and techniques.

As sociologists Mira Crouch and Lenore Manderson have pointed out, with the physical dangers of childbirth mostly removed, "what remains is childbirth as the socially and biologically quintessential womanly act."[4] Indeed, Crouch and Manderson argue that, for many women, the experience of childbirth is increasingly regarded as a culmination rather than a commencement—at least as much an act of "proclamation" as it is of procreation.[5] This tendency is especially marked, they suggest, among the increasing numbers of women who view motherhood not as their central, "socially mandatory and naturally fulfilling career," but as one role among many. So that the less of her identity a woman invests in the ongoing activities of mothering—the full-time, exclusive care of children and home—the more she invests in the one-off experience of childbirth.

This preoccupation is reflected in the nature of the support services provided for pregnant women, which focus almost exclusively on preparation for labor and delivery. It's as if motherhood itself were only a possible side-effect of the birth. This may be one reason why so many pregnant women confess that, although they know they will have a baby, they can't quite believe it, can't quite visualize it. Researcher and educator Margaret Gibson described this peculiar suspension of maternal disbelief as a "common theme" among contemporary women. As one informant explained,

"We can't believe there is a baby at the end of it, we see the pregnancy as an end in itself. The birth was all I thought about. I could not relate to a baby outside my body."[6] Crouch and Manderson report similar findings, perhaps best exemplified by the woman who, upon beholding her newly delivered son, gasped "Look! It's a baby!"[7] My own case was almost as absurd. When the midwife shouted excitedly that the baby's head had appeared, I responded with genuine curiosity, "Where?"

I have been comforted to discover research suggesting that the struggle to transform the "intellectual" baby of pregnancy into an emotional reality is a common experience. Now that I worry less about my own sanity, I have started to worry more about the sanity of the systems and structures that may be exacerbating the problem (if indeed they have not created it outright). How, I wonder, can we have "prepared" ourselves to the point where we can clench our pelvic floor on demand while executing three different styles of breathing, yet still regard the prospect of a baby as a somewhat outlandish contingency? Our generation can boast with confidence that we know everything about birthing babies. It's the stuff that happens afterwards—the experience of motherhood itself—that we find mysterious, inconceivable, even "unreal."

Childbirth is one day, more or less, in a woman's life; motherhood is forever. Yet like gawkers at the empress's new maternity outfit, we steadfastly resolve not to notice. Other observers have noted that we devote more care to the licensing of automobile drivers than we do to preparing adults for parenthood. It's a point worth pondering. Limiting our education for parenthood to prenatal classes is a bit like limiting driver education to defensive strategies for get-

ting out of the driveway. No one would dispute their useful-
ness, but they can only take you so far.

The hidden curriculum of the average prenatal class con-
tains a host of questionable, possibly even delusional, assumptions about the experience of mothering. The first, as
we have seen, is that childbirth itself should be regarded as
the culminating experience of pregnancy. In fact, as anthropologist Robbie Davis-Floyd has pointed out, childbirth is
an act of commencement, a rite of passage that involves the
creation of not just one but four new members: "the new
baby, the woman who is reborn into the new social role of
mother, the man reborn as father—and the new family unit
they form."[8] It's a drama of unprecedented power, not only
in the lives of women but in the life of all humanity. Yet few
women in our society ever anticipate this transition, let
alone receive instruction on how to "breathe through" its
pain. We recoil in horror to think that our mothers and
grandmothers entered the labor ward in utter ignorance of
the ordeal that awaited them. And rightly so. Yet I suspect
the depth of our own ignorance of the afterbirth experience
is greater still, and more dangerous by far.

Yet the ironies do not end here. As we have seen, despite
the increase in knowledge women have gained about the
processes of childbirth, most of us emerge feeling more like
a plucked chicken than a phoenix rising from the ashes. All
the information, all the techniques, all the "understanding"
we have gained, we realize, are no bulwark against the sheer
brute force of the birthing body. What Fiona Place calls the
"fury of childbirth" is what the classes and the books never
tell us, and what women conceal even from their daughters,
their sisters, their friends.[9]

The reason, some maintain, is simply that the experience
is too cataclysmic, too overwhelming, too horrifyingly

unique to convey in words. Yet I suspect the reasons for our collective conspiracy of silence have more to do with the politics of gender than with the poverty of language. Ultimately, our desire to sustain an illusion of control over the bodies of women is greater than our desire to confront reality.

Where previous generations of women approached childbirth expecting the worst—and usually got it—today's generation suffers an even crueler indignity. Having been led to expect the best, we experience the disjuncture between anticipation and reality as a yawning psychic chasm from which we emerge not only battle scarred but angry. For many women, that anger is directed at themselves; it is experienced as guilt, a sense of shame that we have failed to perform to standard. Others experience the anger of betrayal, of violated trust in the authority of experts once implicitly believed.

"This was nothing like the books had said," writes Debra Adelaide accusingly in a powerful account of her own birthing experience.[10] It is a sentiment echoed repeatedly in the fascinating emergent literature devoted to unmasking the experience of childbirth, to which Adelaide's collection *Mother Love* is a notable addition. Another is Anne Lamott's hilarious and moving *Operating Instructions*, a journal of her first twelve months of motherhood. "Lamaze is great," notes Lamott, "and the classes totally educated [my birthing partner] and me about what to expect," but "next time, if there is a next time, I will get the epidural upon registration."[11]

Among other things, this literature demonstrates that it is possible to convey women's experiences in words, and that what has formerly gone unspoken is not necessarily unspeakable. Where clinical language has failed, emotive, metaphorical, and ironic language can prove astonishingly evocative. But we need ears to hear it and a willingness to allow the voices of experience as admissible evidence.

"Twenty-four hours after the first contractions," Adelaide remembers, "I was buried in pain and such palpable emotional exhaustion it was like trying to breathe and move under the dead weight of the earth itself."[12] And it is precisely this that "the books" never reveal: that however sharp and ready and powerful our minds, our birthing bodies are even stronger. They are capable of steamrollering our best-laid birthing plans and whatever confidence we may once have had in the concept of mind over matter. Control is a joke. There are drugs—which many women forgo not out of ideological conviction but because, at the crucial moment, they lack the wherewithal to request them—or there is outrageous agony. So much for managing one's options.

"I am completely overwhelmed by fear and bewilderment," relates the laboring narrator of Fiona Place's short story "Apocalypse Now." "No one ever warned me it would be like this. No one. No one ever told me to expect such fury. In the slightest fragment of a second I pass from thinking someone can change things to realising there is nothing anyone can do. There are no longer any choices. I am locked in."[13] A few hours earlier, exhilarated by the first stirrings of labor, she had made a point of ordering a takeaway Thai feast before settling down to watch a video. Sheila Kitzinger would have been proud. It was all proceeding to plan: uncomfortable but not unmanageable, painful but bearable—just barely, but bearable. Then the bomb hit.

Brenda Walker, another contributor to *Mother Love*, confides truculently that she doesn't attend prenatal classes. "I don't want all their information," she declares.[14] Subversive? Definitely. Arrogant? Maybe. On the other hand,

Walker may be onto something. Which is not so much that ignorance may be bliss but that too much of "their information" may produce its own brand of folly. Certainly the evidence suggests that the tangible benefits of such information are at best elusive, and at worst nonexistent. In a rigorous, population-based study of 800 women, Judith Lumley and Stephanie Brown concluded that prenatal class attendance had no impact whatever on women's experience of pain, use of pain relief, extent of interventions, or level of satisfaction and emotional well-being.[15] Theirs was the second large-scale study to reach this conclusion, which the authors understandably described as "depressing."

It should come as no surprise that women who are encouraged to regard childbirth as a performance, a testing of their maternal mettle, will suffer some degree of performance anxiety. In a study of "the importance of doing a good job during labor and delivery," Marlene Mackey found women equated "managing well" with perceptions of self-control and participation. In her sample of sixty-one women, which did not differentiate between first and subsequent labors, more than 60 percent rated their childbirth performance as poor. Most women did not feel "in control" during childbirth. Most did not believe they adequately "participated in" the experience of their birthing bodies.[16] Either something is dreadfully wrong with these performers, or something is dreadfully wrong with the script they're following.

Many of the women I have spoken to identified loss of control as even more frightening than the physical pain of childbirth. As an informant in Mackey's study put it, "If I started losing control or screaming or whatever—that would be very hard to take. I would be ashamed of myself if that happened; if I wasn't a good patient; if the nurses were saying—'oh my God, shut that woman up.' "[17] The importance of "taking it like a woman"—stoically yet obediently, inoffensively, and with all the rough edges nicely turned in—looms large in the childbirth consciousness of most middle-class women today.

Then again, this same quality looms large in our experience outside of childbirth, too, and perhaps this is one sense in which it is true to say that as we live, so do we give birth. For there is no doubt that we are, par excellence, a generation of consummately Controlling Women. Owing to the nature of the lives we increasingly lead—lives overstuffed with commitment, responsibility, and achievement—we control in order to survive. No wonder it sometimes seems to our partners and friends that we survive in order to control. I am convinced that our obsession with control is part of the fallout of the feminist experiment in which we are all, wittingly or not, the first fully participant subjects. To change the metaphor slightly, the compulsion to maintain control appears to be the fine print of the unspoken social contract giving women full charge over their own lives—a responsibility additional to, and in no way absolving us from, our traditional duties. The net result of all this is that, in the space of a mere forty years or so, we have gone to bed as hired girls and woken up as grown-ups. And not only as some of the grown-ups, but as *the* grown-ups in a social household of men and children clamoring as insistently as ever for care.

To a significant extent, in other words, we are "control freaks" because we have to be—because so much, surely far too much, depends on our ability to keep all the balls in the air at once. For a variety of excellent, empirical reasons (which are explored further in chapter 6), contemporary women have a particular and perhaps even unprecedented horror of the loss of control, and our approach to childbirth is heavily freighted by this fear. Add to this the implicit promises that control is not only desirable but achievable, and you have a tower of false expectations just waiting for an excuse to topple.

Whether a woman "succeeds" in childbirth is nevertheless largely a matter of definition. The question is, whose definition? Somewhere along the line American women have united in the quest for the holy grail we call a "good birth." We all agree that this will entail something empowering, transcendent, and challenging (suggesting something between a revival meeting, say, and a triathlon). Yet when it comes to the nitty-gritty of exactly what the "good birth" should look like and, even more to the point, what it should feel like, all consensus breaks down. When you consider the range of opinion on the matter, both among "experts" and laypeople, this is hardly surprising.

Can a birth still be termed "good" if it makes you feel like your flesh is being roasted from your bones? And what about if it doesn't hurt at all? Does that still count as "good," or is it just the first in what will probably be a long line of maternal sell-outs?

At one end of the spectrum are those who equate a "good birth" with a pain-free birth. At a certain level, it's a definition with which it seems almost ludicrous to take issue. After all, if a man passes a kidney stone, does he try to breathe through the pain? And if did, would we regard him as heroic and worthy of emulation or just plain dumb? Epidurals and other forms of anesthesia are there to help us, our doctors assure us. And who are we to argue? Indeed, *how* are we to argue? For reasons that are screamingly obvious (with the emphasis on *scream*), most of us have needed precious little persuading that science might be a better way forward than clutching the sheets and shrieking for Mammy. After all, given a safe technological means of reducing or even eliminating the hard labor of laboring, who in their right mind would choose to do otherwise?

Well, lots of people, actually. At the other end of the spectrum are those for whom the conjunction of the words "safe" and "technological" implies an obvious contradiction in terms. According to this camp, the good birth is not "pain-free," but rather (and rather confusingly) "pain relief-free." Self-righteously, they describe themselves as adherents of "natural childbirth," implying that anything less is "unnatural," "artificial," and therefore physically (and probably morally) dubious. Proponents of managed childbirth tend to regard devotees of natural childbirth as members of a kind of lunatic maternal fringe (like women who breast-feed their first-graders or who treat infant colic with aromatherapy). Proponents of natural childbirth, for their part, tend to regard their opposite numbers as politically incorrect opportunists who have not only sold out to the patriarchy but are wusses to boot.

Although I'm caricaturing a bit here, the point remains valid: As a culture, we are divided and ambivalent about what constitutes "the good birth." (In our grandmothers' day, the issue was much, much simpler. Back then, the only good birth was a live birth. Period.) I am convinced that this confusion has engendered a keenly felt insecurity and an unprecedented level of "performance anxiety," particularly in first-time mothers. One unfortunate consequence is that we have become increasingly judgmental and downright bitchy about other women's choices. Another is that we are secretly every bit as judgmental, if not more so, about our own performances, suffering untold anguish, disappointment, and even self-loathing as we struggle to negotiate the inevitable gap between the real and the ideal (whichever ideal we happen to have chosen).

One thing is certain: under either of the prevailing definitions, the vast majority of women will "fail" at childbirth. For the incidence of truly "natural" births is probably roughly equal to that of truly painless births—which is to say, negligible. Most of us will experience some form of intervention whether we start out resisting it or insisting on it. And virtually all of us will endure some form of suffering—even if it is "only" the first penetration of the epidural catheter, or the nausea and vomiting that may set in immediately postpartum.

The woman who has given birth with an epidural or via cesarean section will worry that she has somehow cheated. By contrast, her sister who endures the full nine yards of biblical travail—having bought into the mythology that all you really need for the pain is breath control, a sincere partner, and batteries for the Discman—will feel that she has *been* cheated. ("How could they have told such lies?" she'll bristle one moment and, in the next, berate herself for her perceived failure of nerve. "If only I'd been woman enough," she'll ruminate, "I would have not only borne it—I would have grinned and borne it.")

Both of these women entered the labor ward assuming confidently that the experience of childbirth was something they, or their medical attendants, could control. And both emerged with that assumption (among other things) in tatters. It is not really difficult to understand why. In fact, for all their differences, both childbirth models share a common core. Essentially, both define a "good birth" as a controlled birth—whether that control is imposed externally (via medical interventions) or internally (via breath control, creative visualization, or what-have-you). A "bad birth" is one that has somehow gotten out of control: one that refuses to progress according to plan, that pitches a curve where it's least expected, that defies our best efforts to rehearse and predict. A "bad birth," in other words, is what most of us have and none of us expects.

The ways we assess and "score" our birth performances can tell us much about the values we hold dear. And among women who report positive birth experiences, it is clear that the issue of (perceived) control is valued highly indeed. We seem to need to feel in control so badly that we will accept any scenario, however illogical or downright grotesque, that will allow us to preserve the illusion. Which is why a woman rendered semi-paralytic by an epidural block, whose baby needs to be forcibly extracted by vacuum suction, can remain convinced that she has successfully maintained control over her childbirth experience. In such cases—increasingly the norm in American maternity hospitals—childbirth is rendered a virtual spectator sport, with the woman a distanced onlooker in the struggles of her own flesh. As anthropologist Robbie Davis-Floyd has noted, "So common is the use of epidurals today that many childbirth professionals are calling the 1990s the age of the 'epidural epidemic'"[18]. In Davis-Floyd's own study, conducted in 1992, some 60 percent of women received epidurals. In other recent research, the figure has been as high as 80 percent.[19]

The trend itself could not be clearer. What it portends—particularly for women undergoing the challenging transit to first-time motherhood—is nevertheless fraught with ambiguity. Or so it seems, at least, to this observer. As the word "epidemic" suggests, there are many who view the epidural option as yet another attempt by institutionalized medicine to gain control over women's bodies—to anesthetize (as it were) not only our pain but the power with which nature has endowed us to survive that pain and to emerge triumphant. Almost against my better judgment, I must admit that I have a great deal of sympathy with this view. Personally, I found my three births—all of them epidural-free—to be the most powerful and the most empowering experiences of my life. They were also revoltingly painful and frequently downright terrifying. Well, go figure. When I ask myself "Okay, so was it worth the pain?" I am sure of only thing: that this is the wrong question. In my experience, what I gained from childbirth that was "of worth" was inextricably bound up with the pain—and literally unimaginable without it.

Having said all that, I can see with equal clarity that forcing (or perhaps even simply encouraging) women to undergo truly "natural" childbirth may be simply another way of reinforcing the machisma myth: that "taking it like a woman" means pretending it doesn't hurt, that you don't need help, that no sacrifice is too great for the sake of the family (meaning everybody else except you). The epidural experience may give a woman a false sense that she is "in control" of childbirth; but there is nothing false at all about the connection between epidural anesthesia and pain relief. Say what you will about their political correctness, epidurals work. And missing out on a little potential ecstasy seems to many a small price to pay for eluding certain agony.

For myself, I remain a card-carrying agnostic in the childbirth wars. On the issue of "natural childbirth"—despite moments when my faith has seemed strong—I remain unsure whether I really believe in it or not. On the subject of the "epidural epidemic," however, I must confess to an equal skepticism. I remain passionate in the conviction that women need to be presented with real choices (rather than being shunted toward one foregone conclusion or another), and that the diversity of our experiences needs to be acknowledged at least as urgently as our common core. But beyond this, when it comes to the subject of childbirth, I remain decisively, indeed almost militantly, ambivalent. I suspect I am not alone in this.

In a study I conducted in 1995 on the transition to motherhood among older (age twenty-eight and up) professional women, one participant, Sarah, confided during a postnatal interview that her only anxiety about childbirth was "when to ask for the epidural." When Sarah's doctor reluctantly decided to induce her, he felt guilty and full of regret. But she was euphoric. "He kept apologizing [about the epidural], but I said, 'Don't!' I'd heard so many stories about people asking for it too late, and then it's no good. I was scared about not having it soon enough!" Sarah passed most of her laboring hours in pleasant conversation with the attending midwife, who related the story of her own "horror" birth (a twenty-four-hour ordeal culminating in an emergency cesarean section). By contrast, Sarah was so relaxed that she was able to catch a quick nap between the crowning of the baby's head and the arrival of her doctor some twenty minutes later. With the baby literally poised between two worlds, Sarah's birthing partners, including her husband and both her parents, took the opportunity to adjourn for a tea break. They reassembled on arrival of the doctor, who, waking Sarah from her peaceful slumber, instructed her to hold her breath. Sarah felt "one little pull" as the vacuum extractor did its work.

Sarah later described her childbirth as "perfect." She had experienced about thirty minutes of active labor before the epidural took effect, and maintained that she was glad to have had "this half-hour of knowing what it was like." "But," she added firmly, "that was enough." Yet, compared with the "high" of her labor, the birth itself was a disappointing anticlimax. In fact, far from experiencing "this great overwhelming feeling of maternal love," Sarah reported feeling "incredibly tired and just dreadful." The five hours of epidural anaesthetic left her in a state of physical shock: cold, clammy, and shaking so violently that she was unable to hold the baby, let alone attempt to feed her. Later, when the physical symptoms had subsided, her emotional response remained flat. "I kept waiting for this great wave of maternal—I don't know what—that was going to hit me. And I kept thinking, 'I don't feel any different to what I was before—just a bit woozy, that's all.'" By 9:30 that night, when she went to bed, Sarah was still connected to a catheter and her left leg was still numb and heavy. She was not allowed out of bed the next morning.

It was interesting to me that Sarah, a high-ranking bank executive in her early thirties, could describe in such glowing terms a childbirth experience that left her physically and emotionally numb for days. Apparently, the desire to feel in control and "organized" (a repeated theme in her interviews)—a desire gratified by the scheduled, orderly induction process—was for Sarah the definitive dimension of the childbirth experience. Really, she had no wish for a transcendent birth, and no patience for the practice of "spiritual midwifery." She simply wanted it over and done with, and was thrilled to have achieved this with a minimum of drama. As far as her subdued response to the baby was concerned, she was disappointed but not overly alarmed. She was sufficiently well-read to know how variable such reactions can be, and she chose to ignore the possible link between the disembodied nature of her labor and the emotional aloofness she experienced afterwards. Overall, and despite the myriad medical interventions along the way, Sarah felt she had given birth "her way." And who am I—who is anybody?—to say she hadn't?

In an in-depth anthropological study of childbirth in the
United States, Robbie Davis-Floyd identified a significant
minority of women like Sarah, who "seem to judge most
situations by the degree of control they feel they can maintain."[20] Overwhelmingly, such women rate the experience
of epidural birth in positive terms, and report feeling no
need to give birth actively. They are happy instead to "bear
witness to the birth with their conscious and highly valued
minds." Not surprisingly, such women tended to be older,
more highly educated, and professionally employed—
increasingly the profile of the contemporary primigravida.
"They seemed to find their personal fulfilment in their professional identities, in mothering their children, and in their
relationships with their husbands."[21] As one woman commented, "I'd rather see the finished product than [experi-
ence] the manufacturing process."

Another participant in my own study, a self-described
control freak and high-achieving academic, was fascinated
by the experience of childbirth under epidural anaesthetic,
and was amazed and impressed at the efficiency of her birthing body. At the same time, she was alive to the irony that
she was a bystander in her own drama, and that, thanks to
the epidural, childbirth had become almost literally an out-
of-body experience. "They all kept congratulating me on
my progress," Jacqueline remembered with a giggle. "And I
kept saying, 'It's nothing to do with me!'"

At two-and-a-half hours, Jacqueline's labor was only half
the length of Sarah's, and she was also able to attempt some
of her own pushing. She succeeded only in expelling some
faeces (to her intense embarrassment) and was grateful
when an episiotomy was performed and the baby finally delivered by vacuum extraction. Unlike Sarah (who expected
to feel a great gush of maternal feeling), Jacqueline (who

expected "to look at the baby and think, well, nice, but now get me clean and organized") found the experience of beholding her newborn daughter to be "totally mind-blowing . . . I was really, really over the moon from the moment she arrived."

The experiences of women like Sarah and Jacqueline are something of an embarrassment to feminist researchers. According to prevailing theories of the patriarchal appropriation of childbirth, obstetric interventions like epidural anesthesia and planned cesarians cheat women of their "birthrights." For many researchers, the finding that a significant number of women actually welcome such interventions has proved a bitter pill to swallow. Davis-Floyd, for example, found that nearly three-quarters of the 100 birth experiences she studied involved willing (indeed, even enthusiastic) acceptance of what she terms the "technocratic model."[22] A staunch advocate of natural childbirth, she was understandably chagrined by this, the most significant finding of her study.

She admits, with impressive candor, "I have come to understand that even if those interventions come in forms that appear to me to disempower women as individuals and as birth-givers, they do nevertheless make women themselves feel not only powerful over the caprices of nature but also most fully participants in their culture"—a culture that celebrates not only the supremacy of technology but the associated values of predictability, orderliness, and control.[23] Ultimately, Davis-Floyd argues, the positively perceived childbirth experience of women like Sarah and Jacqueline is the result of "false consciousness." Basically, they only think they got it right. For myself, the issue seems far less clear-cut. After all, if a woman thinks she got it right, and feels and acts that way too, then what exactly is the problem?

As we have already observed, for women giving birth a mere forty or fifty years ago, the issue of "getting it right" was considerably less tortuous. If her labor and delivery produced a live, healthy baby, a woman had succeeded. The quality of her own personal experience tended to go unexamined, to the extent of repression and denial of the painful details. While no one would advocate a return to those dark ages of childbirth consciousness, with their reckless disregard for the dignity of women's experience, the "progress" we have made is at best an equivocal one. Today, we accept childbirth as inherently meaningful in its own right. Yet how, and to what extent, and for whom it is meaningful—on these critical matters of interpretation we remain uncertain.

Crouch and Manderson go so far as to argue that "dominant images of birth are no more effective now—in terms of their benefits for women—than they have been three decades ago."[24] Women's anxieties about childbirth, they suggest, are just as intense as ever. Far from being eradicated, they have merely been refocused. So that where our mothers and grandmothers worried about physical survival, we obsess about emotional style. Our mothers worried about whether they'd cope. We're more concerned with the quality of our coping, about how our performance rates. We worry about achieving the elusive ideal of the "good birth" or, as Crouch and Manderson put it, the experience of "immaculate parturition."[25]

And, now that we know about the importance of "bonding," we worry about the possible psychological fallout of a rotten birth experience for our babies, too. In fact, recent studies suggest that bonding with one's newborn is a good deal more complex than achieving a magic postpartum moment. The fabled surge of maternal feeling which women have learned to expect in the immediate postpartum period is highly variable, even among women who have experienced the most "natural" of natural births. Even more to the point, there is no evidence that an immediate bonding experience is a precondition for the growth of maternal feeling over time. Yet Crouch and Manderson found that the concept of bonding remains a key element in contemporary folklore about birth, "and many women feel disappointment and guilt in relation to the perceived shortcomings of their own birth experience and accomplishments in this respect."[26]

At the same time, research does suggest a link between uncomplicated births that require little medical intervention and the early experience of the kind of instant maternal rapture described by Jacqueline as "mindblowing." This is hardly surprising. A woman who has been ravaged by hours or even days of excruciating pain and anxiety, or one who has been so thoroughly anesthetized that (depending on the drug of choice) either her body or her mind is numb, is hardly a likely candidate for ecstasy. More common feelings range from simple relief that it's over, to indifference, to active resentment and rage. For women who have been conditioned to expect a soft-focus swoon, such responses are complicated even further by self-administered injections of guilt. It's a classic lose-lose situation, in which the only "reward" for a woman's physical ordeal is a further emotional ordeal.

"So?" I can hear my mother say. "It's unfair. Whoever said that motherhood was fair?" In her generation, probably no one. But in our generation, a lot of people—from Sheila Kitzinger, Ina May Gaskin, Dr. Lamaze, and a raft of other birthing gurus, to the teachers in the prenatal classes, to the editors of those relentlessly upbeat parenting magazines.

"Nowadays," writes Kitzinger in *The Experience of Childbirth*, "there is no reason why childbirth should involve suffering for any woman . . ."[27] Well, who could argue with that? Of course we shouldn't suffer. Heaven knows we don't deserve to suffer. But the brute fact is that the majority of us *will* suffer, either from pain or a surrender of some degree of control—to an extent that appears to have precious little to do with how conscientiously or thoroughly we did our birthing homework. Why is it that the experts never mention this? Why, in their repeated emphasis on control and "accomplishment," do they ignore altogether what is probably the most crucial factor of all in the experience of childbirth: luck?

When all is said and done, childbirth is largely a lottery. And "success" probably has more to do with the vagaries of timing, the baby's positioning, and the woman's innate physical endowments—matters of pure chance, all of them—than any of the variables we can control. I recognize that it is pure heresy to say so, and the ultimate in bad news, but there it is. Better by far to accept how "out of control" the experience of childbirth is, than to browbeat ourselves for our phantom failures or to wax complacent over some semblance of success. All other things being equal (and of course they very rarely are, but that's another subject), a woman who gives birth easily deserves as much credit for her "accomplishment" as a woman who moves her bowels easily. Which is not to suggest that the experience of childbirth is a purely physiological affair. Clearly—for human beings at least—it is not. Nor should it be. At the same time, however, we seem inscrutably reluctant to admit that childbirth is primarily something our bodies do. And that, inexorably, some bodies will be more equal to the task than others.

I speak as someone who—for very few reasons which

have anything to do with my mind or spirit—has had the good fortune to experience three "ten out of ten" births in a row. Each followed a similar and disgustingly uncomplicated trajectory, with intense but extremely regular contractions building to a nearly-but-not-quite-unbearable climax at transition, followed by a second stage of no more than five minutes' duration. Three or four good pushes and a few ear-splitting, guttural shrieks later, and it was all over. No drugs, no tears, no stitches. Each baby was happily breastfeeding within minutes. And yes, as the icing on the cake, I bonded like a bandit, gushing enough maternal emotion to service the entire neonate nursery. Makes you sick, doesn't it?

Naturally, the first time around I took full credit for this astounding performance (even the midwife was in tears). I knew very few women who had given birth, and, like most American women, I knew most of what I did from books and classes. Despite my "success," I was still astonished at the extent to which my sources had underestimated the pain, particularly that associated with the volcanic eruptions of the second stage (for which the insipid term "pushing" is probably the most ludicrous euphemism since the nuclear warhead "The Peacekeeper"). I was also shocked by the sheer volume of blood and gore, which the books had coyly termed "loss," and by the fierceness of my need for solitude. (To achieve this in a hospital setting is difficult, and in the end I was forced to barricade myself in the bathroom—hardly the ambiance I had pictured in my birthing fantasies.) My sources had depicted childbirth as a sort of social occasion, with lots of handholding and massage. I anticipated a get-together, not Gethsemane.

Nevertheless, I emerged from that first childbirth of mine with a profound sense of pride (which I attempted to conceal, I'm sure unsuccessfully) at having gotten it right, at having redeemed the disaster of my impossible pregnancy with a virtually immaculate parturition. With the wisdom of hindsight (a hindsight that has been informed by years of research, experience, and observation), I have grown considerably more modest. While my estimation of my cleverness has plummeted, my gratitude for the fateful toss of the dice that landed me with such a resilient body for childbirth has magnified immeasurably. I was blessed with a uterus that needed little prompting to do its stuff, a cervix with rather few nerve endings (internal examinations, for me, simply do not hurt) and a naturally stretchy perineum. (The midwife assumed this was the result of a rigorous perineal massage regime, an impression I mischievously failed to correct.) I was blessed, too, with babies whose size and shape was fortuitously proportioned to my own. All three babies were the same sensible weight, within an ounce of each other, with considerately compact head circumferences. What's more, they were, all three, in "textbook" position for birth, with heads and noses all pointing in the prescribed directions. As far as anesthesia was concerned, I was simply too wrapped up in my pain to consider it. My "bravery" was nothing more than the dread that someone might lay hands on me and make it even worse.

Other women, I have since learned—though their numbers are few—are even luckier. Some do not experience pain at all, only "pressure" or "movement." My friend Mary's first birth was like this. I remember the utter disgust with which she was regarded when, in an informal chat about our experiences of labor, she asked a group of friends "Would you really use the word 'pain' to describe it?" There was a steely silence. "No," someone finally answered. "I would use the word 'torture.'" The birth of Mary's second child, while much swifter, conformed more closely to the norm: it hurt like hell. She was aghast and, later, abject in her apologies. "I just had no idea," she kept saying to whoever would listen. While there were probably many factors that contributed to the difficulty of this second labor, Mary's degree of "preparedness" was not one of them. Heaven knows she was completely lacking in anxiety, given the ease of her first birth.

To a large extent, the illusion that childbirth is an experience that women can shape and control is just that—an illusion. It may be a slightly more attractive illusion than that under which our mothers and grandmothers labored (that childbirth is a necessary torment, God's revenge for Eve's original sin, best suffered and forgotten as quickly as possible). Yet it has the potential to wreak equal or even greater havoc on women's self-esteem, and on their confidence as new mothers. By attempting to extract forcibly the mystery that lies at the center of the childbirth process, we cheapen our experience. Being at the mercy of our bodies—as women in previous generations have had to be—is, thank heavens, no longer inevitable. Yet the "mind over matter" approach of Lamaze and related techniques can induce a false sense of security that the body and its primal powers can be (and should be) "conquered." Perhaps ironically, the more control we bring to bear, the more literally insensate we render ourselves. We may feel less ghastly for all this. But gone too may be some of the grandeur—the drama that comes of being caught in the grip of a lifeforce that is huge, inexorable, and utterly contemptuous of our puny attempts to rein it in.

Contemporary discourse on childbirth, in contrast with its exhaustive anatomical explicitness, is curiously cagey on the subject of pain. Indeed, a woman could read all the definitive popular texts, conscientiously attend her prenatal classes and listen with minute attention to her obstetrician's every word, and still come away with the impression that having a baby won't hurt much, or at least not terribly much. The notion is, of course, absurd. Normal childbirth is excruciatingly, outrageously painful, and ever since Eve every generation of women has known it. Except, possibly, our own.

There is no doubt that the increasing (and increasingly well-documented) medicalization of childbirth over the last century has played a significant role in this conspiracy of silence. As sociologist Vivien Nice has pointed out, "the once female territory of labor and childbirth has become more and more the domain of male 'experts'."[28] While such experts have amassed an extraordinary depth of knowledge through observation and analysis, their structural ignorance of the experience of childbirth remains fathomless. Increasingly, of course, women themselves are taking on the mantle of expertise, as both commentators and practitioners. Yet the legacy of centuries-old male medical dominance remains evident throughout even the most contemporary discourse; indeed, these deeply embedded assumptions continue to serve as the template for all but the most ardently feminist alternatives. The result is that a great deal of the information we receive about childbirth continues either to come directly from, or at least to be filtered through, authorities who really don't know what they're talking about, and who (often with the best of intentions) devalue and belittle those who do. Researcher Marlene Mackey relates the experience of a laboring woman frustrated beyond endurance by her doctor's unshakable insistence that he knew what she was feeling better than she did herself. "The doctor kept coming in there and saying, oh, you're not in that much pain. I was taking it pretty good, too, but when he kept saying that I got furious; I just started screaming, so I screamed all the way through until I had [the baby]."[29] An extreme example, perhaps, but one with which many woman can identify.

Medical expertise tells us everything we want to know about childbirth, except what most women want to know most of all: which is what it feels like. It is obvious to the point of banality that the experience of childbirth is something only a woman can know. Yet it is equally obvious that the women who want to know aren't asking, and women who do know aren't telling. When it comes to childbirth, the mask of motherhood has been as effective as any anesthetic in distancing what our minds can know from what our bodies can do. It ensures that, in our social discourse of childbirth, we conspire to hear no evil, see no evil, and speak no evil. It is relatively easy to answer the questions, "Why didn't my doctor tell me?" or "Why didn't the textbooks, the manuals, and the pamphlets tell me?" or even "Why didn't the prenatal classses tell me?" But the truly searching questions, the truly poignant questions, are "Why didn't I listen?," "Why didn't I look around me?" and finally, as Fiona Place asked: "Why didn't any woman tell me?"[30] Why indeed.

One answer—but certainly not the whole answer—is that we have capitulated to the siren song of the patriarchal obstetric establishment. "Trust me," they have whispered seductively. "Trust me and only me." And, like out-of-towners in a slick used-car yard, we have found ourselves doing just that. One woman I interviewed, a sophisticated, well-travelled, and rigorously educated professional in her mid-thirties, admitted that she found her obstetrician's arrogance "rather comforting." On her first office visit, he gave her explicit instructions to "ignore what other women might tell you." "If you have a question," he continued, "ask me. You have no idea how much needless anxiety these old wives' tales can cause." "Weren't you offended?" I asked. (After all, this was a woman who had had no hesitation describing herself as a feminist.) "Offended? No, I was relieved!" she replied. "It is confusing when everyone gives you a different story. I was just happy I had someone who was up on all the research, someone I could trust." At thirty weeks into her pregnancy, with her prenatal classes in full swing, she admitted somewhat sheepishly that she had never asked her mother about her own birth or those of her two siblings. "It just never occurred to me," she explained. "I don't know why."

Folklore has it that it was not always thus, that in the bad old days women were all too eager to regale both young and old with horror tales from the birthing chamber, the bloodier and the gutsier the better. I know of no research that has attempted either to verify or to refute this view of the way things were. Yet I find it difficult to believe that our mothers and grandmothers could have maintained so staunch an ignorance of childbirth if it had been freely and volubly discussed by their mothers and grandmothers. At the same time, it is probably true to say that, where previous generations may have publicized the pain in ignorance of the process, our own generation has not so much redressed the imbalance as simply reversed it. To reduce the experience of childbirth to a sex-linked trial by torture is a cruel disservice to women. Yet the fact remains that most women do suffer in childbirth, and suffer greatly. And most find that their pain is not peripheral to the experience, but its too, too solid core.

Acknowledging that unsettling truth may prove frightening, but how much more frightening it is to be struck unawares. Then we face not only the unspeakable physical pain, but the searing anxiety that something has somehow gone drastically wrong. I have never experienced any sensation more shocking than the contractions of active labor, with the possible exception of the second-order panic that what I was feeling couldn't possibly be normal or right. In that first labor, I remained standing in the delivery room bathroom for some five hours, clutching the cool porcelain basin, staring at my face in the mirror between contractions in dumb amazement that it hadn't yet melted away. I could hear my partner, my teenaged stepdaughter, and the midwife chatting outside.

I had made it as clear as I could, through teeth ground to a virtual powder, that I wanted no "coaching" or laying on of hands from anybody. It would have had as much effect, I could see, as loosening the victim's shoelaces at a hanging. Yet my sense of abandonment, of exile really, was nevertheless overpowering. I felt exactly as I had felt the time I nearly choked to death on a piece of steak in a dark, noisy, and incredibly crowded room, in which, even if I'd been able to scream, no one could possibly have heard me. I had the same sense then, as I did in labor, that I was going to die, and that everyone around me was too busy partying to notice.

What saved me from choking was intervention (thankfully, somebody finally did notice). But what saved me from childbirth was insight. I still can't say where it came from (heaven knows, not from my reading or my prenatal classes), but at some critical moment when I still had a couple of neurons firing I realized, complete with mental italics, that this was the way it was supposed to be. That the conspiracy of silence surrounding the pain of childbirth was just that: a con. That all the talk about "powerful urges" and "rushes of force" and "pressure" was mere poetic bullshit. The reality was not what they had said at all. The reality was this: childbirth was torment—not because my mind or body was doing it wrong but, astoundingly, because I was doing it right.

Strange as it may seem, this epiphany of hopelessness (which I now regard as one of the few moments of genuine insight it has ever been my good fortune to stumble upon) is what ultimately gave me hope. Without it, I could never have mustered the stamina and the will to continue that labor. I clung to the conviction that the pains in which I was drowning were not death throes but life throes—not a sign of something going horribly wrong but of something going no less horribly right. "I" was no longer in control, and I had been a fool and a dupe ever to believe that I could be. Something larger and infinitely more powerful than myself was pulling the strings. I could either let it do so, or I could die fighting. So I let it.

Ultimately, and unexpectedly, childbirth did prove a profound and transcendent experience for me. I was one of the lucky ones. Lucky, as I said earlier, in being blessed with a body as naturally good at bearing children as it is naturally bad at carrying them. But perhaps my greatest stroke of luck was penetrating quickly to the central paradox of childbirth: that the only way to gain control is to lose it, and that the courage to name the pain must precede the courage to bear it.

As I say this, I am acutely aware that the word "courage" has an old-fashioned ring to it. Heaven knows it's a concept you never read about in the birthing textbooks, a "strategy" they never mention in class. Yet confronting the experience of childbirth is arguably the most courageous act a human being can undertake. Precisely whom do we think we are protecting, let alone "preparing," by neglecting to mention this? Euripides' Medea—a woman for whom motherhood was rather spectacularly lacking in masks—made the point without mincing words. "They say that we lead a life without danger at home, while the men go to war," she observed. "But they are wrong. I would rather stand in the Hoplite ranks three times than give birth once."[31]

For all the promises of the pain-free, high-control, technologically assured birth of our own generation, the enormity of the childbirth challenge looms as dauntingly as ever. "In the long gullet of this labor," writes Anna Maria Dell'oso, "I have come to digest a contempt for the puny world of men. Even for the strongest of them, the marathon is only two hours, weightlifting but a few seconds of exertion. The average woman in her first labor will go six times the two hours of the marathon to give birth. There is no turning back, no dropping out of the race, not even the option of simply collapsing: once a woman steps into the great gullet, once she is squeezed in there by the big fist, something must be spat out, an outcome which is never any less than life or death."[32]

Today, our sensible, official discourse of childbirth assures us to the contrary that the labor ward is no place for heroics. Like Anna Maria Dell'oso, I beg to differ. Indeed, I am convinced that the labor ward (or the bedroom, the birthing center, or the neighbor's Jacuzzi) is precisely the place for heroics. And I am filled with despair that so few are brave enough, or bold enough, to say so.

The inexorability of childbirth to which Dell'oso alludes—basically, the fact that one does not so much "ride" contractions as get steamrollered by them—is yet another taboo in the official discourse of childbirth. Yet it is the single quality of the experience on which most women, speaking informally, seem to agree. The spooky sensation of being held hostage by one's own body—of being helplessly digested in a "long gullet" of pain—is precisely what the books and the classes try so strenuously to prevent us having. So that when we experience the inevitable, we feel we've failed.

Nowhere is this sad dynamic more evident than in the second stage of labor, with the onset of the "pushing" contractions that will ultimately (if one is fortunate) propel both baby and mother to release. A volcanic eruption is the nearest metaphorical approximation to a pushing contraction I can think of—at least as I experienced them. For me, the second stage was decisively signalled by an utterly uncontrollable and humiliatingly indelicate urge to grunt, a sound that bellied its way upward, as irresistible as orgasm and as pleasurable as a third-degree burn. I remained standing throughout much of this onslaught, although at the peak of each contraction my body was literally dragged to a squat, as if by some huge magnetic forcefield concealed below the blood-spattered tiles. I continued to cling to the basin like a life raft until a midwife, no doubt alerted by the accelerated fury of my grunts, bustled in to check "my progress." "Remember that enema I didn't want to have?" I gasped. "I want it!" She ducked her head under my gown and did something unspeakable with a gloved hand. "That's not a poo, love. It's the baby's head."

The fiction that the "urge to push" can be controlled and directed by sheer force of will (or brilliance of technique) is another bill-of-goods which women have been persuaded to accept—and a further arena for guilt and self-recrimination. In Marlene Mackey's study, one of the reasons women cited for their perceived "poor performance" in childbirth was "an inability to control the urge to push or an inability to push correctly and effectively."[33] By way of apology, one woman explained, "It's harder than what they say. Because your body is doing it; it's like, hey, I'm trying but my body is doing it, I can't help it."

I also experienced "pushing problems" in my first labor, and was instructed "not to push" for about 20 minutes because I was "not ready." (My "readiness" coincided precisely with my obstetrician's arrival on the scene—a construction of serendipity I was too confused to detect at the time.) Of all the mindless and unworkable instructions given to a laboring woman—including the invitation, mid-contraction, to "just pop up on the table, dear, and we'll have a quick look"—the withholding of permission to push is surely the most perverse. It's like admonishing an earthquake to stop throwing its weight around, or telling a tidal wave to take it easy. How deep in us must the desire to obey run that so many can even make a show of complying? In my own case, while all around me—including two male doctors, one of them my partner—chanted "Don't push! Don't push!," a wise and wily midwife leaned her face down to within inches of mine, locking my eyes in a mesmeric stare. "Breathe!" she hissed savagely. "Breathe!" This, I found, was something I could try to do—something for which my body could dimly perceive a precedent.

I have since learned that many women experience the urge to push in precisely the same unsavory terms: like shitting a pineapple, a basketball or, as novelist Kathy Lette once suggested, an entire block of flats. Yet this metaphorical richness has somehow eluded the official discourse upon which most women now, sadly, depend. Like most, I only discovered how "normal" I was in retrospect (which is when I needed it least).

I wondered, and wonder still, about the defiant persistence of misplaced modesty in our childbirth discourse. We can massage our perineums with glee; yet to suggest an experiential link between childbirth and defecation is clearly beyond the bounds of prenatal etiquette. In official settings, the ones dominated by medical models and clinical language, this failure of nerve reflects more than mere squeamishness. It suggests once again that what women happen to feel is a peripheral concern compared with what experts "know."

As long as this state of affairs persists, it seems to me, we will continue to fight a gallant but doomed battle for the elusive "good birth," however we have chosen to define it. Indeed, our determined willingness to suspend disbelief whenever the neat, official version contradicts the messy data of our own experience makes a mockery of the very notion of informed choice. Without realistic, accurate, and abundant information about how real women experience real labor, there is little point talking about "options" and "choices." As long as most of us remain consumers of rather than collaborators in a shared discourse of childbirth, the illusion that we are "in control" will assuredly remain just that—an illusion.

In childbirth as in the rest of life, it's not exactly that there is no justice. It's just that there's not a lot of it. (Heaven knows there are no right answers either, although under some circumstances we may be eligible for partial credit.) I suspect that acknowledging the tenuous relationship between even the best-laid birth plans and their clinical "outcomes" may prove more empowering than we think. And finally, I suspect that our grandmothers (bless their little cotton socks) were on to something after all. What is ultimately "good" about any childbirth is a well baby on the other side of it—and anything more is just icing on the birth-day cake.

In my own prenatal classes, our last session was reserved

for a "special guest"—a real live woman who had successfully given birth to a baby boy in that very hospital only a
week previously! Like every other woman in attendance
that night, I was on the edge of my seat as she told her story.
It was a decidedly upbeat one, to be sure—she had of course
been handpicked by the instructors—but the tale included
enough harrowing details to make it seem thrillingly "real."
She even brought along her baby as proof (I still remember
his name: Thomas). It did not strike me then as odd that the
first, and only, detailed labor story I had ever heard from
another woman came in the context of a hospital service, for
which my medical insurance would reimburse me. Seven
years and three babies later, I am convinced it is not only odd
but delusional. It is further testament to the bleak power of
the mask of motherhood that the extraordinary silences surrounding childbirth could ever have seemed otherwise.

Penelope Leach Meets Godzilla
A Chaos Theory of New Motherhood

> *When she becomes a mother, it is as if a woman must go deep in the bowels of the earth, back to the elemental emotions and the power which makes life possible, losing herself in the darkness. She is like Eurydice in the Underworld. She is pulled away from a world of choices, plans and schedules, where time is kept, spaces cleared, commitments made, and goals attained, to the warm chaos of love, confusion, longing, anger, self-surrender and intense pleasure that motherhood entails.*

—Sheila Kitzinger

> *Maternity, like housewifery, is a great leveller among women.*

—Ann Oakley

THE CUTTING OF THE UMBILICAL CORD is the official starting line both in the life of a newborn baby and in the identity of its newborn mother. It is hard to say for whom the adjustment will be greater, for whom the break with the past will seem more abrupt and the booming, buzzing confusion of the present more bewildering. Both newborns are recent survivors of a joint biological crisis of becoming. Of the emotional juggernaut that lies before them, they remain (for the moment) blissfully unconscious. At the same time, an awareness is dawning, however dimly, that a metamorphosis of indeterminate magnitude has already, irreversibly, begun.

The gaze of the smaller newborn locks into that of the larger one, the one from whom she's just been untethered. For many women, the bliss of that first meeting can be so blinding that nothing else seems to matter. The sense of exhilaration, of pride, of sheer amazement dominates everything. While there is much that remains bewildering in the background, one thing is certain: a miracle has occurred. And if the birth of a new baby is a miracle made flesh, the spent body of the mother is (for this moment at least) hallowed ground, a sacred site.

But not every woman experiences this thrill of transcendence. Many have been too medicated to feel much of anything. There are others who simply take longer to "switch on" to the good feelings, who are deeply disappointed (usually secretly) by the baby's sex, or whose life circumstances are too grim to admit much joy of any kind.

To describe the birth of a child as an "accomplishment" is a gross understatement. Ultimately, it is not a matter of how (or whether) a woman "manages" the birth, but the astonishing evidence of her body's creative genius: the exquisite perfection of newborn life. "Now I knew how God felt, after the sixth day of creation. Why he had done it," writes Debra Adelaide. "Had I also blasphemed?" she adds guiltily.[3]

This is typical. We have seen how the the mask of motherhood can muffle the voice we women give to our pain, our anger, and our frustration as mothers. Yet it works equally to mute our joy—to modulate and deny the wildness of our rapture, the powerful swelling of our pride. One way or the other, the mask dulls the intensity of our experience, allowing us to feel (or to be seen to feel) only so much and no more. When in fact the only blasphemy we can commit is to deny our entitlement to such feelings and to hesitate to celebrate—to broadcast—the enormity of what we have achieved. It seems to take as much daring to face and to name the ecstasies of mothering as it does the sorrows.

It's not really hard to see why. As the mask of motherhood unceasingly reminds us, motherhood is supposed to equal selflessness. (Is not childbirth itself literally an emptying out of self?) Celebrating a self that's not supposed to be there in the first place presents serious logistical difficulties. Yet, as Debra Adelaide's outrageous metaphors suggest, the "joys of motherhood" are no tepid affairs of sentimentality. They are fierce—and at times most fearsomely immodest. As Adelaide confesses upon beholding her newborn for the first time, "Together we had written the complete works of Beethoven, scaled the Himalayas, flown to the moon and back, then around the earth several times for good measure"; and again, "I was a god. I was a goddess. I was God. I had commanded creation, said *Fiat Lux*, and witnessed life in all its glory."[4]

The sheer intensity of such imagery is almost shocking. It's no wonder Adelaide muses on the possibility of blasphemy, for a more direct challenge to established authority is hard to conceive. For one thing, it asserts that the creation of new life is *ipso facto* something that women do, rather than something that happens to us ("falling" pregnant, as the English say, or "getting knocked up," to use our own vernacular) or something that is done for us ("Which doctor delivered your baby?"). Equally shocking, it suggests that childbirth is not simply a kind of endurance test (although it certainly is that as well) but a genuine act of heroism— indeed, that it is possibly the original, definitive act of heroism. So that instead of a new mother daring to compare her act of creation to the magnum opus of a "great master," it should perhaps be the other way around.

It is not that women have never before felt such things, I

suspect. Rather, what is new is the audacity to give voice to such feelings. The confidence, at last, to make much of what we have done, to refuse to take the miracle of motherhood in our stride and to rejoice noisily in its power instead of murmuring modestly that it was really no big deal. To see motherhood properly, I am convinced, is to see it heroically, which means making full acknowledgment of the pain, the dangers, and the risks and taking the full measure of glory for its exquisite rewards. When we consider the inaugural maternal experience—the journey we call childbirth—the epic nature of the undertaking emerges with startling clarity. The drama of childbirth foreshadows both the pain and the power implicit in the journey ahead. Thus, it can function as a kind of prism through which the wider experience of motherhood is refracted.

All human groups celebrate the birth of a newborn baby, which is absolutely right and fitting. Yet in our own culture, acknowledgment of the newborn mother remains perfunctory at best. "This distinction," writes Kathryn Rabuzzi, "seemingly so obvious, demands attention. Worldwide, this difference informs symbol systems otherwise vastly different from each other. Being born is everywhere celebrated in myth and ritual. Giving birth is quite another matter. Often it is simply ignored."[5] The implications of this cultural "oversight" are profound. Richard Seel, among other researchers, has suggested that the lack of "reintegration rituals" for new mothers may be a major cause of postpartum depression.[6] It is a view with which many women would instinctively agree. The problem is not the enormity of transition—or, more accurately, not simply the enormity of the transition. It's that the transition is experienced as enormous in personal terms, yet it remains socially invisible. The point is that women pay a huge price for motherhood (albeit usually willingly and even happily), yet we allow our contribution to be seen as trivial or worse. So that instead of acquiring the prestige of the philanthropist or the power of the big-time investor, we adopt a collective and apparently transcultural cringe.

Like the biblical merchant who gave all to obtain the pearl of great price, most women offer up to motherhood nothing less than their lives. Yet to hear the things we say — and equally importantly, to note the multitudinous things we don't — you'd think we were getting away with something. (Consider for a moment the widespread complaint that single mothers choose to bear children in order to increase their welfare payments. Admittedly, it's an extreme example. But there is nothing exaggerated in the assumptions it reveals: basically, that motherhood is some kind of females-only racket, an unfair biological advantage that boils down to an excuse for not pulling your own weight).

The claims of postnatal aerobic instructors notwithstanding, a woman's body is irreversibly altered by the processes of pregnancy and childbearing. (Author and mother of four Vicki Iovine identifies five sites of "irreparable damage": breasts, feet, navel, belly, and stretch marks.[7] If that sounds bad, try this on for size: A friend of mine swears that, after giving birth to her third, she can hear her labia clap as she walks down the hall. And I don't think she means in appreciation.) The adaptations to mind and spirit that will be made in the processes of rearing that child are no less violent. This transition, writes journalist Nina Barrett, is — like labor itself — far "longer, more complicated and much more painful than any of the books indicated. Just as my body had stretched and ached to bear this child, so my whole life — my relationships, my ambitions, and my self-image—would have to rework itself around the baby's presence."[8]

In her brave (and deliciously titled) *Motherhood: What It Does to Your Mind*, psychiatrist Jane Price emphasizes the universality of the experience of maternal rebirth. "Having a baby changes everything, both within and around a woman," she writes. "Nothing is the same again and that overwhelmed unfamiliarity is frightening to even the most capable and supported of people."[9] This trauma of reorganization, as the growing literature in the field forcefully attests, is a predictable and utterly "normal" response to the demands of new motherhood. Yet our reluctance to name the experience (except in diagnostic, stigma-laden terms such as "postpartum depression" or "baby blues") remains monumental, and our efforts to ready ourselves to meet it negligible.

For most contemporary women, then, the transition to motherhood is like some arcane initiation rite to a secret society to which the price of admission is (as with the birthing process that preceded it) an oath of silence. Only in this case, the silence is maintained not only outside the group but to a large extent within it as well, where communication, to the extent that it can be detected at all, proceeds obliquely in a kind of assumptive code only rarely decipherable in full. Motherhood in our society is, in short, a club so clubby that even its own members remain significantly estranged and ever anxious about their status, their entitlement to "belong." It strikes me that our collective response to the motherhood club is much like the Groucho Marx quip about not wanting to belong to any club that would have him as a member. Only in this case, rather than face our ambivalence about being accepted into the club, we deny to one another that there's anything there to join.

As a result, most of us are left to experience our transit over the great divide as a personal journey, a solo flight. For many women, although the significance of the journey remains unclear, the sense of having somehow "arrived" is unmistakable. As a participant in Robbie Davis-Floyd's study put it, "Some of the pride I had was having felt that I'd crossed a barrier, that I had joined the rest of the mothers in the world, and that I had joined my mother, in a sense. And that was an experience that nobody could ever take away from me."[10]

Indeed, often the first and deepest of the epiphanies of new motherhood involves a recognition of the irreversibility of one's changed status—that, as philosopher Kathryn Rabuzzi puts it, " 'Mother' is no longer her own mother—someone else—but she, herself," and there is no going back.[11] Sociologist Stephanie Brown and her colleagues found that the eight hundred–odd new mothers they studied needed no reminding of this primary fact. Overwhelmingly, these women—all of whom reported valuing the work of mothering highly and feeling responsible for its successful outcome—reported an acute awareness that "in becoming mothers they experienced irreversible changes in their own lives and their sense of themselves."[12]

The notion of irreversibility does not sit easily with a generation bred to exalt the virtues of control and the necessity of keeping one's options open. Indeed, to suggest that any aspect of human experience—even death itself—is not definitively irreversible challenges our most deeply held assumptions. We live in an increasingly deletable world, in which our lives—rather like beds—are made and unmade with often bewildering ease. Compared with any previous generation, we enjoy an unprecedented freedom to invent ourselves, to assume, in any given lifetime, serial incarnations. Marriages are formed and dissolved. Professional identities are chosen, discarded, or reworked, and economic realities follow suit. Even our physical sense of place has become diffuse, with ties to community or ethnic identity flexible to the point of negligibility. We move around a lot, shifting houses, moving interstate, traveling overseas for definite or indefinite periods. Whether one chooses to laud our adaptability or to condemn our restlessness, the trend towards a lifestyle dominated by options management is clear. Americans are not alone in this. In a news report I read recently, it was found that, for the first time since anybody's been keeping track, more Australians prefer to own cats than dogs. A dog, it is now perceived, is a big commitment. Is it any wonder that we find parenthood so scary?

After the birth of my first child, I remember a twice-divorced friend proclaiming (somewhat dramatically, it seemed to me), "Men come and go. But your children are forever." The more I think about it, the more I see her statement was not nearly dramatic enough. In the lives that most of us lead, almost everything comes and goes: partners, careers, finances, furniture, you name it. Our children, and our children alone, remain the only inviolate tie that binds us. Nor is there any doubt that that tie is infinitely stronger for women than it is for men. In this sense, motherhood is uniquely, and for many women disturbingly, non-negotiable.

Research into the transition to motherhood consistently indicates that women perceive a "loss of individuality" as they struggle to accommodate the continuous demands of newborn life. It's not hard to see why. The rigors of round-the-clock feeding, changing, cleaning, and comforting a new baby are shockingly underestimated in the official discourse on child rearing. The effects of prolonged sleep deprivation barely rate a mention in the standard texts (although chapter upon chapter is devoted to "sleep habits," it is only the baby's, never the mother's, that are deemed worthy of discussion or concern). Yet the problem of sleep is virtually epidemic among the mothers of young children. I am convinced that there is a direct, empirical link between widespread sleep deprivation among mothers and the stereotype of the "scatterbrained female." Not getting enough sleep, or getting sleep that is repeatedly broken, *does* scatter the brain. What's more, it confirms incontrovertibly a woman's lurking fear that she no longer has a place in her own life.

Of course, until very recently, few women ever expected to have a place in their own lives. The luxury of autonomy, the satisfaction of "calling the shots," the privilege of managing options—these were simply not a woman's lot. As long as women were born and bred to a life of service to others, the demands of motherhood presented no dramatic break with the past at all; they were continuous with it, a culmination rather than a crisis of expectations. One cannot experience a loss of self, as we have had occasion to observe elsewhere, unless there is a self to lose—or, to put it less crudely, if one's definition of self revolves around loss in the first place. Where "losing oneself" in the needs of others has been deemed socially and psychologically appropriate, it is experienced as intrinsically gratifying. To the extent that women of old were socialized to accept the "loss of self" as a precondition for feminine identity, in other words, they were admirably prepared for a seamless transition to the mothering role. To the extent that women of our generation have escaped such socialization—an extent that varies markedly according to socioeconomic status, ethnic origin, and level of educational attainment, among other factors—we approach the milestone of motherhood like strangers in a strange land. It follows that the greater the autonomy a woman enjoyed in her life before motherhood, the more acutely she will experience its loss once the great divide has been crossed. At the same time, such women love their babies every bit as fully and as fiercely as mothers have always done. Yet their perception of this attachment as a highly mixed blessing is both more conscious and more acute.

Experiencing ambivalence about motherhood is one thing. Expressing it—and, by extension, legitimizing it—is quite another. The mask of motherhood ensures that the face of ambivalence, however widely or keenly felt, remains a guilty secret. For women today, writes postpartum depression expert Carol Dix, "ambivalence is a large part of the game."[13] Equally striking is our reluctance to admit it, our skill at "skirting the issue." Yet Dix found that when she implicitly offered women permission to express their ambivalence—when she framed it, in the context of her questioning, as a "normal" response—their masks could disintegrate with disarming speed. "Have you begun to realize yet," she asked one woman, "that all you wanted was to see what it would be like to have a baby, play the game a bit? But you never appreciated the twenty-four-hour a day, seven-day a week commitment?" "Don't worry," came the quick response. "I've thought it already. There are times I wish I could send her back. Yet I don't. You know what I mean."[14]

Dix stresses that this woman was not depressed. Indeed, she seemed to be coping remarkably well with her new baby and her own new identity. On the contrary, the evidence suggests that the willingness to acknowledge ambivalence and uncertainty—the courage to let the mask drop—is not, like John Wayne's apology, a sign of weakness, but an indicator of unusual maturity and resilience. In a broad-based study of first-time motherhood, researcher Ramona Mercer found that it was only among older mothers (age thirty to forty-two) that such feelings were openly expressed. "It doesn't register that I am a mother," confessed one new mother of a baby girl. "And it doesn't really register that she is here to stay."[15]

Mercer notes that "statements like these are not easily made by those who don't have a strong ego and much self-confidence,"[16] adding that there were no comments of this type among the teenage mothers she studied. What she did not consider was the possibility that the teenagers did not express such feelings because they did not experience them, that the virtues of "strong ego" and "much self-confidence," which younger people tend to lack, may in fact impede adjustment to the mothering role. As it happens, other research has tended to confirm this hunch. More mature mothers will have the edge later on, as the child passes out of the turbulence of babyhood and its demands become less physical and more emotional. But in the initial period of adjustment, there is evidence to suggest that maternal maturity—as defined by strong ego boundaries, a clear understanding of one's own needs, and associated habits of autonomy and independence—can be downright disabling.

With the age of first-time mothers continuing to climb throughout the industrialized world, the problem takes on particular urgency. In our society, recent figures suggest, the onset of motherhood is dangerous to women's mental health. And it is likely to become even more so with further increases in maternal age and achievement, which are in turn associated with expectations of adulthood that are in many important respects inimical to mothering small children. On the far side of the great divide, in other words, women who have managed to "get a life" before motherhood are especially at risk. Those who have not, those whose expectations are either lower or more traditionally "feminine" (depending on one's point of view), will find the transitional terrain far friendlier and less fraught with hazards.

A woman accustomed to taking autonomy for granted may find the experience of newborn motherhood strangely claustrophic as she struggles to fit two people into a space formerly reserved for one. "In a very profound way, a woman who gives birth to her first baby is not 'herself' for a very long time afterwards," writes Nina Barrett. "No matter how much you wanted the baby, no matter how much joy you felt in her arrival, no matter how much household help you have, you still must, at some point, shed the skin of your old individual self and grow a new one with enough room for this small person-who-isn't-quite-an-individual yet." This skin-shedding, Barrett notes, while potentially "full of warmth and wonder," is fundamentally "abrasive and irritating."[17] Yet I suspect that guilt is the most painful abrasion of all—the creeping fear that, because such feelings are so rarely acknowledged and spoken of among women, because they contradict the prevailing mask of motherhood so completely, there must be something dreadfully wrong with those who experience them. Psychologist Paula Caplan observes that women continue to believe that "every mother except herself is serene. Each is certain that the rage, the physical exhaustion, the desperate wish for two consecutive hours of guiltless privacy are feelings that only she has—and that her women friends would believe something was disturbed or bad about her if they knew."[18]

Yet, as researcher Carol Dix insists, feelings of entrapment are "a normal, obvious, common experience after childbirth."[19] The perception that one has become in some ways both emotionally and physically disabled is no delusion. What is delusional is to deny, against all the evidence to the contrary, that such constraints "ought to" exist or even that they exist at all. "After the birth of my second child," Dix writes, "I felt as though I had literally grown another limb; a limb that was deadweight and had to be dragged around behind me every waking minute. I could not run to the store, go to an exercise class, or choose to meet a friend without arranging, planning, negotiating my time."[20] "Do I dare to eat a peach?" queries the narrator of T. S. Eliot's "Love Song of J. Alfred Prufrock." In what I now think of as the dog days of my own early motherhood, when even going to the toilet required advance planning, I used to muse on that famous line frequently. "Do I dare to have a poop?" I would find myself wondering bleakly.

When we celebrate the birth of a new child, we pay joyous tribute to the enlargement of the human circle. Yet with every "new addition" there are new subtractions as well, inevitable diminishments, "contractions" (to use a particularly apt metaphor) of a woman's life and range of experiences. In order to gain new life in motherhood, she must lose life. To mask the magnitude of this sacrifice with silence, guilt, and denial is to trivialize a genuinely heroic journey into selfhood.

It is also a direct cause of mental illness, ranging from mild depression to full-blown psychosis. Psychiatrist Jane Price has estimated that, using strict psychiatric criteria, 15 to 20 percent of mothers are affected by new episodes of mental illness within a year of childbirth. When those criteria are relaxed somewhat to include more transient experiences of distress, the rate rises to between 30 and 40 percent. In other words, women in the first year of motherhood are five times more likely to suffer mental illness than at any other stage in their life cycle and a horrifying sixteen times more likely to develop a serious, psychotic illness.[21] Research also shows that mothers of preschool children who lack supportive partners are at greater risk of clinical depression than any other adult group. Estimates of the incidence of mild depression among mothers with preschool children range from 30 to 80 percent.[22] Ann Oakley's research in the United Kingdom confirms the higher figure. Fully four out of five new mothers, she found, go through a reactive depression (often patronizingly dismissed as "the blues"). Seventy-five percent of the women she studied reported episodes of being "overwhelmed by anxiety," and two thirds admitted feeling "ambivalent" about their babies.[23]

There are several logical deductions that can be made from this alarming evidence. One is that the majority of women in English-speaking countries are simply too unstable, too selfish, or too immature to be good parents. Rather more plausibly, we can deduce instead that it is perfectly normal to experience some degree of "baby shock"—to feel anxious, depressed, isolated, and overwhelmed—in the early stages of mothering. Statistically, there is no disputing this conclusion. You can call the behavior undesirable, shocking, or unfortunate (or anything else you wish), but on the basis of these figures you can't possibly call it aberrant.

"What we have to consider is just what degree of abnormal behavior is really normal after birth," suggested a lay participant in Dix's study.[24] So far, however, the paradox has proven too subtle for the experts to grasp. Ironically, even the recognition of "postpartum depression" (PPD) as a distinct diagnostic category—a surprisingly recent phenomenon—has tended to pathologize women's experiences of motherhood, driving a false, clinical wedge between those who appear to be coping, and those who don't, between those for whom the mask of motherhood remains successfully in place and intact and those who (for whatever reasons) have let it slip.

Public recognition of PPD—indeed the very existence of the diagnostic label—has proven to be a two-edged sword for women. At the same time as this has bestowed legitimacy on the more acute forms of suffering, it has tended to pathologize the full range of baby-shock experiences. By elevating such experiences into a bona fide "disorder," we take them out of the realm of the everyday, encouraging the misguided belief that baby-shock is something other women have (and therefore, given our drive to get it right, something every woman fears). To this extent, the very existence of the diagnostic label has tended to drive the normal abnormalcy of early motherhood even farther underground. So that we cling ever more tightly to the mask, insisting to each other—and even to ourselves—that we've got it all under control, and that this awesome developmental drama, this tumultuous rite of passage toward female adulthood that we call early motherhood, is for us (though possibly not for some "depressed" other) a mere hiccup in the smooth progression "from here to maternity."[25]

"I can remember only too well wanting to throw my first baby out of the window," confessed one woman to researcher Carol Dix.[26] Research suggests that such destructive impulses are probably as universal among new mothers as shapeless days and sleepless nights. Yet to admit as much publicly remains a deeply subversive social activity. Indeed, even admitting to such feelings privately is more than many of us can manage. In my own case it was left to my uncon-

scious mind to expresss in dreams the thoughts I found literally unthinkable during the day.

In one dream, which I still recall vividly, I found myself
in a second-story bedroom hurling a pile of indistinct little
bundles one by one out the window. Eventually, it dawned
on me that the bundles were in fact neatly swaddled babies.
I was surprised, naturally, but determined to keep on with
my work. "It's a sad business," I remember thinking to myself in the dream, "but it simply has to be done." Even under
the veil of the dream, I found it essential to pass the emotional buck, comforting myself with the age-old excuse that
I was "only following orders"! Although I never forgot the
dream, it frightened me, and I was deeply ashamed of it.
Years later, when I finally had enough emotional distance to
talk about it with my friends, their reaction—to my amazement—was not revulsion at all. It was relief. Everyone, it
seemed, had had a similar experience, whether in the form
of a conscious fantasy or an unconscious one. None of us had
ever been clinically depressed; none of us, heaven knows,
had ever acted on any of our destructive impulses. At the
same time, each of us worried secretly about our "deviance,"
convinced that we were the only ones who had ever felt this
way.

The conclusion was a logical one, of course—thanks to
the efficiency of our masks. Despite our honesty in other
areas of our lives and relationships, when it came to guarding the illusion of motherhood, our vigilance was absolute.
It was as if we believed that by protecting the mask we were
somehow protecting ourselves. In fact, as many of us are beginning finally to learn, nothing could be further from the
truth. Wearing the mask of motherhood offers us about as
much "protection" as swaddling ourselves in plastic wrap.

The odds of being saved are much lower than the odds of being suffocated.

We have seen that, in our society at the present moment, the transition to motherhood is for most women a demanding developmental stage, punctuated by disturbing episodes of "normal abnormal" impulses and behaviors. The sooner we accept this truth, and the more willing we are to share honestly what we experience, the less vulnerable we will be. Our only protection, in other words, is to stop trying to maintain our invincibility. At the same time, however, it is necessary to examine the issue of what is normal and what is not from a wider perspective. We can say with certitude that there is nothing "wrong" with women who find the transition to motherhood a frustrating and difficult experience. We can absolve ourselves absolutely of individual guilt. But what of our collective responsibilities? Can it be "right" or "normal" that, as a society, we have constructed the mothering role in a way that quite literally makes women sick?

What distinguishes one experience of motherhood from another has little to do with "the way things are" and almost everything to do with our notions about the way things should be. In other words, it is not the behavioral routines associated with motherhood that are intrinsically problematic. Rather it is how we collectively choose to assign meaning and value to those routines. From this point of view, the enormous stress suffered by women in the transition to motherhood, while it may be statistically "normal," is in fact a form of acute cultural deviance. The lack of fit between expectations and realities of mothering may be experienced as a personal crisis, but it is ultimately a social tragedy.

Although comparative data are hard to come by, the available historical and cross-cultural evidence suggests that the meanings and values surrounding motherhood in our own society are riddled with contradictions, inconsistencies, and inaccuracies. All in all, our present "social construction" of motherhood is a fast-crumbling edifice that has rendered the central human enterprise of family-making uniquely unworkable. Yet our understanding of these structural imperatives that are not of women's own making has been persistently obscured by the stubborn or resigned silences that most assuredly are. As Stephanie Brown and her fellow researchers point out in their study of the transition to motherhood, the efficiency of women's masks of motherhood simply reinforces "the belief that there must be something the matter with them, rather than something the matter with the circumstances of their lives."[27]

What, exactly, *are* the circumstances of our lives as mothers? Studies of both "normally" and "abnormally" depressed women indicate three broad areas of concern. The first is the fact that mothering young children is carried out in isolation from what most of us have come to consider "the real world." This isolation is physical—entailing a virtual entrapment in one's own home—as well as emotional and intellectual. Its result is to render motherhood a socially invisible enterprise. The second condition of contemporary mothering is closely related to the first. The majority of women who mother young children, regardless of their marital status, function primarily as sole parents, assuming full charge of the demanding, continuous physical tasks associated with childcare and domestic duties. Several decades of feminist rhetoric notwithstanding, in most families the "help" that fathers provide remains exactly that: occasional assistance provided on request and often under sufferance. This is particularly so in the early years of a child's life, when its physical demands are most insistent. Third, because few women in our society have the opportunity for practical, hands-on preparation for motherhood, our knowledge base tends to be hopelessly abstract and theoretical. As a consequence, new mothers face a steep learning curve as they struggle to reconcile expectations with practical realities. For many women, the result is a lethal cocktail of loneliness, chronic fatigue, and panic. Under the circumstances, it would be amazing if we didn't freak out.

As sociologist Jesse Bernard observed more than two decades ago, "it is as though we had selected the worst features of all the ways motherhood is structured around the world and combined them to produce our current design." The result, she argued, was dangerous not only to the mental health of women but ultimately to that of our children as well. The isolation of full-time mothers and children into discrete domestic fiefdoms ensured that children had few or no responsibilities, drastically restricted mobility, and few safe public places to play. What's more, the emphasis on "child-centered" mothering seemed to be producing not happier, brighter, or more fulfilled children but brattier ones (at least in the short term). The result was still more emotional work for mother, Bernard argued. "Now that the mother's physical work within the home occupies relatively little time, the child makes correspondingly more demands upon her for attention. Responding to these demands can be as stressful as scrubbing a tub of laundry once was."[28]

For today's new mothers, who generally come to the task after a signficant period in the paid workforce, the stresses are even greater. Young women speak glibly of "giving up work" to care for their families, and may look foward to maternity leave as a kind of vacation. With enough household help and a cooperative baby, a period of "playing house" can indeed be a welcome break from the frantic pace of professional life. Yet for those with less involved partners, limited purchasing power, and more fractious infants—that is to say, for most of us—the sheer physical work of full-time motherhood more often proves overwhelming.

Brown and colleagues, in interviews with more than eight hundred new mothers, found that "caring for children was much harder than most women would ever have imagined prior to starting their own families . . . It took up practically all their waking hours—if they were not also employed outside the home—and often some of their sleeping hours as well, yet it so often went unacknowledged by their partners or anybody else."[29] Although women drastically underestimate the hard slog of motherhood, it is not the drudgery as such that drags us down; it is the fact that the drudgery is so thoroughly taken for granted. As Brown et al. observed, what women found really distressing was that their work at home "was only noticed when it did not get done."[30]

Recent research on postpartum depression has emphasized that it is not babies that "cause" women's depression. Rather, depression, whether clinical or otherwise, should be framed as a rebellion against the conditions that make mothering so extravagant a drain on our resources. In one study, for example, more than one third of the women identified by researchers as depressed did not wish to call their experience "postpartum depression." These women did not see their distress as linked directly, or even primarily, to their babies or their relationship with their babies. One woman, for example, spoke of her experience as "post-marriage depression." Another admitted readily to being stressed out by her baby's crying (the baby was eventually diagnosed as lactose intolerant) but recognized that this was only an added factor in the difficulties she was having in her marriage and with her stepson.

I suspect that, for many women today, it is not the experience of gaining a baby that proves unbalancing so much as the experience of losing their professional identity and the routines and perks associated with life as an autonomous, wage-earning grown-up. In our mothers' and grandmothers' generation, women (if they worked at all outside the home) tended to retire from the workforce upon marriage. Indeed, in many, many professions, they were required to do so. When in due course a woman produced her first baby, she had already had ample time to adjust to the slow and largely solitary rhythms of domestic life. Even before the appearance of the first baby, a woman was well and truly reconciled to the role of service provider and caretaker. She "looked after" her house and her husband. (In those days, people didn't talk about women "looking after themselves," let alone anyone else doing so. A woman didn't need looking after, presumably because she had no needs of her own to fulfill.)

Today's prevailing cultural mythology tells us, in the pithy language we reserve for bumper stickers and commercial sloganeering, "Girls Can Do Anything!" Maybe so, but the stubborn and politically incorrect fact remains that we cannot do everything. And more specifically, we cannot mother young children at the same time as we pursue a life of our own devising, or at least not in the way we have been encouraged to devise it.

Ann Oakley's observation that motherhood, like housewifery, is a great leveler among women is true not only at the sociological level but historically and cross-culturally as well. It is an uncomfortable truth that women in our age and our culture have conspired to deny. We delude ourselves that we will be different. We will buy our way out, we tell ourselves, with nannies and fast food and housekeepers. We will think our way out with positive affirmations of our own self-worth, or with child-rearing theories that promise to reveal "the secrets of happy children" or "the path to positive parenting" in ten easy lessons. We will love our way out, with revolutionary marriages and partnerships that promise liberty, equality, and justice for all.

Yet we find, most of us, that our most heroic efforts to remain in charge and on top of things are as nothing compared to the juggernaut of a young child's needs. The fact is, once a woman becomes a mother, her life will never again be quite her own, or in quite the same way. It's something few of us want to believe, let alone to discuss, let alone—dare I say it?—to celebrate. But it remains, nevertheless, the single defining feature of a woman's life on the far side of the great divide.

Many researchers have spoken of the transition to motherhood as a period of grieving for the "lost self"—the autonomous, center-stage life that most childless women have enjoyed and taken for granted. With the drastic changes that full-time motherhood entails, women feel their old selves have been somehow swallowed up or ensnared. Novelist Meredith Jelbart used the metaphor of "free fall" to describe the peculiar postnatal experience of disorientation and panic, and the same theme echoes in the growing academic literature. "I felt as if I was falling into a hole much like Alice in Wonderland," explained one informant. "Nothing made sense any more. I was not the boss, had no control, could make no decisions and every second seemed full of something or somebody apart from me. Within two weeks I had lost any sense of who or what I had ever been, and I began to feel as if I had died. My tears were a form of grief at losing the me I was familiar with."[31]

As we have already observed, it is those women who have been accustomed to being "the boss," to "having control"— and who mistakenly carry those expectations over into their new role—who tend to be the hardest hit. Yet, in my own study of the transition to motherhood among high-achieving, professional women, I found plenty of evidence of a host of other, equally predictive variables. Among the most obvious, yet least often examined, of these is the baby herself. The fact is, although all healthy babies are created equal, some are a good deal more equal than others.

Much nonsense is spoken about "good babies" (which in our social context means babies who sleep a lot), and there is no doubt whatever that women systematically misrepresent to one another the real labor involved in caring for even the most placid and undemanding of infants. Having said that, some babies really are easier to mother than others—and the range of "normal" infant behavior in the key areas of crying, sleeping, feeding, digestion, and social interaction is huge. Tragically, though, most new mothers have been schooled to believe that an infant's behavior is primarily a reflection of the quality of mothering it receives—again our obsession with control, rearing its ugly and altogether inappropriate head. As a result, women who have been dealt a particularly trying hand work overtime to keep their baby's real habits (or lack thereof) a closely guarded family secret, while women fortunate enough to have come up aces smugly take credit where none, or precious little, is due.

Sociobiological research is finally beginning to catch up with the wisdom of our grandmothers (which was, as it happens, also based on repeated empirical observations), and to "reveal" that our babies come to us as surprisingly self-contained little genetic packages, with in-built propensities toward good cheer or gloom, wakefulness or drowsiness, "self expression" (that is, crying) or relative containment. All babies cry, eat, and sleep, but how much, when, and with what degree of predictability are all very much in the lap of the genetic gods. Yet our entrenched modern belief that mothering maketh the baby persists against all evidence to the contrary—bolstered largely by the expert advice of childcare authors who, were they to discard the assumption that nurture will necessarily triumph over nature, would find they had a lot less to write about.

The result of all this is a veritable epidemic of maternal performance anxiety, coupled with a touching faith that there is a "solution" for every "problem" the child presents. "Where have I gone wrong?" was a question formerly reserved for guilt-stricken mothers of difficult adolescents. Today, our guilt begins virtually from the cutting of the cord. Does the baby cry "too much" or sleep "too little"? Is he sucking "improperly"? Has he developed a politically incorrect relationship with his pacifier? If so, we tirelessly examine our technique, consult our textbooks, and search our souls for the reasons. We cling to the belief that it is we who pull the strings. So if something is going wrong, we'd better pull them better or differently.

On top of the stress of our babies' demands, we take on the added burdens that come with assuming that we have somehow, ourselves, created these demands. Consider, for example, the now-prevalent notion that a baby's cries are necessarily a form of communication—a kind of urgent, though unfortunately inarticulate, message about unmet needs. As Penelope Leach puts it, "A baby cries for a reason; he needs something. If you can find out what it is that he needs, and provide it, the crying will soon stop."[32] It follows logically that mothers who can't find out what the baby needs, or can't provide it, are either incompetent, uncaring, or ignorant.

A couple of generations ago, most people believed just as firmly that babies usually cried for no good reason at all; and even that crying was healthful for infants, a way of "exercising the lungs." Thus, a crying baby was simply a baby doing what babies were supposed to do. One did what one could to soothe it—within reason—and when all else failed, one pushed the pram to the back of the garden and got on with the housework. There was guilt, of course—a bit. But there was also the sustaining conviction that "babies will be babies" and that life, in the meantime, must go on.

Interestingly, the latest clinical research on early infant crying behavior confirms these "old wives's tales." Pediatrician and best-selling author T. Berry Brazelton describes the colicky baby's cry as a signal that she is experiencing "sensory overload"—a physiological response that, given the infant's immature nervous system, is almost inevitable. According to Brazelton's figures, fully 85 percent of infants experience some form of so-called "three month colic." In direct contradiction to Leach, he goes so far as to imply that such "pointless" crying is actually beneficial for babies, allowing them to "blow off steam" at the end of a hard, developmental day.[33]

Lest parents be lulled into a false sense of security about any of this, the daily media are full of contradictory findings by a range of medical and behavioral experts. In one recent report headed "Tears a warning," a child psychiatrist claimed that "inconsolable" crying in infancy "could indicate parents who were not coping because of psychological problems or unresolved childhood trauma of their own, such as childhood abuse or neglect."[34] The only decisive conclusion one can draw from this range of expert testimony is that colic may or may not be a genuine physiological condition, which may or may not mean anything. For cryin' out loud, indeed.

Yet, as the anthropological record clearly indicates, there are other cultures in which babies hardly ever cry. During the day, they are carried about in slings and passed from hand to hand. At night, they sleep curled against their mothers' breasts, where they can suckle at will. In such societies, needless to say, there are no concerns about nap times or feeding schedules. There are also no cars, clocks, or "jobs," and people tend to concentrate on subsisting rather than on "achieving." Such a way of life has been shamelessly glamorized by certain pro-breastfeeding organizations, and by "alternative" experts who see no difficulty in grafting a third-world childcare ethos onto post-industrial, nuclear-family life. For me, the point is not that mothers in such cultures somehow "do it better" than our grandmothers did. But I would argue that both of these extremes of mothering are superior to our present angst-ridden agenda. For all their flaws, each offers a more coherent and efficient framework for integrating motherhood into the broader context of adult female life.

For women today, that integration is noticeably and alarmingly lacking. Mothering young children mixes reasonably well with full-time housewifery, especially to the extent that girls are socialized to adopt a service mentality. Motherhood also fits seamlessly into a traditional or tribal domestic economy, in which strict divisions of labor along gender lines are reinforced by economic necessity and ritual observance. For women in our society, however, although the urge to perpetuate the species is no less insistent, the place of motherhood in the wider social drama is increasingly unmoored and uncertain. Women mother because they want to mother, because they have to mother. Yet more and more they suspect that "real life" is elsewhere; that what they are doing in their work as mothers may be biologically and psychologically necessary, but somehow socially anomalous. The proportions are wrong. The balance is off. Yet the harder we strive to find a solution, the more elusive it seems.

Researcher Mary Boulton believes that most middle-class women continue to find motherhood meaningful, but have ceased to experience it as intrinsically rewarding. We harbor no doubts that mothering our children is infinitely worth doing. It's only that we'd really rather be doing something else. Perhaps this explains why so many of us are seeking a compromise, however uneasily, between our professional and maternal identities—between the "real world" of work, which is generally rewarding (though often not transcendentally meaningful), and the work of mothering, which we accept as meaningful (but experience as, at best, only intermittently rewarding). Interestingly, it was only the working-class (that is, non-professional) women in Boulton's sample who described childcare as "interesting" and their children as "enjoyable companions." Their better educated, better salaried sisters of the middle class tended to find motherhood less satisfying, and felt more alienated and in conflict in their roles. Yet, despite their dislike of the actual tasks of childcare, these women still described motherhood as a deeply fulfilling experience. The reason, Boulton argues, has to do with their depth of commitment to the "meaning" of the enterprise. Although the realities of mothering were grim, the theory, as it were, remained glorious.[35]

For these middle-class, educated, relatively high-

achieving women, rearing young families proved the ultimate test of their capacity to defer gratification. Although
they loved their preschool children passionately, most did
not really "enjoy" life with them. Yet their inner conviction
that the hard and often lonely work of mothering them was
an infinitely worthwhile endeavor never wavered. To me,
there is something both profound and gallant about this admission of ambivalence, and something enormously liberating as well. That it's possible to experience motherhood as
redemptive at the same time as one grapples (often badly)
with the tedium, frustration, and chaos of a child-centered
life. The fact that we can do this, that we *do* do this, is for me
evidence of the intrinsically honorable nature of womanhood. There is nothing particularly honorable about getting
on with a life that is rich in what Boulton calls "intrinsic
rewards." But beyond the rhetoric of greeting cards and
other cheap, mass-mediated sentiment, motherhood is not
such a life. The fact that we pursue it so conscientiously and
with such ardor anyway reflects powerfully both the will of
the species to survive, and the heroic capacity of women to
defer short-term gratification for long-term gain.

Women will confess things to researchers they wouldn't
be caught dead saying to each other, let alone to the uninitiated. As a result, most women begin their careers as
mothers with buoyant and extravagantly uninformed optimism. Although our society no longer preaches that women
will find ultimate fulfilment in mothering their children,
we now peddle the myth that motherhood is fun—a "lifestyle option" that will enrich, but certainly not revolution-
ize, our lives. Today's women are less and less likely to
regard motherhood as a "career," let alone a "vocation."
Rather, it has come to be viewed by many as time-out—

even a sort of holiday from the workaday drudgery of a "real" job.

"I'll give it three years," they say (or one year, or two, or six months)—as if at the end of this period the child will be somehow off one's hands and ready to drive itself to daycare or preschool. As if motherhood were a period of further study, or a year overseas, women increasingly enter into it with a sort of false conscientiousness. We start out determined to make the most of it while it lasts—and end up stunned to discover that the lifestyle option we meant to pursue is in fact pursuing us. This is no holiday. It's more like full-scale migration. As one informant observed in Ann Oakley's classic study *Becoming a Mother,* "It's really like living in a different world."[36]

Women grope for words as they attempt to explain the scope of the changes motherhood brings. We are still not used to speaking publicly about such matters. "I think it's more dramatic, the whole thing," one woman began. "It's changed everything more than I thought. I thought I would carry on as normal, but with a baby. But I feel different about lots of things . . ."[37] Research that has attempted to classify and dissect such changes presents a sobering and painfully precise picture that should be required viewing for every intending mother. Stephanie Brown and colleagues, for example, found that the majority of new mothers they studied did not have time to pursue their own interests (59 per cent), did not have an active social life (57 per cent), needed a break from the demands of the child (55 per cent) and were less confident since becoming a mother (55 per cent). More than a quarter bluntly admitted "they did not like their lives."[38]

Among new mothers who worked full-time for pay, Dr. Lorraine Walker of the University of Texas found the most common coping mechanism to be "a pattern of self-neglect."[39] The sacrifices such women make include not only leisure time pursuits, but such basic needs as sleep, food, and exercise. A similar study of the transition to motherhood among professsional/managerial mothers by University of New Mexico sociologist Beverly Barris came to equally depressing conclusions. Said one informant, a medical technician, "It was horrible . . . a horrible adjustment to make. I almost had a nervous breakdown. . . . I now know how a person feels when they're going through retirement—they feel useless." Another informant, a mother of two, admitted feeling, "If I were at home all the time, I'd be a child abuser."[40]

Even Sheila Kitzinger, more widely known for the celebratory tone of her manuals on natural childbirth and breastfeeding, flatly describes the experience of mothering young children in our society as "an ordeal, an endurance test."[41] A major reason, she argues, is that our society remains almost fiendishly baby-unfriendly. "Anyone who has ever dragged a stroller over kerbs, up and down steps and in and out of public transport, or breastfed a screaming baby in smelly lavatories or surreptitiously on a park bench or in a public library, will be only too well aware that our society is not geared to mothers and children."[42] Heaven knows this is true, and that we conduct our public affairs as if babies and small children were unpleasant social anomalies (like crippled beggars, say, or prostitutes), who have no business interfering in "real life." At the same time, it is easy to be glib about "our society," as if the conditions we create for ourselves were entirely somebody else's doing. If we continue to sustain the view that children are socially negligible, we need to examine the extent of our own collusion in that myth. So long as we continue to cling to a mask of motherhood that radiates composure and compliance (where, as often as not, irritation and anger are due), we simply reinforce the prevailing assumption that "nothing is too much trouble," that mother will manage.

Perhaps the greatest shock of the immediate postpartum period is the realization that motherhood is no more likely to "come naturally" than the baby itself. In technical terms, becoming a mother is "processural";[43] it happens by degrees, with the slow accumulation of experience and observation, of the wisdom of others and of confidence in oneself. And in our own society, the learning curve is especially steep, its rate of progress uniquely sluggish. Many observers have noted the irony that we assiduously prepare women for childbirth, yet treat childrearing as if it were an afterthought, or an anticlimax or (probably more to the point) so screamingly obvious that, like a celebrity guest, "no introduction is necessary." As Crouch and Manderson put it, "Women cease to be of sustained professional interest once they have delivered successfully and left the hospital grounds."[44]

Yet what most of us know about the real tasks of caring for a new baby would fit into a disposable diaper. Most of us have had strikingly little contact with babies before having our own. Ann Oakley found that three-quarters of the women she studied had never held a newborn, even for a few moments. Less than a quarter had ever babysat, bottlefed, or changed a baby's diaper.[45] She concluded that, for many contemporary women, doll play constituted the only apprenticeship for childrearing. "Adoptive mothers may be carefully scrutinized for their mothering abilities," she observed, "and nannies and children's nurses are professionally trained, yet women who give birth to babies may not know one end of the baby from the other."[46] Mary Boulton found that less than one-fifth of the middle-class women she studied had had any experience at all in looking after young children (compared with almost half of the working-class sample).

These figures are astounding, and they suggest that the degree to which we have succeeded in marginalizing motherhood from the mainstream of everyday life is probably unprecedented in both historical and cross-cultural terms. Once, children were meant to be seen and not heard. Today, non-parents are lucky even to catch sight of any, let alone to get down and get dirty caring for them. Smaller family sizes, increasingly isolated nuclear family units, and greater reliance on institutional childcare have combined to segregate children from the lives of their collective, non-parental elders. No other society in the history of humanity has had to worry about "training" women to be mothers—not because mothering comes naturally or instinctively, but because, up until the present, it has always been so visibly and unavoidably part of the fabric of social life.

I once asked an elderly Aboriginal man how he had learned to fish and trap for game as a young boy. He looked genuinely puzzled. "No one taught me, if that's what you mean," he finally answered. "It was just something everybody knew, like you were born knowing it." In some cultures—in most cultures—mothering is exactly the same. Girls and young women absorb the skills and wisdom of mothering effortlessly, almost helplessly, by a kind of epistemological osmosis that begins so early, and continues so seamlessly throughout life, that it does not even feel like learning. While all the biological evidence refutes the existence of a "mothering instinct" (at least in the "how-to" sense of the term) in homo sapiens, in many, many human societies mothering "feels" instinctive. The knowledge of what to do and how to do it has been so thoroughly internalized that it really seems to be something "you were born knowing".

In our society, the situation is exactly the reverse—to the extent that when the opportunity to observe mothering in action does arise, we have enormous difficulty "seeing" it at all, let alone believing that what we see might tell us something important about who we might become. Women without children complain that they "can't relate" to "this obsession" with motherhood. Care for young children simply does not fit within our collective, cognitive framework. As one woman, the last in her group of friends to have a baby, explained to parenthood educator Margaret Gibson, "no one could have told me how much time a baby takes up, and I've seen it over and over and I still couldn't believe it. They used to say, 'I can't make lunch' or 'I can't do this or that,' and they would arrive hours late, and I used to think they just weren't organized enough—I never believed it till I had to experience it."[47] Beverley Barris found that the managerial/professional mothers she interviewed were especially unsettled by the disorganization that is an inevitable part of life with a young baby. These women spoke repeatedly "of their feelings of being 'out of control' upon being pregnant and having babies."[48] "I have not been on time once since this baby was born," confessed one informant, a manager. "I need to feel in control and . . . there's three loads of laundry sitting in the living room. It gives me a vague sense of being out of control, and I feel sort of seasick and I don't like that."[49]

At the same time as we fetishize the necessity to be "in control" and to "organize" ourselves—adopting a sort of managerial metaphor for motherhood—we continue to hold to the contradictory notion that mothering is (or ought to be) both natural and instinctive. In fact, it is neither. "Motherhood is earned," writes Adrienne Rich, "first through an intense physical and psychic rite of passage— pregnancy and childbirth—then through learning to nurture, which does not come by instinct."[50] Women who mistakenly believe that it does will feel frustration at their inevitable failures. They will feel not only foolish and inept (which is bad enough) but deeply guilty. "I just thought everything was going to fall into place," explained one new mother to researcher Amy Rossiter, "so when it didn't, and I didn't know it's not supposed to yet, that's when I felt inadequate. It works for everyone else, what's wrong with me?"[51]

This woman was fortunate enough to discover relatively early in the piece that, as she so poignantly put it, things were not "supposed" to "fall into place." Many others are so busy keeping their own masks in place that they never notice that everybody else is wearing one too. Most of us are soon faced with the truth that "maternal instinct does not arrive by magic to coincide with the first birth"[52]—yet we persist in the irrational belief that this is evidence of personal inadequacy. That in some deep, scary sense we were not cut out to be mothers, that we are not "like the other girls." In fact, most of the other girls are exactly like us, and they face precisely the same terror that somebody might find out. Which is how we all landed in this mess in the first place. The minority who do seem to take to motherhood like so many maternal ducks to water are the exceptional ones.

The research suggests that, even in the case of these fortunate few, "instinct" has nothing to do with success. The variables that do seem to matter are experience with babies; solid, practical support from partners and other family members; and a baby genetically predisposed to relatively settled behaviors. We should all be so lucky—but precious few of us ever will be. Women who lack practical experience in babycare are apt to compensate by consuming prodigious quantities of secondhand knowledge—usually in the form of "expert" texts and manuals. In most cases, the results of this self-education are disastrous. Rather than gaining insight, women who (often in sheer desperation for a handle on things) "mother by the book" generally end up even more anxious and unsure about their competence.

It has often been observed, lightheartedly, that parenting would be a lot easier if babies came with an instruction manual. (Hence the title of Anne Lamott's delightful journal of her son's first year: *Operating Instructions*.) The strange thing is that these days they usually do—in the form of popular bibles by childcare experts such as Penelope Leach, Arlene Eisenberg (and daughters), Sheila Kitzinger, T. Berry Brazelton, La Leche League and many, many others. The problem is not that these writers do not know what they're talking about. On the contrary, they tend to be exceedingly well qualified, both in academic and practical terms. Most of the advice such experts impart is truly "good"—humane, positive, and (most of the time) based on sound scientific and/or psychological principles. The only problem is that the good advice rarely works. Well, why should it? Babies are individuals; so are mothers; so are fathers, other family members, the houses we all live in, the clothes we wear, the milk we produce or buy, the food we eat, the priorities we set, the language we use . . . need I go on? In short, the variables that contribute to shaping infant behavior and relationships are numerous and ever-shifting. Beyond the most basic of basics—diaper folding, say, or how to sterilize a bottle—there are frighteningly few hard and fast rules a mother can cling to. The problem with the books is that—without saying so in so many words—they insinuate that precisely the opposite is the case: that mothering is some kind of learnable sequence, that infant behavior is (or can be, with proper handling) predictable and, above all, malleable.

Consider for a moment the standard advice on "demand feeding," a simple, straightfoward notion if ever there was one. Feeding on demand, as most of us are aware, is now the universally preferred option—at least publicly—to the four-hourly "schedule feeding" method on which most of today's adults were reared. The formerly widespread practice of letting a baby scream, possibly for hours, until its next feed was due is now regarded with horror and disbelief. This is no longer the done thing. (If, indeed, it ever really was. Most women I know who came of age as mothers in the schedule-feeding era confess now that they "cheated"—a lot—concealing the whole charade behind their own generation's mask of motherhood.) Today, women are taught a simpler and more humane method: to feed the baby whenever it is hungry.

But when one moves from the idea of demand feeding to the realities of feeding a baby, alas, things change. Most women find that the "simplicity" of the notion evaporates on contact—which is where, unfortunately, most babies habitually reside. The problem is that a baby cannot "tell" you when he is hungry. (Indeed, we are not entirely certain that he even "knows" when he is hungry, as distinct from feeling undifferentiated distress.) The baby can cry, certainly—but the grown-up is left to "decode" the cry. Is it hunger, or is it pain? Or is it a call to be picked up and noticed? It could be that the baby's too hot or too cold. Then again, maybe it's frustration. Maybe it's boredom, or sleepiness. And maybe—just maybe—the cry means nothing in particular at all. Many women brag that they can tell absolutely the difference between a hunger cry and, say, a wet-diaper cry, and possibly some of them are even telling the truth. But to many, many others, their babies' cries all sound roughly alike, and the process of "translation" is a tedious business of continual trial and error, punctuated by confusing advice from inlaws and onlookers. All too often, by the time you've more or less figured it out, the baby is ready to be weaned.

In my own case, I decided to play it safe by offering my first baby a feed regardless of the tenor of her cry. Because she was the kind of baby sometimes described as "sucky," this suited her well enough. For the first six months of her life, she fed at least two hourly (and often more frequently), twenty-four hours a day. She spent much of the time not at the breast—quite understandably—spitting up the over- flow. For my part, I suffered continuous bouts of mastitis, and my nipples were so cracked that one of them nearly de- tached (leaving a fat, wormlike scar still menacingly visible today). My "bible" was *The Womanly Art of Breastfeeding*, a book published by the international organization La Leche League. I had learned from this book that feeds should never be timed, but should last for as long as it took the baby to drift into a contented, milk-drugged sleep. My daughter's feeding pattern, according to La Leche League, was simply "an indication that the baby is lively and grow- ing and is not a cause for worry. 'Ad-lib breastfeeding' can be very relaxing. You should not worry about putting baby to breast 'too often.' "[53] Ever the conscientious student, the re- sult was that I often fed my daughter continuously for four, five, and six hours at a clip in the early weeks. Suffice it to say, she was rarely hungry. And I was rarely sane.

Eventually, through the wise intervention of an experi- enced nursing mother (who took one look at my nipples and admitted she was way out of her depth), I was referred to a lactation consultant: a real, live mother of five who gently pointed out the lunacy of my fundamentalist approach. Her first piece of advice was to get the baby a pacifier. (A pacifier?! I was horrified. Hadn't La Leche League implied that the use of a pacifier was only a notch above child abuse? Didn't this woman realize that a mother's breast "is the best soother in the world from the baby's point of view."[54]) Her second sacrilege was to scale back from six-hour-long feeds to ten-minute ones: five minutes per side. Then there were lots of technical bits that I had read about but that simply made no sense without a hands-on demo—the positioning of lips and tongue, the "biscuiting" of the areola into a more suckable shape, techniques of manual expression that might eliminate the need for a nipple re-tread. In one three-hour consultation (during which my daughter, for the first time in her four-week-old life, steadfastly refused to feed, or even to wake up), I went from a lactating Kamikaze pilot to a woman more or less in charge of her own anatomy, if not quite her own destiny.

The biggest revelation, for me, was the shock of realizing how poor my own instincts had been (including my instincts for personal survival), and how fundamentally "unnatural" an act breastfeeding really was anyway—how much art, how much technique, how much sheer uncommon sense it took to do it right. No one could come into the world "hardwired" with that kind of knowledge. (Or, as Arlene Eisenberg diplomatically puts it in *What To Expect When You're Expecting*, "Though nursing does come naturally, it comes naturally a little later for some mothers and babies than for others."[55] I remember my brother-in-law, an anthropologist, chuckling over the La Leche League book as he hefted it off my desk one day. "A whole book on breastfeeding?! How many words does it take to say, 'Put baby to breast.

THE MASK OF MOTHERHOOD

Allow to suck'?" I was just beginning to realize that I had obviously (although secretly) agreed. Deep down, I was convinced there was really nothing to it. And then my nipples began to shred. This can be a strong motivation to rethink your assumptions.

Of course, I was also shocked that a book widely regarded as an authoritative source could offer such spectacularly fatuous advice. With hindsight, I now recognize that while the La Leche League advice proved unworkable for me, my experience was (thank God) atypical. It is not the books that are so dreadfully wrong, in other words. It's the attitude with which we approach them. And my own attitude was a classic: a mixture of naivete, arrogance (I was going to do it right), and vulnerability—combined with a willingness to suspend disbelief in exchange for a comprehensible, or any, solution.

Among the many cultural contradictions about mothering that we collectively harbor, none is more harmful than this: that we believe on the one hand that for every parenting problem there exists some technical or technological solution; and on the other that mothering is a fundamentally instinctive, intuitive process. It's a problem that's been with us ever since Spock. The first of the modern childcare gurus, and in many ways the template for them all, Dr. Benjamin Spock began his immensely influential *Baby and Child Care* with the famous sentence: "You know more than you think you do."[56] More than three decades later, these words were applauded and augmented by no less a personage than Penelope Leach herself: "You know more than you think you know and a great deal more than anyone else."[57] In its "pocket" edition, Spock's book runs to some six hundred pages, and Leach's definitive work is only slightly shorter. We may know more than we think we do—but what we don't know is clearly the stuff that publishers' dreams are made of.

It's a classic case of what the psychological literature calls the "Be Spontaneous" paradox. "Trust your instincts," the experts exhort us—then proceed to direct and control our every maternal move. The very existence of these texts implicitly (and often explicitly as well) undermines the new mother's confidence not only in her own judgment but in the accumulated wisdom of her own peers and elders. We are taught to shun such "old wives' tales," even when they are demonstrably effective, in favor of scientific or otherwise politically correct solutions that may not be. Sooner or later, of course, most of us become "old wives" ourselves, painfully reinventing the same old wheel as our mothers and grandmothers. The only thing really new is the shamed silence we keep about what we have learned—about the efficacy of anything from diapering to discipline.

Ours is possibly the only civilization in the history of humanity in which the handing down of mothering wisdom from mother to daughter is seen as a breach of familial etiquette, a form of "bad taste" strenuously avoided by both parties. Indeed, our mutual fear of "interference" has escalated to phobic proportions. One woman I interviewed lived literally next door to her mother, yet was scrupulous to avoid consulting her on any matters related to infant care. Instead, Vanessa relied on her collection of textbooks and a variety of local "hotlines," staffed by women who had had the "proper training" she believed her own mother lacked. Vanessa claimed, "Mom didn't cope very well with us as babies. We used to cry a lot, she said, and she could never get us to sleep. Nothing went right, basically." Vanessa saw her mother's frank disclosures about such difficulties as evidence of maternal failure, and decided that—despite their closeness in

other ways— "Mom is not the right person to give advice."
Vanessa's own baby was also colicky and wakeful, as it happened. She, too, "failed" to modify her baby's behavior, despite having tried a veritable arsenal of expert advice—
from the use of a "flow regulator" to baby massage and
"papoosing." She found, as her mother had before her, that
the first three months of her baby's life were a trial that
simply had to be endured. Her readiness to brand her
mother an "untrained" incompetent gained her nothing, in
the end, but a pile of unused gadgetry. For the mother's part,
she dutifully accepted her role as observer, not participant,
in her grandson's young life. A softly spoken career housewife, still youthful in her mid-fifties, she seemed grateful to
be entrusted with jobs like driving to the drug store to purchase the orthodontically correct pacifier, or the wind drops.
She seemed almost awed by her high-powered daughter's
"positive" (yet ultimately futile) approach to infant care, yet
one can only guess at her private thoughts on the matter.

Although Vanessa represents a somewhat extreme case,
recent research confirms that middle-class women are rely-
ing less and less on family, and more and more on classes,
books, and institutions in the transition to motherhood. Researcher Raymond DeVries believes that "the most striking
feature of the transition to parenthood is the enhanced control of institutions over the experience. Because today's parents are having fewer children and are waiting longer to
have them, they cannot look to their own parents for advice
on parenting. Instead, new parents must rely on institutions
and their representative 'experts.' "[58] Yet other studies have
shown that the single best predictor of maternal confidence
is the frequency of contact between a new mother and her
own mother.[59]

To an extent, there has probably always been a legitimate

psychological need impelling new mothers to exert their autonomy, to establish dominion over their young in their own way. Heaven knows, the perceived problem of "interference" from relatives (particularly in-laws) as a woman begins her mothering career is nothing new. What does seem to be new is the notion that the accumulated wisdom of mere mothers—those lacking medical credentials or PhDs in psychology or social work—can tell us anything worth knowing for our own parenting. We are, after all, so very different from our mothers, on so many objective measures. And this is true for the present cohort of young women to an extent unequalled by any previous generation.

We are better educated, more highly skilled, and better paid. We see ourselves (and, for the most part, live our lives) as autonomous agents in the world, rather than as support systems for the autonomy of others. And we are, perhaps above all, children of the Information Age: trusting implicitly in the maxim that knowledge is power, and that the more objective and scientific the knowledge, the greater that power will be. As a result, we tend to approach motherhood as a series of problems to be solved. We forget that, even in our own drastically changed circumstances, motherhood remains in essence precisely what it has always been: not a "phase" or a "challenge," not a "hurdle" or an "opportunity," but a way of life. It just so happens that it is a way of life utterly subversive to contemporary values stressing achievement, control, and autonomy as the highest of adult aspirations.

Our mothers and grandmothers may have known nothing of sudden infant death syndrome or slings or "controlled crying," but they knew more than perhaps we ever will about acceptance, forebearance, and humility. All of which, it seems increasingly clear, are the only "techniques" of motherhood that are ever truly foolproof. Ironically, we of the present postfeminist generation seem to have lost respect for the wisdom of women who have travelled the path of motherhood before us. Like all cases of throwing out the baby with the bathwater, this is an incalculable loss. To some extent, what we don't know about motherhood is what we refuse to hear and refuse to see in the lives of women around us, in the arrogant presumption that we are unique, that we will be different. Ultimately, we will pay dearly for our hubris.

It is a short step from performance anxiety—the "false conscientiousness" that suggests motherhood is simply another arena for achievement and mastery—to guilt and despair. Our masks will never concede defeat. Yet "failure" lies at the very heart of the mothering enterprise, as it does of every other form of human intimacy. As psychiatrist Jane Price observes, "Psychological failure is a normal part of all relationships because we can never be more than an approximate 'fit' to each other. Mothers cannot 'fit' each of their babies with anything more than imperfection. Mothers are not shapeless expendable blobs that can merge effortlessly with whatever genetic fate happens to throw at them, and we do neither mother nor baby any good by holding out unrealistic expectations that they would be if they were 'good' mothers."[60] The demographic reality of shrinking family size continues to exacerbate the problem. Most of us begin in the knowledge that we will have only one or two shots at "success," and that those will come relatively late in our reproductive lives. It's a case of now or never—of raising the stakes while diminishing the margin for error.

The result is often a severe case of maternal martyrdom, and a family structure in which the child takes on a psychologically uncomfortable and socially inappropriate center-stage role. Not surprisingly, the baby develops a whim of iron—necessitating ever-escalating cycles of maternal preoccupation. Somehow or other, our guilt gets the better of us. Often, it is the guilt we feel about our perceived differences from our own mothers: guilt about working (or, often just as potently, guilt about not working); guilt about feeling unfulfilled, ambivalent, or just plain bored by motherhood; guilt that, despite our successes in the "real world," here, where for the moment at least it really counts, we are in over our heads.

Although you'll never read about it in the glossy magazines or the expert texts, the feeling of being buried alive by early motherhood is now a commonplace experience. Postpartum depression researcher Vivienne Welburn has observed that "after we have given birth it is as if we wake up to discover that a mountain of sand has been deposited in front of the door of our home. Some women get to work energetically to dig routes out . . . They find marvellously inventive ways to cope with the situation . . . Some try to dig a way through and get buried, others just look at it, feel defeated, retreat within their four walls and give up."[61] Yet virtually all of us will experience an initial period of claustrophobia. Given our expectations, our priorities, the structure of our family units, and the abrupt shift in lifestyle that new motherhood increasingly entails, it would probably be irrational to feel otherwise. Yet individually each woman is convinced that the inevitable claustrophobia of new motherhood is somehow aberrant, personal, shameful: maybe if we don't talk about it, it will go away. Most of us find that eventually it does go away—but in spite of our silences, not because of them. In the end, our masks have served only to prolong and intensify the misery.

Mothers are supposed to be serene, the mask of motherhood reminds the world and its wearers. But, as Paula Caplan has written, "mothering an infant actually produces some of the most intense feelings of panic, fear, rage, and despair that adults can experience."[62] Whether or not we collectively choose to deny this truth, sooner or later babies do grow up, and the crisis of new motherhood eventually resolves itself into a more or less steady state of routine. Yet the goal of "getting back to normal" remains, for most women, a stubbornly unattainable ideal. "In truth," writes Penelope Leach with reflective candor, "they cannot get back to normal at all, because birth shakes up lives as children shake kaleidoscopes, leaving the patterns of the past in pieces."[63] When women who mother fail, ipso facto, to qualify, there is something wrong with our definition of "normal."

Lactation Intolerant
The Worst of Breast Is Best

It is important to recognize just how much the early experiences of breastfeeding or bottlefeeding are important in the development of the woman's self-esteem as mother. If she fails she has failed such an early hurdle she may well become increasingly uncertain of her abilities across the whole spectrum of mothering activities.

—Jane Price

I need one of those . . . what do you call them? Alert Bracelets, which reads 'Brain-Dead Breast-feeder. Handle with Care.'

—Kathy Lette

IN THE NEW YORK MATERNITY HOSPITAL in which I was born, new mothers were routinely medicated to suppress lactation even before it began. Such was middle-class America circa 1958. Bottle feeding was not just the preferred option, my mother recalls; it was the only option. Breast feeding was regarded as "animalistic," unhygienic, and "common." "It was something poor women had to do," mother has explained, "because they had no choice and couldn't afford sterilizers and formula." Although she and her three siblings had all been breast fed, to my mother's way of thinking this had been a grisly necessity of the Depression era, like wearing hand-me-down clothes and sleeping three to a bed. In America in the feel-good 1950s, thank heavens, such deprivation was a thing of the past. Breasts were everywhere being fetishized—this was, after all, the decade of Marilyn and Barbie and *Playboy*. Yet the notion that breasts might be functional was regarded as faintly pornographic. Breast feeding her babies would have been, for my mother, a bit like plowing over our immaculate suburban lawn to plant vegetables.

In the maternity hospitals in which the present generation of new mothers is giving birth, notions about feeding are no less rigid than they were in 1958. Only now, of course, we know that Breast Is Best—and we endorse breast feeding with precisely the same vehemence and precisely the same condescension with which my mother's generation championed the bottle.

As late as 1970, just over a quarter (26.5 percent) of babies born in U.S. hospitals were being breast-fed at birth. By 1996 this figure had almost doubled.[3] In today's maternity hospitals, the social outcasts are the bottle feeders—the socioeconomically disadvantaged, the teenage moms, the unwed, the smokers and others regarded as too ignorant or too selfish to "do the right thing." In many maternity wards, it has become standard practice to require new mothers to sign a permission form for each and every formula feeding the baby takes. ("I felt like I was signing my life away every time I fed her," one harassed new mom confessed to me.)

Breast milk, we have come to understand, is nutritionally superior to formula and more easily digested, too. Breast-fed babies are less likely to become obese and will have stronger immunities against a range of infections. They will also, according to recent research, be more "intelligent" than bottle feeders. Breast feeding is believed to aid in "bonding," due to the frequent skin-to-skin contact between mother and child, and to accelerate postpartum weight loss. Today, it is breast feeding that is touted as the more convenient and hygienic option. Above all, we now understand that breast feeding is the "natural" way to feed. When one objectively considers the options . . . well, there really are no options. Breast is Best, and anything less is a halfway measure, a capitulation, an admission—let's face it—of maternal incompetence.

Yet the fact remains that fully half of women who do breast-feed give up entirely within six months—and many of those much, much sooner. And the ones who do soldier on often do so with an ambivalence increasingly incorrect to acknowledge. Most women, in other words, ultimately perceive themselves as "failures" at breast feeding, with predictably disastrous results for their self-esteem. They have been brainwashed to believe that breast feeding will come naturally, even effortlessly; that as nursing mothers they will experience profound physical and emotional satisfaction; that their "perfect" milk will produce "perfect" babies: robust, contented, settled.

Indeed, they believe the theory so implicitly that when experience contradicts it, they assume that they (and not the theorists) must be the deviants: that they must have erred somehow or proceeded in some obscure way in the wrong spirit. Writes psychiatrist Jane Price, "sadly, many mothers do not realize that there is such a discrepancy between what is taught (the ideal) and what they will achieve (the reality), and so begin to develop mothering guilt from their earliest days of interaction with their baby."[4]

The reality of the breast-feeding experience is that it is as diverse as any other human relationship. There is no doubt that this diversity is systematically denied in the way breast feeding is currently pitched to pregnant women, both through the medical establishment and other sources we consider expert and authoritative. There is no doubt that, for many women, breast feeding does feel natural and joyous and "empowering." Yet, for at least an equal number, breast feeding feels more like hard work for which there is little apparent reward.

Women in the latter group discover that breast feeding can be technically tricky, physically painful and/or fatiguing, and emotionally draining. To add insult to injury, some even find that their babies don't seem to have read the literature and don't particularly enjoy the breast; instead of feeding lustily they do the infant equivalent of "picking." (Other, more forthright babies may reject the breast altogether, screaming whenever it looms into view.) Women who feel modest or awkward or embarrassed about their bodies will almost inevitably have difficulty breast feeding, and it does no good at all to maintain that they "shouldn't" feel this way.

Many others who feel comfortable enough as far as body image goes may still be highly equivocal about the continual flesh-to-flesh contact that breast feeding requires. For these women, breast feeding presents less a problem of modesty than of sheer tactile overload. Others find that the free-form schedule of breast feeding simply fails to keep tempo with other, equally insistent life demands, whether those of other children, partners, or professional commitments. To others, breast feeding is just mindblowingly tedious. They hate having to sit "doing nothing" while the rest of the world spins on, presumably productively, around them.

All things being equal, breast milk is best for babies. Yet all things are not equal, not by a long shot. Most women, sooner or later, find this out for themselves. Many continue on anyway, either because the pluses in the end outweigh the minuses or because these women are willing to make a substantial sacrifice in time, convenience, and energy for what they presume to be their baby's best interests. Eventually, every woman who attempts to breast feed will discover what the mask of motherhood never reveals: breast feeding is not merely an "option" but a way of life. In the context of the orderly, autonomous way in which most of us have been socialized to live our lives, the breast-feeding lifestyle is fundamentally subversive. It is not surprising in the least that so many women decide that it is not for them—and to blame them for not trying harder is not only facile but cruel. Yet by clinging to this particular mask of motherhood—by upholding the official discourse that minimizes or ignores the commitment that breast feeding entails—we make everything so much harder than it needs to be. We make breast feeding into another wilderness experience, another maternal proving ground in which it's every woman for herself. By refusing to tell what we know, to share what we have learned, we increase our arrogance (if we "succeed") and our guilt (if we "fail") at the same time as we diminish our chances for wisdom.

Like many of life's great achievements, breast feeding is easy once you know how. Yet most new mothers are entirely unprepared for the physical challenges of breast feeding, let alone its complex emotional and social demands. The propaganda tells us that breast feeding is "natural," and from that we conclude that it will also be effortless; that the way forward will be obvious, if only we trust our instincts. It's no wonder most expectant mothers are so blithely optimistic about their prospects for success. The boob is there, the baby sucks, and Mother Nature does the rest. After all (as I myself used to say) that's what the word "mammal" means, for heaven's sake. What could be easier?

We forget, of course, that while, as *Homo sapiens*, we still

possess mammalian equipment, we are no longer reposito-
ries of mammalian instinct except in the most vestigial
sense. What our fellow mammals "know," we must learn.
That's what having a human brain means, for heaven's sake.
We do not suckle our young by instinct any more than we
experience labor like the family cat. Any woman who has
not given silent, unattended birth to quintuplets, or noncha-
lantly consumed her own afterbirth, should not expect to
breast-feed instinctively. Yet we do so expect. If it were not
so insane, it would be hilarious.

It is possible to affect a stoicism about breast feeding, just
as with childbirth. It is possible to pretend that it doesn't
hurt, that you don't need any help or support, that you are
not sometimes overwhelmed or just plain at a loss. Yet the
extent of our deceptions aside, the overwhelming majority
of women who breast feed face a steep learning curve if they
are to continue successfully, or even to endure for the first
few weeks. Because few women expect to have to learn to
breast-feed, they find the process not only arduous but de-
moralizing. The assumption remains that if only one were
"more maternal" none of this fumbling around would be
necessary.

Most women pick up the rudiments of breast feeding in
the do-or-die, pressure-cooker atmosphere of the maternity
ward. "Trust your instincts," the first staff midwife advises,
"and make sure you do everything exactly as I tell you." So
does the next midwife—only her advice contradicts that of
the first and probably that of the third as well. The only
constant factors, a woman soon realizes, are those damned
instincts—if only she had a clue as to what they were. In the
meantime, the advice and the contradictions continue to
avalanche her. A recent survey found that more than 70 percent of first-time mothers complained that they received

"conflicting" advice about breast feeding in the hospital. "Never feed a screaming baby. Wait until she settles," one learns, only to be told at the next shift, "It's about time you fed that baby, can't you hear her screaming?" The length of feeds is another hotly contested issue, with "authoritative" advice ranging all the way from "As long as she wants, dear—it'll build up your supply" to "Not more than ten minutes per side, unless you want to end up with cracked nipples." Some staff, it turns out, are vehemently opposed to even the occasional "top-up" bottle of formula; others to nipple shields or pacifiers or heat lamps. Some insist that you wake up the baby and feed it to prevent dehydration, jaundice, or (heaven forbid) "lazy sucking." Others are equally insistent about letting sleeping babies lie. "One of the most distressing things in the hospital after the baby was born was to do with feeding," reported one recent initiate in a postnatal interview. "I had 101 different bits of advice and did not sort out the problems until I got home."[5]

Now that the practice of "rooming-in" has become the norm in maternity hospitals, the problem of physical exhaustion for breast-feeding mothers can become particularly acute. Women experience pressure, both subtle and not so subtle, to "go it alone," without a break in the caring or feeding regimen, and with no guarantee of even three or four consecutive hours of sleep. One woman I interviewed was made to feel "dreadfully guilty" when, after five exhausting days of breast feeding, she requested that her baby be kept overnight in the nursery and given one bottle of formula. "Oh, I don't think that's such a good idea," she reported the midwife as saying. "She sat on the bed right next to me and said, 'I really think it's not a very good idea that you give your baby formula during the night-time, because Breast Is Best. By switching to formula you're not going to improve her jaundice at all.' " (In fact, many doctors believe it is the intake of fluid, not of breast milk per se, that can help flush away the bilirubin—a yellowish by-product of the breakdown of red blood cells—that causes jaundice. Nor do they feel jaundice is some sort of illness needing to be "cured" anyway but a natural, normal condition for a new-born baby that, in the vast majority of cases, corrects itself within a few days.) In other hospitals, it is policy to refer to bottle feeding as "artificial feeding"; the obvious implication is that those who resort to it are "artificial mothers."

Stephanie Brown and colleagues found breast feeding to be a major arena of struggle for postpartum women. "A few people reported good experiences" during their stay in hospital, they found, "but critical and negative accounts were much more common."[6] The lack of consensus about basic breast-feeding technique played a major part in this dissatisfaction. The feeling was widespread that, as one woman put it, "With medical advice like this, who needs in-laws?" Either there's something wrong with the midwives, something wrong with the mothers, or something wrong with all those babies. (As one woman reported to me "I was doing everything right; he just wasn't sucking correctly.") Or possibly, just possibly, there's something wrong with how we're defining the enterprise.

If breast feeding is a natural, instinctive response, there should be one right way to do it, we seem to believe. And if it isn't—if it is in fact a learned set of techniques or routines—well then, there should *still* be one right way to do it. It is not usually until women leave the hospital that they begin to realize that breast feeding is, strictly speaking, neither of these, and that there are many ways to do it "right," just like mothering itself. That as much as one needs support and advice, trial and error are not only appropriate but absolutely necessary. We find out eventually that, just as different midwives will have different ideas, we too will have different physical and emotional capacities as breast feeders—and so, in fact, will our babies.

"Yes, I had blisters, and then they turned into blood blisters," recounted one "artificial mother," as she reminisced about her four-day battle with breast feeding in the hospital. "Then I couldn't feed him because of the blood, so I expressed for twenty-four hours on the electric pump, then that just made them worse. Then I had the ray lamps as well, but my boobs felt like they were sunburnt, and my whole chest was throbbing . . . It would sometimes take the midwives an hour to get him on, and then he'd pull away and we'd have to start again . . . And then I tried the nipple shields as well, and we tried dunking them in solution and all sorts of things, but he just ripped the whole shield, because he wants to look around the other side of the room . . . In the end, one of us had to hold his hands and everything down while the other one tried to latch his head on. One person couldn't do it. He was so strong! And I said, how am I supposed to do this when I get home?!" She found that even when she switched her baby to a bottle, he was exceedingly difficult to feed. It took months for his "head tossing" to settle down, and even after he started on solids it was a matter of following his mouth around with a spoon.

For their own obscure and ultimately unknowable reasons, some babies simply resist feeding of any kind. Much more common is the baby who seems to need days or even weeks to get the hang of it all, which would not, of course, be a problem if we didn't expect it to be otherwise. Babies are supposed to know how to suckle "instinctively"—all the books tell us so. So when our experience tells us otherwise, we cast around for someone or something to blame. Being women, usually we blame ourselves. And if we are determined, achievement-oriented women, our "failure" makes us even more determined, even more driven to "succeed." Recalled one new mother, a thirty-ish teacher with self-described perfectionist tendencies: "For the ten days in hospital, I had to have a midwife every time I fed her, and it was just a screaming match: her screaming, me screaming . . . it was really much more painful than the birth—and that baffled me."

Why the pain of breast feeding should be "baffling," or even downright frightening, to women is no mystery once you consider the source. For one thing, relatively few of today's new mothers were themselves breast fed as babies (a variable consistently related to breast-feeding success—although obviously neither a necessary nor sufficient condition for that success). As a breast-feeding generation, we are treacherously short of role models. We lack access to the informal, accumulated wisdom of experience that breast-feeding women in other cultures and at other times could consult as a matter of course. The medical establishment has attempted to compensate for this loss of wisdom with a torrent of information.

National and transnational groups like La Leche League International, the Association of Breastfeeding Mothers, and the Nursing Mothers Association have been formed in a conscious effort to redress this imbalance. Such organizations are run by breast-feeding women, for breast-feeding women, on the laudable assumption that expertise without experience is a contradiction in terms. Typically such groups provide an impressive range of information resources and support services (especially telephone counseling) that can provide genuine and much-needed mentoring for new mothers. At the same time, however, such groups are widely perceived as propaganda machines, a confederation of "Big Sisters" intent on weeding out dissenting voices and uncomfortable experiences—a kind of Milk Police who separate out the maternally pure from their fallen, formula-feeding sisters, and who systematically withhold information that might prove damaging to "the cause."

Admittedly, such judgments are often made secondhand, on the basis of somebody else's bad experience. But while the slur may be unfair, the fear it expresses is genuine. Such groups, whatever their good intentions, have done at least as much to alienate and divide women as they have done to empower them. By drawing such sharp and uncompromising lines between insiders and outsiders, they continue to play a significant role in keeping in place the masks behind which most mothers (however they choose to feed their babies) still find it expedient to hide.

Ordinary, nonaligned women normally discover in the course of things (through their own experience, and by talking to other ordinary, nonaligned women) that they have been given a hopelessly sanitized version of the physical travails involved in normal breast feeding. The first thing that has been censored is pain, which is not to be confused with "minor discomfort" or "a slight ache" or any of the other euphemisms routinely adopted. Even the word "suck" is a misnomer. "Clamp down" is more accurate, as every woman who has ever curled her toes during an early attempt at "attachment" can attest. The force of a baby's gums in action is astoundingly disproportionate to its size and putative helplessness. Even if there is no cracking, bruising, or blistering of nipples (all of which we are led to believe are unusual conditions, and none of which is), the first few weeks of "attachment" can be quite gruesomely painful.

Added to all this is the rarely discussed matter of

"afterpains"—the powerful, postpartum contractions that cause the uterus to shrink and descend to its normal position in a matter of days after childbirth. These pains are triggered by the same hormone that controls the let-down response; consequently, they begin within moments of the baby's latching on (just when you thought it was safe to uncurl your toes, in other words). Although variable in frequency and duration (they are more intense after second and subsequent deliveries), the incidence of afterpains is usually noticeable for at least several days. They feel exactly like early to mid-labor contractions or very severe menstrual cramping, and pain relief is usually essential. (In my own case, I managed to get through labor without drugs, but not the afterpains.) Women who bottle feed experience only mild afterpains, if any.

The business of the equipment a woman brings to breast feeding is another taboo subject among the Milk Police. "All women can breast-feed," they assure us; "the size of your breasts has nothing whatever to do with it." While this seems true, like most propaganda it is as significant for what it omits as for what it asserts. In fact, although breast size does not appear to be an issue in successful breast feeding, the size, configuration, and sensitivity of the nipple area most certainly is. All women can indeed breast feed. But for some it will hurt so much, or prove so damaging, that the price in maternal suffering may prove far too high. One does read about the relatively rare problem of "inverted nipples" but almost never about such widespread equipment problems as small nipples, "inflexible" nipples (ones that resist the requisite stretching), insufficiently pigmented nipples (basically, the paler they are, the more sensitive they are) or "mismatched" ones (leading to the baby's forming a stub-

born preference for one at the expense of the other and caus-
ing many a breast-feeding mother to list dangerously in the
favored direction). Any of these idiosyncrasies can make
breast feeding problematic and more than usually painful,
especially in the initial establishment period.

Women also learn—again, correctly as far as it goes—
that every woman is capable of producing enough milk to
nourish her baby. What we don't often hear is that for some
the time and energy required make lactation virtually a full-
time job. Sure, such women *can* feed their babies; but quite
possibly that's all they'll be able to do. Many, many women
find lactation to be a physically depleting ordeal, making
them feel tired and dazed most of the time. And virtually
every woman who breast feeds—even those who produce
milk copiously and without appreciable physical exertion—
will experience more fatigue, and get less sleep, than her
bottle-feeding fellows. This is simply a fact of lactating life,
and anyone who tries to deny it or minimize it does all mothers a gross disservice.

Research that somehow never makes it into the popular
Breast Is Best literature shows conclusively that breast-fed
infants are far more likely to disturb their parents in the
early hours of the morning (from midnight to 5:00 A.M.),[7]
while "mothers who elect to bottle-feed their infants from
birth will find that the feeds which occur in the early hours
of the morning are dropped at a significantly earlier age."[8]
One study found that nursing infants slept in nighttime
bouts of four to seven hours compared with nine to ten hours
for weaned babies.[9] Some researchers have suggested that
breast-fed babies may come to expect more attention when
they experience any discomfort on waking: on-demand
feeding (surprise! surprise!) will tend to create babies who

demand more.[10] Even more sobering, the demands for nighttime attention associated with breast feeding have been found to persist right through to the preschool years.[11]

Women who breast feed feel more tired because they *are* more tired. Their babies not only demand more frequent feeding, especially at night, but those demands are centered exclusively on mother's body. When it comes to breast feeding—the occasional bottle of expressed milk notwithstanding—there is no substitute. Breast is not simply best; breast is it, and "it" happens to be attached to you and no one else. The pro–breast-feeding lobby emphasizes the benefits of this unique feeding relationship: the enhanced opportunities for mother-infant bonding; the impressive biological economy that develops between "supply" and "demand." Yet the constraints of this symbiosis are real, too. And for many women, already strained to their emotional and physical limits by the trauma of childbirth, the tyranny of proximity can prove overwhelming.

Studies of the psychology of breast feeding have tended to focus almost exclusively on the relationship of the child to the breast, while the responses of the person to whom that breast happens to be appended have been taken for granted or ignored outright. In the literature it has become a commonplace to emphasize the interactive nature of the breast-feeding relationship at the biological level (that is, the cycle of supply and demand in milk production). Yet our understanding of the emotional realities of breast feeding continues to be naively unilinear. We are very, very interested in the impact of breast feeding on babies, yet have hardly taken notice at all (except in the most one-dimensional and highly sentimentalized terms) of its impact on mothers. This remains unexamined and unremarked.

"Is breast feeding more or less the way you expected it

would be?" I ask a new mother who has just described herself as "completely besotted" by her four-week-old daughter. She hesitates, and seems to grope for words. "It's a good
thing," she begins, "but it's too intense . . . To me, it's like a
kind of devouring . . . like I'm devouring her as she's devouring me. I anticipated, in the back of my mind, that I
might find it boring, that I might be dying to get back to
work. But it's not like that at all. It's not the boredom, it's
the . . . , the weight of it. It's difficult to describe." She told
me about the overwhelming sense of elation, of freedom, of
"refreshment" she felt the first time her husband bottle fed
the baby and she was able to walk away for an hour by herself. "Just to go and walk across to my office and just sit there
and read my e-mail, which I'd forgotten how to get into. Just
to sit there and not have that responsibility for her, and every
little cry you've got to figure out what's wrong . . ."

Yet in an interview conducted during her pregnancy, this
same woman had expressed amazement that "an entire
three-hour prenatal class" had been devoted to the topic of
breast feeding. "Maybe I'm a little naive, but I just think,
well, what's the big deal? I just think I'll go with the flow,
basically," she added gaily. Although she had never observed a woman breast feeding at close range, she watched
with interest the instructional video shown during her class.
"It looked technically quite complicated to start with," she
admitted, "but I imagine that once you've got the pattern
and the way the mouth and the nipple have to be so it's not
choking or it's not giving you all those diseases you can
catch—that once you've got the technique down pat, the
rest might be quite easy."

For compassionate reasons, I chose not to remind her of
these words two months later. This was when, while maintaining her desire to continue breast feeding, she admitted

bluntly, "At this stage, it's too much for me. I intuitively feel that, for my mental health, having a break from it all now and then is important." Such feelings, I suspect, are not only normal but probably universal among breast-feeding mothers. Yet they are so rarely voiced, so seldom acknowledged either in the literature or even among women in private, that they are perceived as perverse, "unmaternal," an admission of inadequacy. "Someone else who's perhaps stronger emotionally or mentally could be with the baby twenty-four hours a day and be able to maintain a balanced approach" was how this woman phrased it. "Then again," she concluded thoughtfully (and, as I heard it, hopefully), "maybe that person doesn't exist, anyway."

Among the growing number of women for whom a sense of well-being is tied to achievement, autonomy, and an orderly, organized lifestyle, there is no doubt that "that person" is becomingly increasingly hard to find. To the extent that we deliberately mislead women about the havoc breast feeding may wreak on their hard-won independence, we are making a difficult situation well-nigh impossible. The woman quoted above abandoned breast feeding altogether three months later, when she returned to work part-time. "How did you feel about it?" I asked her. "I don't even think I was sad," she began with a guilty laugh. "I think I was relieved." "Why should you be sad?" I inquired. "Yeah, true, why should I be? It was a nice thing, I guess. Or was it just in theory a nice thing? I think maybe it just was in theory."

As she warmed to her subject, one could see the mask of motherhood fairly melting. The will to fake it was gone—with a vengeance. "The whole hormonal thing, that you feel hot and flushed—the fact that you're in public and it's always dripping. Oh no! I don't regret that at all! In fact, I hated it." Overall, she explained, the cost was simply greater than the benefit. "The actual experience once she's there drinking was okay, but the whole process surrounding it is just awful! You can't do anything, you can't go out. Even a coffee shop experience becomes complicated. No, I didn't like it. I was very relieved, and maybe so was she, to get onto the bottle."

There is a common perception that women who abandon breast feeding do so out of a misplaced sense of shame, that they are not, as the saying goes, "comfortable with their bodies." Yet many of the women with whom I have spoken express exactly the opposite view. If anything, in today's generation, young mothers seem to like their bodies prodigiously. So much, in fact, that the notion of interfering with their usual smooth, dependable functioning is understandably anathema. Having been raised in the historically and sociologically novel belief that our bodies do in fact belong to us and to us alone, we contend less with issues of shame than with issues of control.

Another woman I spoke with, who had no problems at all with breast-feeding "technique," gave up after a week because it made her "really tired and spaced out." She explained, "All I seemed to do was feed and sleep, and that part of it I didn't like because I felt as if I couldn't get organized. I mean, I couldn't even have a shower when I wanted one, because either she'd be just about to wake up, or I'd just sort of put her down, and then I'd be so tired I'd think, 'Oh, blow the shower! I'll have one when I get up.' And then when I went to get up, she was ready for a feed . . . And of course I couldn't go anywhere." The expectation that women will want to go anywhere, that they'll have anywhere to go or any means to get there even if they did, is a revolutionary one—and an enormously complicating factor in settling down to a breast-feeding lifestyle.

Women who do persevere with breast feeding past the chaotic first few weeks are quick to point out that a routine can be established, and that it can prove much easier to breast feed on the go than to lug bottles and their associated paraphernalia. There is no doubt at all that this is true— some of the time. It was true for me with my first baby, who was so single-minded at the breast that it was possible for me to eat dinner, talk on the phone, take notes, and even teach classes and keep her firmly and contentedly attached. Yet my second child was completely unimpressed with my care-free attitude towards public, take-out-style feeds. I was not in the least squeamish about my body. Unfortunately, he was: he refused to take any nourishment at all unless concealed in his own darkened bedroom—and no visitors allowed.

Other women find that breast feeding in public poses not a moral problem but an aesthetic one. There's nothing "shameful" about having a wet stain creeping stealthily across your T-shirt, but it's not exactly chic either. Similarly, most women who have told me that they dislike breast feeding in restaurants, at social gatherings, or in meetings have cited loss of concentration rather than loss of modesty as the reason. It's their own state of mind they worry about, not anyone else's.

The mental vagueness of the lactating female is no myth perpetrated by evil formula manufacturers. As virtually any breast-feeding mother formerly accustomed to using her brain will tell you, lactation produces a dense hormonal fog that can cloud reason, judgment, and recall (especially of numbers, it seems) to an alarming extent. The Milk Police remind pregnant women that breast feeding will help them get their bodies back, but they omit to mention that it will take their minds (at least temporarily) for ransom. This is one reason that so few women can work outside the home (or even, often, within it) and continue breast feeding.

Another reason has to do with the physical constraints of lactation, including the delicacy of the supply-demand cycle, the unpredictability of the let-down reflex, and the sheer effort and tedium entailed in most forms of manual and machine-assisted expression. Many women are surprised and disappointed to find that they cannot express their milk at will, at their convenience. (Breast milk may travel well, but in most cases it "decants" poorly!) Expressing by hand is relatively kind to the nipples but hard on the shoulders and neck; most women find it a slow and uncomfortable process. Using a hand-held pump is more efficient but a good deal fussier: the various bits and pieces require sterilization and must be assembled, disassembled, and packed away with each use. Often women find that, though they seem to have plenty of milk when their babies suck, there is little in the way of leftovers. Others simply can't get the let-down reflex happening without the baby's expert assistance. Either way, it is often a challenge to express enough milk to fill a syringe, let alone a full bottle. Despite all these obstacles, so many women blame themselves when their dreams of returning to work (even part-time) while still exclusively breast feeding begin to dry up along with the milk. Yet, as Jane Price has observed, it is not the experience that is aberrant—it's the expectation. "Theories that suggest that the mother is in charge or in control of the [breast-feeding] situation or can make of it what she chooses not only miss the point but also encourage a further sense of guilt and failure in the mother," she writes.[12]

Women who expect to be more or less in charge of their lives—which is to say, most of us—will find breast feeding a particularly disorienting experience. In a successful breast-feeding relationship, it is the baby who calls the tune and the mother who dances the jig. It is the baby whose "judgment" must be trusted, whose pace must be respected, whose needs determine the style, frequency, and context for feeding. Breast feeding is without doubt empowering for babies. ("Don't call us," say our breast-fed infants, "We'll call you.") Indeed, some researchers have argued that the much-reported link between breast feeding and IQ advantage has nothing to do with the nutritional superiority of human milk and everything to do with the fact that breast-fed babies are permitted to "call the shots" in this distinctive power imbalance.

"The extent to which the environment is contingent on the actions of the infant will determine the strength of his belief that his actions can affect the environment. The infant with a strong expectation of mastery will expect his interactions with the environment to be rewarding, and will be motivated to achieve control through all the means open to him."[3] Nothing strengthens a child's "expectation of mastery" more effectively than breast feeding on demand. And nothing diminishes his mother's expectation of mastery more effectively either. It would not surprise me in the least to learn that the short-term IQ advantage enjoyed by breast-fed babies is matched by a short-term IQ disadvantage in their mothers.

The point is not that there is something wrong with allowing a mere infant to exercise command over its own environment, or that control is something only grown-ups should be allowed to exert, or that the exercise of tyranny is a divine right of parenthood. It is not an error to allow a baby to set its own pace, in breast feeding or in any other sphere of activity. What is an error is to ignore the consequences of this empowerment for the women who mother such babies. The politics of breast feeding place women in a reactive, essentially subservient position in relation to their babies. And whatever else we may say about it, this will make a difference, and a profound one, in the day-to-day management of women's lives.

In breast feeding, the question "Whose body is it, anyway?" takes on a special urgency. For every woman who experiences the merger between her own flesh and that of her baby's as sensuous and fulfilling, there is another who finds it abrasive if not downright intrusive. "Real women," "maternal women," are meant to revel in the flesh-to-flesh intimacy that breast feeding demands. Yet my own informal polling suggests that the numbers of "artificial women" out there are legion. Many of them continue feeding anyway, because they believe it is in their babies' best interests to do so; yet, for themselves, breast feeding is more like an endurance test than a sensuous indulgence. Despite their success at feeding, such women often feel like failures—like the woman in the Woody Allen movie who claimed she had an orgasm once but was told by her analyst it wasn't the right kind. These days, women scoff at such absurdities. But many of us who wouldn't dream of faking an orgasm continue to regard faking motherhood as if it were a sacred public duty. Pretending to enjoy breast feeding when you don't, upholding the myth that it's all a simple matter of "going with the flow," feeling secretive and shameful about the resentment and frustration you may be feeling—these are all small but telling testimonials to the continuing power of the mask.

There's another small detail that the publicists for universal lactation fail to mention to intending mothers; namely, the impact of breast feeding on breasts. Only in a society that has a huge stake in keeping the realities of motherhood a deep, dark, and subversive secret could so many women remain so ignorant for so long about so obvious a process. I remember reading during my pregnancy that "it is an old wives' tale that breastfeeding reduces the size of your breasts." That's funny, because a lot of the young wives I know say exactly the same thing. Their observations about their own bodies may be lacking in scientific rigor, but they're not blind for heaven's sake. Nor are they ignorant, mischievous, or prone to superstition. So why do we have such a hard time hearing them, let alone believing them? At the same time, it needs to be said that many women do not experience a reduction in breast size following breast-feeding. Yet virtually all who breast feed will end up with breasts softer, flatter, and droopier than they were before. It is possible that breast "mass" remains the same, but it is certain that this mass gets drastically rearranged. I remember asking my mother why the women in *National Geographic* had such droopy breasts. "It's because they don't wear proper bras," she answered. I believed it at ten, and some women still believe it (to judge by their shock when it happens to them, too).

The propaganda encourages pregnant women to believe that, as breast feeders, all things will be possible — that, with just a modicum of planning, life will go on exactly as before. We are led to expect further that breast feeding will add a newer, richer dimension to our lives as women. And it can, I believe. Yet there is a price to pay, and for every dimension added there is a dimension subtracted or diminished. This is common sense. This is life. Yet our persistence in upholding the fantasy of "having it all" is stronger than our will to confront the most basic of our own realities.

Like most choices in life, the decision to breast feed will close off at least as many options as it will open. Recognizing that at the outset is essential for new mothers if they are to avoid undue frustration and self-blame. Yet for the present generation, the prevailing mask of motherhood has effectively muffled a dispassionate, woman-centered examination of the breast-feeding way of life. In the contemporary caste system of maternal correctness, breast-feeding mothers are our "sacred cows," in every sense of the term.

Breast feeding ties a woman to her child in a way that is much easier to sentimentalize than to operationalize. Indeed, in many ways, the lifestyle demands of breast feeding could not be more alien to the expectations of everyday, adult life that today's women increasingly share with men. Breast feeding is essentially a vestige of a hunter-gatherer way of life. The wonder is not that it grafts so poorly onto industrialized minds and bodies, but that we persist in trying to graft it at all. To my way of thinking, women who succeed at breast feeding demonstrate a heroic capacity to defer gratification and to survive repeated violations of contemporary cultural assumptions about the proper regulation of time and space.

It is no mystery at all that women who do manage this feat may perceive themselves as in some way special or set apart. In a world in which human beings prefer to maintain both physical and emotional autonomy, where "getting things done" is a measure of personal worth, where time is compartmentalized into neat, observable divisions, where extended families have been geographically dispersed, breast feeding is nothing less than a culturally subversive activity. None of which is to suggest that breast feeding is not—despite all of this, and even perhaps because of all this—eminently worth doing, or without compensatory rewards. At the same time, we need to understand how ridiculous, how shallow, and how ultimately dishonest are most of our attempts to sell breast feeding to a naive and unsuspecting public.

The Juggled Life

. . . it takes all the running you can do to keep in the same place. If you want to get somewhere else, you must run at least twice as fast . . .

The Red Queen in *Alice in Wonderland*

AS THE CLASSIC BUMPER STICKER reminds us, "Every Mother Is a Working Woman." It can be hard to remember how radical that observation once seemed. As recently as the 1970s, recognizing mothering as "real" work was almost as challenging to our shared assumptions about womanhood as acknowledging that "real" working women could also be mothers. Today, by contrast, three quarters of all American mothers are currently in paid employment, including a majority of those with children under the age of one. What's more, women who do drop out of the paid workforce to pursue full-time mothering are increasingly likely to regard their decision as a sacrifice (in terms of both economics and personal growth). Today, in other words, the rallying cry has achieved the status of historical relic. Or has it?

Nearly thirty years on, the working mother debate rages every bit as fiercely and as fulsomely as ever. While there is no doubt at all that a huge proportion of mothers are working, there remains a great deal of residual uncertainty about when, to what extent, and even whether they should be working. A look at the "Women's Issues" section of any bookshop confirms that while our workforce participation may be at an all-time high, our anxiety about it is apparently even higher. The proliferating number of paperback titles containing the words "women" (or "mother") and "work" is an index not only of our society's abiding interest in the issue but also of our accelerating insecurity about it.

A generation ago, the "right" of mothers to participate in paid work was subject to regular and rigorous questioning in the culture at large. Today—despite all the statistics on women's workforce participation—we are questioning it still. This was one thing (indeed, possibly the only thing) that the Louise Woodward case demonstrated beyond a reasonable doubt: that lurking just beneath the brittle surface of recent social changes lie vast and murky reservoirs of resentment, uncertainty, and fear. A woman who hires a nanny to look after her young child while she works outside the home for pay may no longer be a statistical anomaly. Yet in many ways she remains a sexual suspect—one whose status as either responsible mother or responsible professional is at best probationary and provisional.

Oddly, however, the status of her full-time homemaking counterpart has plummeted lower than ever, and our society seems actually less, rather than more, inclined to acknowledge her contribution as bona fide "work." As we have seen, we do not feel completely good about mothers who decide to work for pay. We never really have. What's new under the sun in the 1990s is having equally mixed feelings (or worse) about mothers who stay home. Joan K. Peters, for one, states bluntly in the introduction to her recent book *When Mothers Work*, "mothers should work outside the home." "Equality," she adds, "means that women can no longer use motherhood as an excuse to drop out of public life . . ."[2]

Peters call her stance "strong medicine," and no doubt it is. What she has failed to notice, however, is that it is also extremely familiar medicine: that our cultural predilections for telling mothers what they "should" be doing and for apportioning blame when they "fail" have remained a dispiriting constant in our public discourse. We hear so much about the multiplication of women's options that it is easy to forget the extent to which we have at the same time multiplied the risks. Now, instead of only one or two ways in which to fail, we have dozens.

Is it any wonder there has been such a profound closing of the ranks among "working mothers" of all varieties? Although it is not something anyone is proud of, the schisms are there and they are real. Mothers who work full-time for pay do feel (by turns) threatened by, envious of, and superior to those who work full-time at home and vice versa. Meanwhile, those who seek a *via media* by working part-time often feel most sidelined and embattled of all. What unites us is the painful sense that we are missing out, that, like some hapless game-show contestant, we have chosen the wrong door, coupled with a determined refusal to lose face by admitting it.

Which perhaps helps explains why we seem to need our masks more than ever, whichever side of the working mother debate we find ourselves on. The more we anguish over our deficits in private (a Hobson's choice, generally, between the fear that we have sold our families short and the regret that we have sold ourselves short), the more likely we are to parade our assets in public. So that instead of taking part in a genuine conversation, we end up simply trading elaborate justifications for our respective choices. "My kids just adore day care," gushes the work-for-pay mom. "And I really look forward to that quality time at the end of the

day." "Play group is so terrific—it keeps us both stimu-
lated," enthuses the work-at-home mom. "Really, my days
are so full, I couldn't think about going out to work." Both
are likely to protest, if challenged, that they have pursued
their chosen course "for the sake of the family." And they
will also declare themselves "lucky" to have "such supportive partners."

It is not exactly that these women are lying. But the
truths they are choosing to reveal (perhaps even admit) are
highly partial and selective. Ultimately they tell us more
about how women think they should be feeling rather than
how they do feel, more about how they would like their lives
to look than about the effort it costs to keep them that way.

Regardless of our personal striving and public posturing,
there is no "winning" side in the working mother debate—
nor will there ever be. Yet just because we can't win, doesn't
mean we are doomed to lose.

It has often been observed that, when it comes to balancing career and family, there are no "right answers" for
women. I believe the real problem is that there are so many.
(I said "right answers," remember, not "perfect answers.")
We need to accept that finding the one that will work for us
must begin with an honest assessment of our own needs,
capacities, and values and those of our families. But because
all things are definitely not possible, we need also to know
what we're up against, both in terms of the social structures
"out there" and the emotional constructs we carry around
inside of us (often unconsciously).

If all that sounds complex, analytical, and a little exhausting, it's because it is. Which is why so many of us end up
accepting somebody else's prefabricated set of "shoulds" in
the first place. Finding a balance between career and family
is proving to be harder work than any of us bargained for.

Yet when we get around to pooling our resources—to sharing freely the intelligence we've gained from the front
rather than simply slinging the propaganda of our chosen
party line—we may find that the greatest barrier has already been overcome. Really, do we have anything to lose
but our masks?

My twenty-six-year-old stepdaughter is too polite to say so,
but I can tell she thinks I've got the motherhood thing way
out of proportion. It's not that she has a problem about combining kids and a career. To her, in fact, the only problem
would lie in not doing so. Pursuing paid work at the same
time as one pursues motherhood appears, from Naomi's perspective, about as challenging as being able to walk and
chew gum at the same time. A death-defying feat of skill
and daring it's not.

Generation Xers like Naomi represent the first generation of women for whom feminism is not accrued earnings
but inherited wealth. These young women have absorbed
the rhetoric of baseline feminist consciousness: equality of
opportunity in education, work, and play. Now in their
twenties and early thirties, they are beginning to confront
the realities behind that rhetoric: in relationships and in the
media, on the job and on campus, inside (to use the vernacular of the glossy magazines) the "bedrooms and board-
rooms" of contemporary American life.

Their self-esteem is high. Their goals are even higher.
They are women with attitude, so secure in their rights and
privileges that the old labels, including that of feminism itself, seem quaint or redundant. They don't need to "make an
issue of gender."[3] And, perhaps not entirely coincidentally,
most of these women have not (so far, at least) had children.

From the comfort zone of childlessness that such young

women enjoy, motherhood is defined chiefly as an industrial relations issue. "We're still fighting a common perception that if a woman has children she won't be taken as seriously in the workplace," writes Kathy Bail, editor of a recent collection of Generation X feminist thought. Yet as far as she and her peers are concerned, the future remains unambiguously bright, the way forward untrammeled and clear. After all, we are reminded, executives in some large companies "have already acknowledged they have to institute more flexible work arrangements if they want talented women to stay in senior management."[4] But the really "big liberating point" for mothers in the workforce, argues another contributor, is on-site child care. As the Pill made possible sexual freedom for her mother's generation, she explains, on-site child care will create maternal freedom for her own.[5] A third woman, "Alison," an economist, agrees. "The big issue for both parents is the proximity of childcare."[6] Perhaps not entirely coincidentally, none of these women has a child.

Among the five "corporate warriors" interviewed for a piece on the future of executive women, only one, "Julie," is married with children. Julie is a lawyer. As it happens, she doesn't require on-site child care; she employs a nanny. Flexible work hours are not really a problem either, as she works part-time. Corporate warriors like Julie, the authors insist, are "optimistic about their futures." Yet Julie doesn't sound optimistic to me. She just sounds tired, even defeated. Unlike her childless peers, Julie's reflections on the challenges of professional life are strikingly lacking in the rhetoric of workplace regulation. In fact, it's not her paid work as a professional that's the issue at all. Julie is mired in an industrial relations nightmare, all right—but it concerns her other job: her unpaid work as a wife and a mother.

The basic problem, Julie explains, is not work but . . . , well, life:

> I have a very supportive husband, but I still run the household. I still have to make all the decisions . . . Even if Ian does the shopping I write the list . . . I take responsibility for the shopping, for what we're going to have for dinner, to making sure the clothes are done, that all the washing is done. And on top of that I still go to work three days a week. And on the days off, I still have two children to look after — Every morning I still have to think about what we are going to have for dinner, do I need to do shopping for that? My husband just doesn't even think of it. It's a different world to him.

"I don't want to be defeatist," Julie says apologetically. She doesn't want to be — but she is. "At this time in my life I can't do everything and I have to realize that I can't do more at work. I certainly can't think about a promotion. It's just a matter of holding on to the position I've got." Indeed, Julie's problems with time management are so severe that she regards her paid work as a form of recreation. "I can't get time for myself any other way," she explains.[7]

Is Julie a blip in the trajectory of new-wave industrial life, a vestigial life form among the emergent breed of postfeminist corporate warriors? All the demographic evidence suggests that she is not. It suggests that where Julie is now, the rest of her generation will find itself very, very soon. The vast majority of them will marry or "partner," have babies, and settle down to a life of professional compromise, maternal ambivalence, and chronic fatigue. They will find, as Julie has found, that however many hours of paid work they chalk up, their unpaid workload as wives and mothers will remain substantially and alarmingly undiminished. They will find that, in sociologist Arlie Hochschild's phrase, they have come of age as mothers in a period of "stalled revolution."

The ideology of equality notwithstanding, maternity continues to be the great leveler among women and the great disequilibrator between the sexes. Nowhere is this effect more clearly visible than in the division of our labor and leisure.

Working men and working women continue to inhabit "different worlds," as Julie's experience so poignantly illustrates. Yet in a sense, the younger generation of feminists is right. It's not, strictly speaking, a gender thing. Rather, it is—quite literally—a motherhood issue. As the gaps in "equal opportunity" between males and females continue slowly to close, a more subtle fault line has emerged, dividing mothers from all others. The buck stops, as it were, with babies.

Motherhood will not slam shut the doors opened by gains in educational and economic opportunity for women. But it will, and it does, narrow and distort them in significant, uncomfortable, and utterly unanticipated ways. As a result, the current generation of mothers feels not only constrained, torn, and frustrated: they feel cheated, as if an important secret of adult life has been withheld from them. (It *has* been, of course.) All things were meant to be possible. The discovery that only a few of them are achievable, and some of those are mutually exclusive anyway, comes as a nasty shock.

That we could ever have believed otherwise is the legacy of 1970s feminist fantasies, according to Mary Ann Glendon, Learned Hand Professor of Law at Harvard University. "By treating marriage and motherhood as obstacles to women's progress," Glendon argues, first-wave feminist thought "actually helped to reinforce the idea that the only work that counts is work for pay outside the home."[8] As for the rest of life—the "motherhood thing" most emphatically included—well, we were implicitly assured, that would all fall into place somehow. We swallowed this, Glendon suggests, not because it made any sense (it didn't), but because we so badly wanted it to. The fantasy of "having it all" has been so alluring, we have been willing to give up almost everything—even our common sense—in the quest.

Isn't it time we grew up? Glendon suggests sternly. "The grown-up question is not can all our dreams come true," she writes, "The real question is whether we can do better than we're doing now."[9]

No, Virginia, there is no such thing as Supermom. Lots of women may appear to have their cake (as mothers) and be eating it too (as paid workers), yet the net result feels suspiciously like emotional bulimia. The mask of motherhood that women wear as workers conveys the usual deceptions: that we are serene, in control, and coping beautifully. Indeed, if anything, the mask suggests that we are in fact slightly superior, "lucky" in having such supportive partners, such adaptable children, such enviable career prospects. (If I had ten cents for every working mother who has ever said she is "lucky" to have a supportive partner, I could retire before finishing this chapter.)

Working mothers are now striving as never before to keep the cracks in their armor from showing. It's not simply that they are scared to seek special privileges for fear of losing their jobs or their self-respect, for fear of setting a bad precedent and letting their side down. It's that they have grown up believing that they are not entitled to any. Motherhood, they now believe, is not supposed to make a difference.

At the same time, we are all our mothers' daughters, and cannot help but be. In our collective, female unconscious we remember that, only a generation ago, the laws of our land forced women out of the workforce at marriage and, even more resolutely, at maternity. Hence, in our politically incorrect heart of hearts, we continue to regard our workforce participation as mothers to be a privilege. And we accept that we must pay for that privilege by consenting to work a full "second shift" at home, as wives and mothers.

What's more, we increasingly see motherhood itself as a privilege, an option we pursue rather than a necessity we accept. We work harder than ever at "succeeding" as mothers, and feel ever-increasing guilt about our inevitable shortcomings. For many of us, work for pay is a necessary outlet from the emotional hothouse of our own self-imposed standards of maternal excellence. Those who choose to forgo paid work and who also regard motherhood as a privilege often feel an even greater conflict, an even greater failure in "measuring up" to the phantom standard.

It is worth noting that few men, by contrast, see either fatherhood or workforce participation as "privileges." Despite welcome agitation within the men's movement to the contrary, paternity continues to be viewed by most men and most women alike in primarily genetic rather than behavioral terms. With the obvious and telling exception of the long-term unemployed, men do not regard work as a privilege either, but as an entitlement which is seen to carry both rights and responsibilities. Males in our society do not enjoy the luxury, still claimed by many females, of "opting" to work for pay. Either they participate in paid work, or they are regarded (and regard themselves) as deviant. This is both unjust and discriminatory. It means that men are in fact presented with fewer, not more, lifestyle opportunities from which to choose.

At the same time, less choice means less anxiety. Although the choices for men are beginning to expand, along with the growing social consciousness that man cannot live by breadwinning alone, in relative terms the ambiguities remain manageable. There is beginnning to be a bit of room to maneuver—with options like part-time work and house-husbandry now thinkable alternatives—but hardly room enough to get lost in. Men consistently report higher levels of satisfaction from marital and family life than do women. They are far less likely to initiate divorce and separation, report experiencing greater confusion and resentment when marriage does break down, and are far more likely to remarry quickly. For men, family life—which translates almost universally into full-time work and peripheral parenting—still works.

For women, increasingly, it does not. For women, the sudden expansion of options is reaching a kind of critical mass, in which the disjuncture between expectations and realities has grown absurdly and painfully wide. The price we are paying for our newfound "privileges" is enormous both in emotional accommodation and in sheer exertion of energy. Instead of "having it all" we find that we are "doing it all." We never reckoned on that. We married and became mothers in the expectation that our lives of independence and achievement would remain fundamentally unaltered. We expected to share parenting, to share the domestic burdens as well as the financial ones, in equal partnership with our men. We are shocked to discover, and often too ashamed to admit, how far from this ideal we have traveled. Parenthood was supposed to pull us even closer. Instead, we find it has banished us to different and mutually unintelligible worlds. We never reckoned on that, either.

From the start of the baby boom era, women's workforce participation has soared almost as high as our egalitarian ideals. Indeed, according to demographer Howard Hayghe, "The increase in the proportion of women who are working or looking for work that began shortly after World War II has been one of the most significant social and economic trends in modern U.S. history."[10] In 1950, for example, only 12.6 percent of married mothers with children worked for pay. Today, nearly three quarters of them do—and they are earning an ever-increasing share of the family income. Just a shade under half (48 percent) of women in married couples currently provide half or more of joint income.[11] It has been estimated that what we now call a "traditional" family (homemaker mom, sole-provider dad, and kids) accounts for less than 3 percent of American families today.[12] Although labor participation rates for childless women have remained flat since the 1980s, the number of mothers entering the workforce has continued to climb steadily. Between 1975 and 1995, for example, the workforce participation rate for mothers of children under six rose by more than 60 percent. According to 1997 figures, approximately two-thirds (63.9 percent) of women in this category were working for pay. Among mothers of infants under one year of age, workforce participation—which a mere generation ago would have been seen as tragic or aberrant—is now, at 56 percent, the statistical norm. Nor do these trends show signs of abating. Far from it. According to U.S. Department of Labor forecasts, by the late 1990s two thirds of all entrants to the U.S. workforce will be women, a majority of whom will be in their childbearing years.[13]

Not only are more mothers working, but more mothers are working longer hours. Among women in the workforce with children age twelve and under, for example, only 13 percent are currently working fewer than forty hours a week.[14] According to recent findings by the U.S. Bureau of

Labor Statistics, one in every two working mothers is now employed full-time. What's more, we like it that way. A mere 21 percent of American women work part-time by choice.[15] And almost half (48 percent) of us claim that we would still want to work if we had enough money to live as comfortably as we would like.[16]

Amid all of this enormous upheaval in our professional lives, women's reproductive lives have remained relatively constant. True, we are having our first babies later (the number of first-time births to women aged thirty to forty-four has more than doubled in the last thirty years) and we are having fewer of them overall.[17] But for the vast majority of women, workforce participation has been pursued in addition to, rather than as a substitute for, reproductive participation. Evidence suggests a slight rise in voluntary childlessness during this period. Yet our perceptions that motherhood has become "optional" for today's women are nevertheless exaggerated. In the United States, for example, current figures suggest that, among married women age forty-four and younger, fully 88 percent have children. Of the remaining 12 percent, less than a fifth are childless by choice.

Thus our participation in child bearing and childrearing has remained relatively constant. Yet the attitudes that we express about that participation have altered dramatically. In a survey conducted in 1971 — my first year of high school — eight out of ten women agreed with the statement "Motherhood is my most important role in life." In 1991 — the year my first child turned one — seven out of ten disagreed. In that same year, a majority of both married men (85 percent) and married women (91 percent) participating in a family formation project agreed that men should share equally in child care.[18]

Media reports labeling such findings "revolutionary" were no exaggeration. Studies like these demonstrate convincingly that our attitudes towards family life and towards the equitable distribution of labor within it—both paid and unpaid—have undergone genuinely cataclysmic shifts in the course of a single generation. This is the good news of feminism, the stuff of self-congratulation, "special report" coverage, and general banner-waving. Our attitudes are beyond reproach. And they are reflected, for the most part, in our impressive legislative record regarding equal opportunity for men and women in the relevant areas of workplace practices and family law. We know beyond a shadow of a doubt the way things should be. But what about the way things are? Has our rhetoric run ahead of our reality?

On the evidence of every recent examination into "who does what" in American homes, there is no doubt that it has. According to the most extensive and best known of these studies, Arlie Russell Hochschild's *The Second Shift*, even mothers who work full-time still end up carrying approximately two-thirds of the unpaid domestic workload. Adding together paid work plus housework plus child care, Hochschild discovered that women work approximately fifteen hours longer each week than men. Over the course of a year, that works out to an extra month of twenty-four-hour days of domestic slog.

Hochschild's findings, although based on research conducted in the 1970s and 1980s, are unchallenged by more recent work. In a review of the division of domestic labor literature conducted in 1993, social researcher Brenda Major found a clear consensus: that wives typically perform two to three times as much family work as their husbands. Indeed, one research team quipped that men continue to do so little around the house that research in this area is quite literally "much ado about nothing." This is the case whether wives work or not. As Major points out, "Husbands whose wives work outside the home spend about the same amount of time doing housework as husbands whose wives are full-time homemakers."[19] In fact, one study found that, in cases where the wife's earning capacity was greater than her husband's, sharing of household tasks was *least* frequently observed.[20]

State University of New York (Buffalo) researcher Beth Anne Shelton found that men with full-time working wives and men with full-time homemaking wives performed precisely the same amount of domestic labor per week: twelve hours. Only thirty minutes of that total, incidentally, involved "indoor cleaning."[21] Other research has shown that even in dual-career families, wives spend up to three times as many hours per week doing housework as their husbands.[22] Another study, which compared husbands' contributions to housework from the 1960s to the 1990s, found that the so-called "revolution" in the distribution of family labor has boiled down to a measly two hours a week of extra unpaid work for men—currently averaging about thirteen hours a week in total, compared with eleven hours three decades ago. "Men may do a little bit more housework than their fathers. They may help out a little bit more with their kids," concludes David Demo, professor of human development and family studies at the University of Missouri (Columbia), "but these small changes have been exaggerated. The fact of the matter is women still do all or most of the housework; all or most of the parenting" in addition to the work that three-quarters of us now perform outside the home.[23]

In a 1994 study of husbands' involvement in household chores traditionally associated with females (i.e., everything except yard work and home repairs), Marjorie Starrels found only about one-fifth of husbands to be "fully involved."[24] Nor do men make up for the shortfall by devoting more time to child care. In one study of white middle-class families in the Boston area, Grace Baruch and Rosalind Barnett found that working men married to working women spent only three-quarters of an hour a day longer with their kindergarten-age children than did those men married to full-time housewives.[25]

Demographers point out in black and white what the rest of us experience in living color every day: while our attitudes towards the division of labor in families have changed dramatically in the last two decades, our behavior has not. "The times have not shifted the bulk of chores from women," observes demographer Susan Mitchell bluntly. Examining the results of the General Social Survey in 1996, Mitchell found the "second shift" was alive and well in American homes. Indeed, of the five household chores examined in this study, only one was found to be performed "always or usually" by men: household repairs.[26] Starrels found that 54 percent of the men she studied performed no household chores at all.

Many researchers have noted the tendency for men to perform household tasks that are more physically demanding but are also more intermittent and generally less urgent than "women's work." As Hochschild has noted, "Even when couples share more equitably in the work at home, women do two-thirds of the daily jobs, like cooking and cleaning up—jobs that fix them into a rigid routine."[27] Men's work, by contrast—repairs, yard work, automobile maintenance—rarely needs to be done right now. Such jobs can be (and often are) postponed indefinitely, or at least until convenient—which is why, incidentally, they are the stuff of which nagging is almost inevitably made. Researchers have pointed out that the result is that the average male's domestic burden is lighter in both quantity and quality. In a 1997 study, for example, Rosalind Barnett of Radcliffe College and Yu-Chu Shen of Harvard University compared the effects of men's relatively low-pressure, high-control household tasks with those of high-pressure, low-control tasks like cooking dinner or feeding and dressing the kids in the morning. Not surprisingly, the latter were found to be significantly related to symptoms of anxiety and depression.[28] In the vast majority of American households, these daily "stress out" jobs remain overwhelmingly (and often exclusively) allocated to women.

If you think the division of domestic labor among couples presents a depressing picture (and you're right, it does), consider how much worse things become when "baby makes three." One large-scale study concluded in 1991 found that with the birth of a first child, a woman's domestic workload increases by 91 percent to reach a total of fifty-five hours and forty-eight minutes—while her husband's domestic workload (lower to begin with) does not increase overall by a single minute.[29] On the contrary, the male partner typically devotes more of his time to paid work during the baby's first year, a factor that often spells an actual reduction in time devoted to household chores. Following the birth of a first child, in other words, new parents divide the domestic "to do" list in increasingly gender-stereotyped ways. Researcher Marjorie Starrels has put it in the politest possible terms when she observes that "becoming a parent encourages more traditionalism. Indeed, there seems little doubt that the birth of a couple's first child—whatever else it may or may not portend—"represents the high water mark in segregation of paid and unpaid work by gender . . ."[30] To the extent that fathers perform any child-care tasks at all, they will spend a disproportionately small amount of time in the physical care of their children and a larger amount in play. Although mothers will spend even more time playing with their children, "this time is dwarfed by the large quantity of time devoted to less appealing aspects of childcare."[31] Not only do the domestic burdens associated with children—especially cooking, laundry, and cleaning—fall inequitably upon mothers, they actually increase as the baby grows to childhood. The result, observes researcher Michael Bittman, is inevitable: "All in all, mothers find themselves leading different lives to their partners."[32]

There has been a "revolution" in contemporary family life all right, and what it boils down to is yet more work for mother—precious little of which entails pay, professional advancement, or peer recognition. There has been a "revolutionary" raising of women's expectations and an equally "revolutionary" gap between those expectations and the realities we will almost inevitably face. There is nothing shocking about the finding that mothers and fathers inhabit substantially different worlds; they have done so for all human history. The shock is that we thought we were going to be different. We were wrong.

Husband and wife researchers Carolyn and Philip Cowan spent ten years studying the lifestyle changes that occur when couples have children. (The term "great divide," used throughout this book, is theirs.) Their findings in *When Partners Become Parents* echo those of virtually every other contemporary study of the division of labor within contemporary families: "the ideology of the new egalitarian couple is way ahead of the reality."[33] (Or, to put the same thing more bluntly, "wantin' ain't havin'!") Interestingly, the Cowans found that couples they interviewed in the last tri-

mester of pregnancy actually anticipated a somewhat unequal distribution of tasks after the baby's birth, particularly
with regard to primary child care. What they never expected
was the extent of that inequality. And it was the "fallout
from their unmet expectations," the Cowans argue, that
seemed "to convert both spouses' surprise and disappointment into tension between them."[34]

For many women (and for some men, too), the reversion
to traditional gender roles after the birth of a first child is not
only unwelcome but downright mysterious. One day a
woman is conducting herself like an emancipated, autonomous adult, sharing equally in the challenges and triumphs
of public life, and the next day she has turned into Beaver
Cleaver's mother. The metamorphosis is Kafka-esque. How
could something like this hit without warning? (Heaven
knows it wasn't mentioned in the prenatal class; Penelope
Leach and Benjamin Spock never got within spitting distance.) "It's not just that couples are startled by how the division of labor falls along gender lines," observe Cowan and
Cowan, "but they describe the change as if it were a mysterious virus they picked up when they were in hospital having their baby."[35]

Lawyer and author Rhona Mahoney argues that women
who expected that family life would be otherwise have been
kidding themselves. "We kidded ourselves when we
thought that government subsidies to child care centers
would eliminate the second shift. We kidded ourselves when
we thought about our own futures. 'Oh, it won't happen to
me,' we said. 'I have lots of energy and my husband will
help' or 'My mother will babysit and I'll be office manager
in no time.'"[36] Somehow it just doesn't work out that way.
We find that our estimation of the demands of parenthood
(and often of the delights of parenthood as well) was wildly,

even hilariously, ill-informed. We applied additive logic in a situation of geometric progression. It's no wonder we find it impossible to balance the books.

"Before the baby," Mahoney explains, "it is almost impossible to peep over the threshold and see what your life will be like afterwards." It is especially difficult for the current generation of new mothers to imagine life "afterwards." For better or for worse, we are uniquely placed at the crossroads between tradition and innovation—between the values we absorbed in our families of origin and the ideals we have been busily acquiring ever since. At the risk of oversimplifying an historical, cultural, and psychological nexus of truly terrifying complexity, the fact is that our hearts are telling us one thing and our minds another. Which is why what is most "startling" of all about the inequitable division of labor within contemporary families is how quickly we consent to participate in it.

Previous generations of women were much more adept at "peeking over the threshold" of parenthood; consequently, their expectations were better informed, more realistic, less vulnerable to delusion and shock. Traditionally, young women have envisaged motherhood by analogy with the lived experience of their own mothers (and other, older female kin). Among other things, that has meant that women expect their experiences as mothers to turn out more or less like those of the previous generation.

For young women on the brink of motherhood today, however, those familiar lines of gender succession have snapped. In important respects, we have ceased to "think back through our mothers," to use Virginia Woolf's memorable phrase.[37] Our educational opportunities, our professional aspirations and achievements, our notions of entitlement to the privileges of adult life (including, but not limited to, adult sexuality), often bear little or no relationship to those of our mothers' generation. We don't look like our mothers, we don't sound like them, and we don't act like them, either on the job or within our relationships. We have no reason to expect that, when we come to have children, any of this will change. And yet it does. To the best of our knowledge, brute force has ceased to be a factor in a typical family's prospects for economic survival. As Mahoney observes, "The glaciers have receded and mammoths are extinct, but this relic of the Pleistocene still slouches across our living rooms. Mom raises the kids."[38]

Yet supposing, just supposing, "Mom" actually wants to raise the kids—what then? It's a possibility that many commentators simply refuse to entertain. Joan Peters, for example, implies that any woman who opts for more than 50 percent of the parenting burden is either a traitor or a fool. Women who insist on full-time mothering, she argues, can neither "preserve their identities" nor "raise children to have both independent and family lives."[39] Mahoney also accepts the ideal of shared parenting uncategorically; what's more, she assumes her readers do too. Thus, her approach is essentially tactical in nature: a matter of figuring out strategies that will raise the bargaining power of mothers relative to fathers in the struggle to renegotiate domestic responsibilities. The assumption is that women view their unequal burdens in family life as unambivalently unacceptable. That what we are lacking is not will or conviction, but know-how. (Perhaps this is why one critic has described Mahoney's work, half-admiringly and half in scorn, as "very American and a little strange.")[40]

Mahoney argues that women continue to get the fuzzy end of the parental lollipop because—all other things being equal—the slight advantages their partners continue to hold in age, earnings, and cultural status are just substantial enough to tip the scales in their favor in any renegotiation of domestic deployment. Men still earn more, relative to their female partners—according to recent U.S. figures on the university-educated workforce, approximately twenty-three percent more.[41] Yet the effect is exacerbated by the Iron Law of Marriageability, which states, just as definitively in our own day as it did in Grandma's, that women marry "up" and men marry "down." In other words, women are virtually pre-programming inequality into their relationships by choosing men who are both older than they and whose income and earning potential are greater than their own. Thus, argues Mahoney, when it comes down to the question of whose career takes priority—as it often does with the arrival of the first child—it turns out that the real decision was made at the time of the marriage: it is the man's—the more established, the higher profile, the better paying one. Economic reality, it turns out, is notoriously resistant to rhetoric.

The earnings gap may be closing, but the fact that it's there at all continues to exert a massive, disproportionate force on family decision-making. "Sure I'd consider staying home with the baby—if my wife could earn as much as I do. But she can't. It's not my fault that we need the income," explains the understandably defensive New Man. Women who feel trapped by such logic, Mahoney suggests, are "kidding themselves" too. In a very real sense, the trap is of our own devising. It was our doing to marry "up." What we may not have realized is how much traditional baggage that single decision would inevitably drag with it. Under the circumstances of such obvious, structural inequality, it will continue to be women's professional lives, not men's, that will be diminished and delayed by parenting.

It is important to remember that this is the case even among the highest achieving women (who will of course tend to marry even more highly achieving men). In a recent survey of Harvard University's medical, legal, and business alumnae, for example, fully seventy percent reported having reduced their hours of paid work because of their children. Indeed, more than half had changed jobs or even specialties to accommodate childcare responsibilities.[42]

Yet the traps that women set for themselves are not simply economic ones. In our heart of hearts, we are not entirely certain that we want such equality. And we are not entirely certain, either, whether we are glad or we are mad that we don't.

In a study of forty-six high-achieving women with children, Kathleen Gerson found very few who professed a desire for marriage to "Mr. Mom." Not surprisingly, these high-income-earning women considered paid work very important. They did not respect or value homemaking—whoever was performing it.[43] Many other women are ambivalent about who does what around the house for the opposite reason. They do respect homemaking and childcare—so much so that the high standards they impose make it virtually impossible for their partners (or anyone else) to make the grade.

By means both intentional and unintentional, such mothers often sabotage their chances for a more equal distribution of the slog. They cherish a deep-seated belief that "Mother knows best," whether in relation to soothing a baby, scrubbing a toilet, or getting value for money at the supermarket checkout. In this, they are probably right. As we have seen, despite our lately acquired egalitarian ideals, most of us were raised in traditional families in which girls (whether they liked it or not) acquired the skills of nurturance and homemaking, and boys took out the rubbish and washed the car.

A 1993 study by psychologists at Boston University, which followed one hundred new parents for five years, found the problem of maternal sabotage to be nearly universal. Even the most committed feminists among the new mothers had a definite tendency to insist that their style of child- and homecare was best. Their men retreated quickly (whether in disappointment or relief, it is impossible to say). The authors concluded that such "gatekeeping" behavior reflects unconscious assumptions shared by both partners about women's innate superiority for nurturing.[44]

Are such assumptions false? Although a growing body of evidence suggests that they are, definitive answers remain tantalizingly elusive. One study, for example, found that "gatekeeping" behavior is common among lesbian couples, too—a finding that certainly tends to throw doubt on the "gender" hypothesis. Even more persuasive is the growing body of ethological evidence that, in many animal species, males behave as "innately" nurturant towards their young as do females. The tendency is especially marked among our nearest cousins, the primates.[45] Other researchers are equally convinced that women do retain a biogenetic advantage as caregivers. Among humans, they argue, females are measurably more sensitive to touch, sound, and smell, resulting in a slight but significant edge in effective caregiving. Thus, they conclude, "it is the mother rather than the father who is more alert to the nuances and the non-verbal hint, more naturally responsive to the babies' needs."[46]

While the question of our innate capacities remains unresolved, the question of our acquired expertise is no mystery to anybody. When it comes to all-around domestic competence, there remains a painfully evident "skills gap" between the sexes. Yet there is no doubt that women do nothing to close that gap, and may even contribute to widening it, with our eyeball-rolling and our in-jokes. ("How many men does it take to change a roll of toilet paper?" "No one knows. It's never been done.") It is a common complaint among today's women that their partners continue (just as their fathers before them) to perceive their domestic contributions as "helping"—as in "I helped you clean the house all day Saturday. What more do you want?!" Yet we reinforce this delusion more often than we realize by treating men's efforts as "help," and often inferior help at that.

Consider again the example of "Julie": "Even if Ian does the shopping, I write the list." Or of the myriad mothers who "allow" their partners to dress the kids but lay out the clothes beforehand. (I have one friend, a sales rep who travels frequently, who actually hides certain of the kids' outfits before leaving her husband in charge for the weekend. "You just would not believe the color combinations he comes up with," she offers by way of explanation.) "Proper nutrition" is another arena in which the clash between gender-related standards is unnerving for mothers. For a generation raised on the virtues of "Mom and apple pie," the reality of "Dad and junkfood" is difficult to swallow. If Dad's idea of a balanced breakfast is a bowl of sugary cereal with a Hawaiian punch chaser, the chances are that he will find himself sleeping in most mornings. It's not fair, grumbles Mom to her girlfriends, but what can you do?

Well, one answer is that you can simply do a whole lot less—starting with all forms of "gatekeeping." Ultimately, men don't need criticism as much as they need practice—and in chunks of time long enough to allow the feedback loop to complete its full cycle. (That is, make sure the man who insists on subduing a child with sugary treats sticks around long enough to deal with the behavioral burnout that is sure to follow. If he's laissez-faire about bedtimes, let him take responsibility for morning-after care, too.) But above all, women need to be prepared to accept the price of sharing the privileged status as primary caregiver: that when our children need us less, they will love us differently—less single mindedly for sure, and perhaps with less intensity. What a mother gains in "freedom," in other words, she will necessarily lose in "depth." It's a trade-off that many commentators appear to accept cheerfully. I've often wished I could be one of them.

Yet for me, and perhaps for most mothers, that trade-off explains more powerfully than any other factor the tie that continues to bind us to the terms of a demonstrably lousy bargain. Stephanie Brown and colleagues noted in the working mothers they studied an almost perverse "unwillingness to let go of the special, close relationship of mother and child."[47] These women had no difficulty accepting the traditional dictum that Mom raises the kids (although they faced enormous practical difficulties in enacting it—but that's a different matter). Mom is supposed to raise the kids. Mom has a giant stake in raising the kids—not just any old way, not a guy's way, but her way. The "payback" is not just love, and not just power, but some heady fusion of both that transcends the sum of each. Call it false consciousness, learned dependence, or biosocial imperative, the pull of primary parenting remains the strongest undertow of most women's lives. We need more than "strategy" to help us resist. We need to consider whether resistance itself is the appropriate stance. Personally, I suspect that it is not—and that the perversity lies not in women's unwillingness to "let go" of motherhood, but in the expectation that we ought to.

As far as household standards are concerned, Mahoney

argues, a woman who wants both motherhood and a life must learn to bend. If she insists on making her bed to her own exacting specifications, she may find she rarely has a chance to lie in it. "Nearly every chore can be done less often, more simply or just not at all," she advises. "The only real requirement—legally speaking—is that the house remain non-lethal."[48] Full-time professional and mother Adele Horin, who describes working mothers as members of a "Secret Circle" of maternal subversives, agrees. Do you find you have too many morning chores to attend to? Try "the working mother's best-kept secret," she urges: "Put your children to bed in their dayclothes."[49]

Why stop there? one wonders. Why not give the kids breakfast at 9:00 P.M. and be done with it? Why not go to bed yourself in your dayclothes? Come to think of it, why bother to bring the kids back home from school or daycare at all? If the best one can offer one's children is a "non-lethal" environment in which to sleep fully clothed, what on earth is the point of having them in the first place? "I consider myself a good mother," remarked one overworked informant in a recent study. "But my kids aren't having a good childhood."[50] There's something Orwellian about all this—about the greeting cards for parents too busy to see their kids ("Sorry I can't be there to tuck you in," "Sorry I can't say good morning to you"), about 1-800 telephone services like "Grandma Please!", which link kids who are home alone with elderly strangers in the same boat, about daycare centers from which parents can collect both their offspring and a pre-ordered, pre-cooked evening meal.[51] Adele Horin would be the first to admit there's something beyond absurd about such a lifestyle. "You've got to laugh," she says brightly— yet the suggestion is not without irony, nor entirely lacking in bitterness. For women working full-time in dual-career families with children, Horin implies, survival is its own reward. Indeed—apart from the camaraderie of conspiratorial commiseration with one's peers—it may be the only reward.

Relatively few women with young children appear able, or willing, to let go of enough of the traditional unpaid workload to render full-time paid employment a reasonable option—particularly in families with preschool children. Many pursue full-time work anyway; financially, and in some cases professionally, they have no option. For most, however, part-time employment seems the best, indeed the only, compromise. In the United States at present, almost two-thirds (63.9 percent) of women with pre-school-aged children are working for pay. Of all mothers of children under age 18, almost three-quarters are in the workforce—31 percent of them part-time.[52] These rates of employment have been widely interpreted as impressive evidence of large-scale social change. To an extent, of course, they are. The participation of mothers in the workforce has expanded exponentially. How women feel about their expanded participation is a different matter.

In fact, women's attitudes towards their paid employment reveal a much slower rate of social change, particularly among mothers of preschool children. When researchers asked women in this category about their work preferences, only 5 percent actually wanted to be working full-time, compared with 42 percent who expressed a preference for part-time work. The majority of women with young families (53 percent) preferred to do no paid work at all—including one in five women already employed.[53] Among all mothers who actually did work full-time, nearly half (43 percent) reported that they "did not have the energy to be good parents," as compared with 27 percent of working fathers. Either the standards of good parenting are a lot higher for these women than for their partners, or they simply have less energy because they are doing more. As we have seen, there is little doubt that both of these factors are relevant. Together, they constitute the working mother's double whammy, promoting a chronic-fatigue lifestyle in which "keeping all the balls in the air" too often becomes an end in itself. These are women who dreamed of blending marriage, motherhood, and career into a seamless, self-actualized whole. Yet for many, perhaps even for most, the reality feels as "blended" as a head-on collision.

The title of Elizabeth Perle McKenna's top-selling book, *When Work Doesn't Work Anymore*, says it all. In it, Perle McKenna describes the "yearning for balance" among the legions of full-time professional women who do not wish to parent via greeting cards, surrogate relatives, and Huxleyesque daycare centers. She points out that women who are employed full-time and have kids under the age of 13 are "the most stressed people in America."[54] Although such women rate "lack of time" highest on the list of stress factors, it is the underlying struggle with identity that probably hits us hardest of all. "Every professional woman I know with young children has two sets of competing urgencies," observes author and therapist Dr. Lillian Rubin. "It's not just values, but urgencies. These women want and need a professional outside-the-home identity and they want and need an identity as a mother. These women are always caught."[55] The real problem, explains a 42-year-old mother and political consultant whose quest for balance has involved boomeranging from full-time work to full-time homemaking, is that "none of my value systems go together"[56] Like the woman who considers herself a good mother but fears her kids aren't having a very good childhood, there is a serious flaw in the logic somewhere.

The term "the juggled life" suggests an existence characterized by ceaseless activity, awareness, and concentration, in which the real "trick" lies in maintaining the illusion of effortlessness. There is a suspenseful quality to the juggled life, too. Sooner or later, the law of gravity will snag even the most accomplished performer—though precisely when or how or with what degree of destruction no onlooker can ever be quite certain. Ultimately, of course, a juggler is a performer, and aims to please. Yet there is a clownish, absurd, and even tragic quality to this performance. As it happens, the consequences of successful juggling are even worse than the consequences of doing it poorly. The better at it you are, the harder (and longer) you will work. The more accomplished your performance, the more invisible your efforts become. After all, you "make it all look so easy"!

Women who juggle for a living and do it badly—which is to say, most of us—spend so much time chasing dropped balls that they have little energy to observe, let alone to question, the rules of the game. It doesn't feel right, mind you—being too busy to spend time with friends, to listen to music or read, to listen to your children's delightful nonsense, to exercise, to sleep. But the alternatives don't feel right either. The prospect of endlessly renegotiating the division of household labor with an unwilling or unable partner often seems more daunting than doing it all yourself. The option of resigning from paid work (providing that it is an option) is seductive one day and scary the next. It seems to be missing the point of your whole adult life up to now: the education, the goal-setting, the sheer hard work and dedication you've invested. To many women, the thought of being financially dependent on anyone, even someone they love and respect deeply, is repellent. Yet the pull of primary parenting—the desire to put one's children at the pulsing center of one's life, rather than neatly stacked around its periphery—remains an astonishingly powerful force in the lives of women who mother. Succumbing to that pull may feel like capitulation or defeat, while resisting it feels like treachery. Whichever choice a woman makes, "real life" seems to remain elusively, and tantalizingly, elsewhere. Whether owing mostly to nature or mostly to nurture, women continue to have more invested in parenting than their partners do or did. They set far higher standards for achievement, and they suffer more acutely when they perceive that they have fallen short. No one bothers to poll men about their work preferences; it is assumed (possibly incorrectly) that what men would prefer to be doing is precisely what they are doing. The burden of decision about the patterns of family life, along with the burden of proof that those decisions are correct, rests therefore almost entirely with women. This is so even in partnerships that most closely approximate the egalitarian ideal. Basically, behind every "equal" marriage is a woman exercising eternal vigilance to keep it that way. One recent large-scale study found that mothers resuming employment frequently anguished over individual decisions but accepted without question the role of human fulcrum for the family balancing act. Women rarely gave "any indication that the question of balancing employment and family responsibilities might rest on anyone's shoulders but their own . . . Sometimes extra 'help' came from partners or family, but it was almost always mothers who orchestrated the daily symphony, or perhaps cacophony, of family life."[57] Even in families with incomes high enough to hire out a good portion of the domestic load, the tasks of managing the help—finding, communicating with, and paying the nanny or babysitter, organizing the cleaner or ironing person, planning even the takeaway meals—fall almost entirely to the women. The assumption remains firm that it is she who is being replaced by the hired help, her time that is being "freed" by their labor. This same highly traditional logic dictates that the sum of all childcare and housecare expenses is deducted from the wage of the mother. In many cases, the woman is deemed to have earned the privilege of workforce participation if and only if her take-home wage significantly exceeds the cost of replacing her. If this is what we mean by "revolution," we *are* kidding ourselves.

The "problem that has no name" for today's mothers is the struggle to reconcile the rhetoric of equal opportunity with the stubbornly unequal realities of family life— among the most stubborn of all, the unwillingness of women themselves to abandon ship, or even share the wheel, when it comes to their traditional duties. "Having it all" means "doing it all"—and "doing it all" means doing none of it particularly well. I heard a friend remark recently that she was firing her house cleaner. "If I wanted the job done half-assed, I'd do it myself!" she declared stoutly, and without irony. It's how too many of us feel about too much of the responsibility we've agreed, with touching and totally uninformed optimism, to shoulder. The myth that part-time work offers women the "ideal" compromise between paid and unpaid work, family care and self-care, is yet another contemporary delusion—more insidious for being more widely held. In fact, in many respects, the mother who works for pay part-time has the worst of all possible worlds.

In the professional world, she finds herself (even in the most enlightened workplace) a second-class citizen—

almost inevitably taken less seriously for promotion and career advancement than her full-time peers. She is on the "Mommy Track," as Arlene Rossen Cardozo so unforgettably termed it, and everybody knows it. This is so even in cases where a part-timer's productivity is as high as or higher than that of full-time co-workers—which is not infrequent at all, as it happens. Part-time workers, particularly those in professional or management positions, are often driven to make the absolute most of their limited working time. Unlike their full-time counterparts, they have no slack for lunching, socializing, or office politics.

This not only places them outside the mainstream of professional life and reduces opportunities for networking, it imparts a stressful, structural urgency of its own. (This problem also dogs mothers in full-time employment, who struggle to keep their working hours within manageable bounds.) As Adele Horin has noted, "Working mothers make lousy lunch dates. It's not that they cut your steak or wipe the cappuccino froth off your upper lip. It's just that they're tense. They look at their watch a lot. They hassle the waiter."[58] Most of the women I know who work part-time while their children are young regard their paid work as both a treat and a privilege, and they are almost obsessively determined to make the most of it. Nevertheless, the perception that part-time work is more "casual" (in every sense of the word), and that it requires less commitment, continues to belie the reality.

When my first child was eight months old, I returned to work part-time in order to finish writing a book for which I had been contracted only weeks before conceiving her, and whose delivery deadline—by some bizarre poetic justice—fell precisely on my daughter's first birthday. Like most women returning to the workforce after a period of full-time parenting, I was astounded to discover how relaxed, even somnolent, the pace of professional life (in this case, an academic department) now seemed. Didn't these people have anything to *do*? I would wonder, with growing irritation, as I watched my colleagues indulge in all the normal time-wasters I had forgotten about: opening their mail, reading the paper, drinking coffee, trading gossip and occasionally even ideas. For myself, having only four scrawny little hours to fool with (almost a quarter of which were "wasted" on simply getting there), such prodigality was unthinkable. Even today, six years later, I still find myself explaining to perplexed colleagues that I don't do lunch—not ever. For me, and for millions of other part-time workers with young children, work *is* lunch.

Somewhat later, when I had expanded my hours to a 4-day week, a male colleague (himself the father of two young children) remarked enviously on my "long weekends." I pointed out that the privilege could be his, too, for the asking—if he was willing, as I was, to accept a twenty percent cut in pay. After my rage shifted from murderous to merely blinding, I reminded myself that this man (whom I had formerly counted as, if not a friend, then not exactly a savage either) was simply articulating an assumption shared by almost the entire civilized world: that the less paid work one performs, the more leisure time one has to enjoy. In fact, as recent research has demonstrated, the equation does hold water—but only for men.

This unpalatable fact of contemporary marital life forms one of the major themes of Arlie Hochschild's widely acclaimed study *The Time Bind*. Whereas men regard home as an escape from work, Hochschild argues, women increasingly look to work as an escape from home. In a profile of dual-earner parents and partners Linda and Bill Avery,

Hochschild casts an uncompromising light on the persistance of our unstated assumptions about entitlement to leisure by gender. "Both Linda and Bill felt the need for time off, to relax, to have fun, to feel free, but they had not agreed that it was Bill who needed a break more than Linda. Bill simply climbed in his truck and took his free time. This irritated Linda because she felt he took it at her expense. Largely in response to her resentment, Linda grabbed what she also called 'free time'—at work."[59]

The unequal distribution of leisure is a trend researchers have noted throughout the industrialized world. A study conducted in Australia by the Office of the Status of Women, for example, found unequivocally that "among women, reductions in paid work are associated with increases in unpaid work, while for men the trade-off is between paid work and leisure."[60] My insensitive colleague quite reasonably applied the same logic to my situation. He was unaware that reason has nothing to do with it.

When it comes to the division of labor, women increasingly perform as the packhorses of our egalitarian society—yet the bulk of their contributions continue to be unacknowledged, quite literally invisible in the common reckoning. The bleak folk wisdom that "a man he works from sun to sun, but a woman's work is never done" is truer today than it has ever been, yet we seem all of us (men and women alike) locked into a conspiracy of politically correct silence on the matter. When a father's idea of leisure is a game of golf and a mother's idea of leisure is part-time work, we can be sure that the egalitarian family exists largely in our dreams.

As we have seen, the mother who works part-time (often regardless of her productivity or her commitment) is likely to be perceived as less of a contender in the struggle for professional fitness. Nor does her status as part-time worker materially affect expectations—either her own, or those of her family—about her participation in unpaid work. Indeed, that is often the whole rationale for pursuing part-time work in the first place: "I want to work, but I don't want it to affect my family," women explain. The desire is understandable. The reality, it turns out, is unachievable—unless one excludes the mother herself from the definition of "family." In fact, this is precicely what does happen. Mother succeeds in meeting family needs to the extent that her own needs are denied, disallowed, or indefinitely postponed. In this way, the functioning of contemporary family life is increasingly predicated on the dysfunctioning, indeed the quite literal dismembering, of women's lives. And if it seems an outrageous overstatement to say so, this is only because we take such sacrifice for granted. More often than any of us is comfortable admitting, mothers earn the right to work for pay by foregoing not only leisure, friendships, and community involvements but even basic, physical needs—especially sleep.

In *The Second Shift*, Arlie Hochschild noted that many of the women in dual-earner families she interviewed "talked about sleep the way a hungry person talks about food."[61] Indeed, I have no doubt that sleep deprivation is the greatest single contributing factor to women's precarious mental health during the active years of early mothering. It is also the least researched. Publicly, we uphold the myth that once a baby learns to "sleep through" by three or four or six months, the problem has been solved. Privately, the nighttime reality of broken sleep commonly lasts for years—often up to and even beyond school age. In families with two or more children, the period in which a mother can expect to have her rest routinely interrupted can last for ten or more years. While this may be outrageous, it is also perfectly "normal." Yet many mothers never find out about the normality bit. They never read about it in the books, and even the best of friends are anxious to conceal the extent of the problem, assuming that it must reflect accusingly on their parenting.

It may be children who keep us wide awake at 3:00 A.M., but it is we mothers who keep ourselves well and truly in the dark about how little and how poorly we sleep. For mothers who work for pay by day, the invisible handicap of sleep deprivation can become a waking nightmare. Yet most soldier on silently anyway, zombie-like and with an almost continual dull throb in the temples, daydreaming about an uninterrupted night's sleep the way other people fantasize about wild sex or winning the lottery. In any other context, we would condemn such conditions as a form of torture— and hail its survivors as heroic. Yet in the context of motherhood, where the masks women wear are almost as impenetrable to ourselves as they are to others, our efforts are not only unsung, but utterly unacknowledged. Indeed, we collectively conspire to deny that we suffer at all.

For most working mothers with young children, life is a juggling act that keeps them too exhausted to examine the quality, let alone the inequality, of the experience. The stress such women feel is not simply the result of over-work—even though, relative to their male partners, they are overworked. In addition to this, women suffer because they are the meat in the sandwich between contemporary convictions of "equal opportunity" and the unyielding deep-structural realities of family life. These realities include a domestic division of labor that continues to disadvantage women to an extent that is nothing short of astounding in a so-called "postfeminist" world.

Yet when we consider the alternatives to the juggled life, the picture is equally, albeit differently, depressing. There is no doubt that trying to "do it all" leaves women breathless and resentful. As Lily Tomlin once remarked, the worst thing about the rat race is that, even if you win, you're still a rat. Yet the evidence suggests that even a ratlike identity may be better than no identity at all. For many stay-at-home mothers, opting out of the rat race feels exactly as if one has . . . well, opted out. It's not a good way to feel—as the dismal mental health profile of full-time homemakers forcefully attests. Of course, you'd never know this by looking at, or even necessarily by talking to these women. The fact is, women who opt for a traditional, exclusive-care mothering role tend to wear masks at least equally rigid, with smiles at least equally ironclad, as those of their work-for-pay sisters. Just as women in the workforce are too ashamed, or too confused, to admit when "work isn't working anymore," so women at home struggle to conceal their anxiety that home sweet home quite demonstrably isn't.

It is no exaggeration to say that, when it comes to the multiple choices we must make between work and motherhood, the only correct answer seems to be "none of the above." As Sharon Hays, author of *The Cultural Contradictions of Motherhood*, has observed, if a mother "works too hard at her job or career, some will accuse her of neglecting the kids. If she does not work hard enough, some will surely place her on the 'mommy track' and her career advancement will be permanently slowed by the claim that her commitment to her children interferes with her workplace efficiency. And if she stays home with her children, some will call her unproductive and useless. A woman, in other words, can never fully do it right."[62]

Although stay-at-home motherhood offers women a

more leisurely lifestyle, the social isolation and lack of status with which it is increasingly associated create their own difficulties. Indeed, the evidence suggests that the emotional stresses facing today's full-time mothers are even greater than those of their valiantly juggling sisters. Numerous systematic studies of women's work and home lives consistently confirm this: women who manage multiple roles—even those wracked with guilt about managing them poorly—actually feel better about themselves and their lives.

Cowan and Cowan, for example, found that women who returned to work part- or full-time before their child was eighteen months old reported fewer symptoms of depression than their stay-at-home peers. Other research has shown that mothers who work for pay not only have higher self-esteem but appear to have greater emotional reserves for dealing with their children as well. By contrast, women who have "excessive responsibility for their children and who are forced to spend long periods of time caring for them without help and without a break are likely to be irritable and emotionally unstable in their dealings with them."[63]

There is no doubt that the exclusive-care mother has a more intense relationship with her children. Yet, as child psychologist Bruno Bettelheim has pointed out, "intense" has the same root as "tense." Bettelheim's study of kibbutz-reared Israeli children, who are raised by "multiple mothers," found infants lacked "the utter security that may come from feeling himself at the core of his mother's existence"; at the same time, they escaped "the bondage" that such feelings may bring.[64]

It is also worth bearing in mind that both the concept and the practice of exclusive-care motherhood are historical and cultural anomalies. Throughout most of human history, in most places in the world, most mothers have worked outside the home—and choice has had nothing to do with it. This remains the case today. A 1977 study of parenting patterns in 186 non-industrialized societies, for example, found only five in which children were looked after almost exclusively by their mothers.[65] Although in our own society we refer to exclusive-care mothering as "traditional," the term is clearly a misnomer. As Miriam Johnson has noted, "the idea that the rearing of her own children could be a full-time occupation for an adult woman is very modern and without precedent . . . in earlier cultures."[66]

Yet it's possible to be overly glib about these interesting cross-cultural parallels. We need to keep in mind that "tradition" is, first and foremost, a state of mind, not a matter of fact. From this point of view, what feels "traditional" is simply that which we can recall as traditional. And in reality (as distinct from in academia) our memories do not extend much beyond a generation or two. What women are doing now in their mothering lives feels different, even if in historical or cross-cultural terms we can recognize that it is not. As Elizabeth Perle McKenna has astutely observed, rightly or wrongly, the "tenacious image" of the so-called traditional family "is the one centrally installed in most baby boomers' mental wiring."[67]

It's important to recognize too that definitions of both "mothering" and "working" within any social setting are also culturally and historically specific. Our goals and expectations as contemporary mothers bear little relationship to those of genuinely traditional peoples. We may share a sort of collective, universal core of maternal values—yet the standards and methods we use to apply those values remain diverse.

The same is true for the work we perform outside the

home. In almost all societies, women work—as do men—out of economic necessity (or at least the perception of economic necessity). Yet, from one society to the next, the manner of that work is so drastically different that comparisons may prove not only odious but downright silly. A woman in rural India whose "day job" is carting water and making dung cakes bears precious little resemblance to her American sister setting out for the office.

What's more, although both women would probably maintain that they work because they "have to," both the responsibilities they shoulder and the rewards they enjoy are utterly incommensurate. When work outside the home is a matter of family life or death, women squander little energy in anguishing over it. Where there is no alternative, there is no ambivalence either. In our own case, as Elizabeth Perle McKenna has pointed out, "most of the time it's our lifestyles—not our lives—at stake."[68] Although we share the rhetoric of economic necessity, we enjoy the unique and really, truly unprecedented reality of choice. It is this difference that makes all the difference, and no amount of anthropological research can erase it.

In our society, with exceedingly few exceptions, middle-class mothers who work outside the home do so because they want to, because it gratifies their own desires. And this, I suspect, is the unacknowledged root of the contemporary working mother's much-documented anxiety. As women, and especially as mothers, we have not yet ceased to fear that if it feels good it must be selfish—and that looking after ourselves will inevitably mean a dereliction in our first and truest duty: to look after everyone else. Wearing a mask called "Economic Necessity" allows us to pass the buck for our own gratifications every bit as much as wearing a mask called "Exclusive Care." In both cases, the rhetoric of maternal self-sacrifice—"I'm doing it for the sake of the family"—is precisely the same. It's also becoming increasingly threadbare.

Indeed, this insight may explain a great deal about why the so-called egalitarian revolution in family life has remained stalled for the past three decades—why working mothers continue to shoulder a disproportionate share of family work relative to working fathers, and why full-time mothers at home (who in most cases have been privileged to choose exclusive-care parenting) feel if anything even more embattled and embittered about enacting the role of sacrificial lamb in the drama of family life. All of us, it seems to me, are still behaving as if (like our mothers and grandmothers before us) our lifestyles had been foisted on us, rather than freely chosen. It's as if we were uncomfortable with the whole notion of choice—as if the exercise of free will were a form of conspicuous consumption too embarrassing to reveal publicly. Maybe we feel deep down that real choice remains a luxury to which, by virtue of being female, we have no natural entitlement. Possibly we continue to regard it as an "idea beyond our station," best repented for by continual hard labor.

One thing is certain: that we will never attain the goal of living comfortably with our choices as mothers until we acknowledge that we *have* choices and, even more importantly, that we deserve to have them. Women who diminish their own needs "for the sake of the family," by whatever means and however sterling their motives, are living a lie. If families do not begin with mothers, where do they begin? Even more to the point, where on earth can they hope to go?

Superwoman and Stuporman
Parenthood and Partnership

T HE PSYCHOLOGICAL LITERATURE is full to
bursting with discussion of what fathers and mothers can do to children but had remarkably little to
say about what children can do to marriages. Yet, when the
historical realities of family life are considered, the knowledge gap is less curious than it first appears. The fact is, until
remarkably recently, sexual partnership and parenthood
have been so closely associated—both ideologically and in
practice—as to be operationally indistinguishable. In traditional terms, there was no marriage without children, nor
children without marriage. Even the most determined psychologist has a hard time studying a relationship that
doesn't exist.

Throughout human history, sexual pairing has inexorably implied parenthood, to the extent that (other than in
cases of infertility) a "childless marriage" has been a contradiction in terms. Under such conditions, questions about
the impact of children on the marital "unit" of husband and
wife would have been logically meaningless. We need to be
reminded how avant-garde the concept of childless marriage is, in cross-cultural as well as historical terms. It is only
in modern times that sexual relationships between men and
women have had any significant existence in their own

right before, and separate from, the birth of a child. And this has been as true in our own industrialized society as in any traditional setting. A mere generation ago the shotgun wedding was a firmly entrenched cultural institution. Today, with roughly one in three American babies born out of wedlock (a term which suddenly sounds positively medieval), single parenthood seems about as "disgraceful" as writing left-handed. Between 1970 and 1990 the number of single-parent households in the United States nearly trebled.[1] While the figures for babies born to married women have remained constant, those for babies born to unmarried women continue to rise sharply (between 1980 and 1990, for example, by a whopping 64 percent). "What these figures illustrate," writes sociologist Naomi Miller, "is the growing decline of the centrality of marriage and its link to child-bearing in our society. It appears that parenthood (as well as love) and marriage no longer go together 'like a horse and carriage.'"[2]

The abrupt metamorphosis of parenting from bedrock biological necessity to lifestyle option (however widely chosen)—made possible by the advent of reliable contraceptive technology—has precipitated the discovery of marriage as a discrete entity. Other factors have reinforced the impact of technology on the social creation of the married couple. For instance, the expansion of educational and economic opportunities for women can be seen as having propelled sexual partners through the doors that technology has opened. In other words, women are having babies later in their married lives not simply because contraception has enabled them to do so but because they have other (and presumably better) fish to fry first.

For the first time ever, a significant stretch of married life without children is not only achievable but widely perceived as desirable. Underlying these changes is the revolutionary assumption that the core marital relationship—the one that pre-exists and is discrete from the arrival of the first child—has integrity and value in its own right. It is as impossible to underestimate the magnitude of this change as it is easy to forget how recently and how quickly it has overtaken us. In the course of a mere generation or two, we have succeeded in unraveling almost entirely the ancient knot that tradition-ally bound our joint destinies as parents and partners.

In many significant ways, we have re-imagined "the couple" with extraordinary success. Increasingly, men and women come together in marriage expecting to share life and its resources as devoted but equal partners shaping a common future. We factor into this equation our educa-tional attainments and professional goals, our friends and family, our social and recreational pursuits, and our aims for personal and spiritual development. We begin with a sense of our sameness, of how much we share, of our closeness as a couple. And we expect, over the course of our relationship, that that sharing and that closeness will grow even stronger, and that our already minimal "differences" will diminish even further. As partners, convergence at every level—sexual, intellectual, emotional, social—is our aim and our delight. We have no reason to expect that having children should, or will, change this. To the extent that we think about it at all, we imagine parenting as simply another in a series of joint undertakings, as another arena for the exercise of what we have come to call our "mutuality." Having chil-dren, we imagine (not unreasonably), will enrich our part-nership.

Yet, the reality is that parenthood will almost certainly erode the terms of that partnership irrevocably—with the result that we may have a hard time even recognizing ourselves, let alone basking in what we have achieved. Having children may or may not enrich a marriage. But there is no doubt at all that it will put our notions of partnership to a test that will spell failure for many and disillusionment for most. Our success in imagining, and in part enacting, an egalitarian vision of sexual partnership has obscured our failure in extending that vision—either imaginatively or in practice—to the project of parenting.

To those perched on the childless ledge of the great divide, Nora Ephron's description of the birth of a first baby as a hand grenade thrown into a marriage may seem harsh and exaggerated. Yet for those on the other side, the only shock it evokes is the shock of recognition. Although almost everyone is uncomfortable about admitting it, the addition of children to a marriage—however eagerly anticipated, however much loved—will create at least as much stress as harmony, and present at least as many new problems as it may appear to solve. Determining whether the rewards of parenting ultimately outweigh the costs to the relationship is a calculation men and women tend to make separately—and in secret.

"Of course it's been worth it!" we protest, possibly just a bit too loudly. By such means, we assure others (as indeed we assure ourselves) that the choices we have made—choices that just happen to be irreversible—were the right ones. Our mask of motherhood prohibits dissent. Probably our hearts do also. Yet such glib statements belie the complexity, the magnitude, and the sheer destructive force of the changes wrought when partners become parents. Indeed, the story of these changes is among the most closely guarded secrets of our public and private lives as adult men and women.

For previous generations, as we have already observed,

the transit from partnership to parenthood was more automatic than problematic. Indeed the two states were so closely intertwined, and the interval separating them was so brief that they were barely distinguishable. One result of this is a frustrating dearth of historical evidence with which to compare the contemporary experience. Yet enormous changes are discernible even in the short time in which it has occurred to researchers that there is something worth studying here. In a 1965 study, for example, 91 percent of new fathers and 71 percent of new mothers endorsed the statement, "Since the birth of the baby, my marriage is happier and more satisfying than before." Ten years later, the study was replicated using a new sample of first-time parents. This time, only 45 percent of the men and 39 percent of the women believed that having a baby had increased their marital happiness.[3]

It is no wonder that researchers remain convinced that the journey to parenthood is more treacherous today than ever before. Among the best informed of these researchers are Carolyn and Philip Cowan, whose 1992 *When Partners Become Parents* tracked nearly one hundred couples over the first five years of their parenting lives.

The findings from this landmark research convinced the Cowans that "the transition to parenthood is more difficult now than it used to be" and that "the evidence of risks to the parents' marriage and the children's well-being continues to mount." In stark contrast to our publicly paraded complacency about the unalloyed joys of parenthood, the Cowans found "there is a large body of data to suggest that the transition to parenthood is disequilibrating for a majority of men, women and marriages."[4] The fallout is most obviously harmful during the early postpartum period, with the majority of couples reporting many more negative than positive changes. Yet the shock of these early months is only the preliminary round in a long series of emotional explosions.

By the time their babies were eighteen months old, almost a quarter of the new parents in the Cowans' study reported that their marriage was in distress—and this was in addition to the 12.5 percent who had already separated or divorced by this time. These results are consistent with the conclusions of similar, smaller-scale studies: the presence of children does not "enrich" marital satisfaction; it erodes it. In the rather cold-blooded language of one study, "love decreased and ambivalence increased for both partners" following the birth of the first child. The effect was especially evident among mothers.[5] Overall, the Cowans found that fully 97 percent of the couples they studied reported more marital conflict after the baby arrived than before.

Paradoxically, however, as marital satisfaction declines, marital stability actually rises. In the Cowans' sample, for instance, one fifth of couples had divorced by the time their child entered kindergarten at age five. Yet the divorce rate for comparable childless couples was nearly 50 percent. Other research has found that, on average, divorce rates for families with a preschool child are half of what they are for childless partners.[6] When partners become parents, they may like each other less and less, but they stay together more and more. If this is what intending parents anticipate by "increased closeness," they have a definite point. Yet if they have anticipated, instead, a convergence of interests and activities as a couple, they are in for a cruel shock.

In fact, the most apparent effect of children on marriage points in precisely the opposite direction. With the appearance of the first child, there will be a marked divergence of interests and activities between partners—a dramatic widening of the gap between "his" world and "hers." And the direction of this divergence will be dictated to a distressingly predictable degree by traditional definitions of gender roles. However egalitarian the partnership may have been before children, after children the pull of these traditional gender roles will exert a force that in most cases will prove hopelessly irresistible. Indeed, research suggests that the more egalitarian the childless couple, the greater the shock will be—and the greater the damage the partnership will sustain.

The evidence is overwhelming: "As their roles become more specialized, men and women become more different from each other than ever before."[8] For couples who begin their partnership with an acceptance of such differences—a conviction that such differences are "right" (or at least "natural")—the growing pains for the marriage will be relatively minor. A mere generation ago, of course, such convictions were nearly universal. As late as 1977, 66 percent of adults polled in a national survey agreed that "it is better for everyone involved if the man is the achiever outside the home and the woman takes care of the home and family." By 1996, the figure had fallen to 38 percent.[7] Our own mothers and fathers may have begun to question the justice, or even the efficiency, of traditional gender roles within the family. But their explorations remained tentative and philosophical and were only rarely translated into action.

Today, by contrast, young men and women are far more decisive in their rejection of traditional gender roles, which are widely seen as both oppressive and vestigial. In the public sphere of school and work, they have witnessed genuine and substantive changes in these roles. For this generation, "equal opportunity" is not so much demanded as it is simply assumed.

For many, the assumption is carried over with relative

ease from public life into the private sphere of sexuality and relationships. Equality (more or less) within a partnership or a marriage may present unanticipated challenges. Maybe he still balks at scrubbing the toilet, but then again you hate to mow the lawn. He might cook a little less than you'd like, or cut too many corners with the laundry, but basically things seem fair—and compared with the way you remember your parents living, they seem positively utopian. Truly egalitarian marriages are probably a lot rarer than we like to admit, but an increasing number are at least approaching the ideal of down-the-line, fifty-fifty sharing.

Yet, when the first child comes along, most egalitarian couples will hit the wall at high speed. Just when they thought the dangers of gender typing were dead and buried, they find them rising up like unquiet spirits from the wreckage. Suddenly, she is "Mom" and he is "Dad," and— struggle and resist though they might—there isn't a hell of lot they'll be able to do about it. Again, the effect is particularly marked for couples who were sure it would never happen to them. Among working-class men and women, where researchers consistently find greater acceptance of traditional gender role differentiation, the transition to parenthood is rarely experienced as traumatic. In such couples, it has been suggested, expectations regarding leisure and adult autonomy are much lower (or more realistic, depending on one's interpretive angle).[8] Hardest hit of all are middle-class couples, particularly where partners are professionally employed and have their first child later, which, as we have seen, accounts for a growing sector of the population. Evidence suggests that men and women in this age range are more likely to maintain satisfaction with themselves as individuals during the transition to parenthood, but they experience a significantly steeper decline in marital satisfaction than their younger counterparts.[9] The more highly educated those parents are, the worse off they will be. Research shows that, for both men and women, gratification with the parenting role is negatively correlated with educational attainment.[10]

It is tempting to conclude that too much knowledge may be a dangerous thing, at least among men and women hoping to make a smooth transition to parenthood. Less cynically, such findings raise disturbing questions about the relationship between education and efficacy, between knowledge and maturity, between abstract "attainments" and applicable insights. To the extent that the education a society provides is demonstrably disabling to the lives of its future parents, the question "Education for what?" takes on a critical urgency. But I digress.

As the Cowans and other researchers have stressed, the problem is not so much the magnitude or even the multitude of changes that parenthood brings to a marriage: it's the direction of those changes. The core problem is that men and women are "changing in different directions while becoming parents: in the division of household tasks and child care, in social support outside the marriage, in work life."[11] The pattern of divergence is further complicated by the differential pace of change for mothers and fathers. Although both partners will undergo significant shifts in self-concept, attitudes, and behavior, mothers will change faster and further than fathers. "Most women make more than the necessary changes when they have children; most men make none," observes Joan K. Peters, author of *When Mothers Work*. "And when this happens, the family structure moves into a subtle disequilibrium, leaving the women to do it all and the men to pick and choose."[12]

When it comes to our marriages, we persist as individuals

in the hilarious illusion that we are "lucky" to have partners who express an ideological willingness to "help," or even partners who simply refrain from hindering us. ("Finn has been great since we had the baby," enthused one young mother to psychotherapist Stephanie Dowrick. "He never complains if his dinner isn't ready when he gets home. In fact, he says it is really monotonous always to have dinner at the same time. I am so lucky."[13])

Arlie Hochschild believes men and women both kid themselves about the extent to which they are "sharing nicely" in the joint enterprise of child care. She cites the experience of "Dorothy and Dan," a dual-earner couple with a young son, as epitomizing the "subtle disequilibrium" that seems to set in like a bad cold after the birth of a first child. "Dorothy worked the same nine-hour day at the office as her husband," Hochschild explains, "But she came home to fix dinner and to tend Timmy while Dan fit in a squash game three nights a week from six to seven (a good time for his squash partner). Dan read the newspaper more often and slept longer," too.[14] Yet, as journalist Kath Kenny points out, in most cases "the amount of time men spend doing housework is hardly more than the amount of time women spend thanking them."[15] All over America, there are women laughing themselves silly—as women have always laughed themselves silly—recounting sagas of male help-lessness. It's like a familiar Borscht Belt comedy routine: "Take my husband—please! He can't cook, he can't shop, he can't clean"—yet you must greet every incompetent attempt with effusions of gratitude anyway. And if you don't, he'll sulk. Underlying our complaints lies a perverse complacency, an acceptance that is difficult to justify on the evidence given.

Among the evidence not given are women's own feelings

of ambivalence about our entitlements to the bargain of equality. We are still, to a large extent, guarding our turf—or at the very least sending mixed messages about rights of entry. Studies of "gatekeeping" behavior among new mothers confirm that in many ways we are our own worst enemies. Despite our rhetoric to the contrary, most women continue to undermine and undercut the attempts of their men to even up the domestic score. This is particularly the case when it comes to the day-to-day management of our children's lives. As inexplicable or even as embarrassing as it may be, the fact is that most mothers—regardless of our professional status—still insist on non-negotiable oversight of our kids' meals, clothing, homework, television viewing, bedtimes, and a host of other mundane but somehow sacred spheres of domestic influence.

This tendency remains strong even within the 25 percent of married couples in which the woman is the primary wage earner. Media executive and mother of two Doreen Lorenzo, for example, has been her family's sole breadwinner since her husband quit his job as a commercial litigator to pursue doctoral studies and a more active role in family life. But it is Doreen and Doreen alone who chooses the kids' clothes, brushes her daughter's hair, and dispenses "unconditional emotional support" as needed. These, as she explained to journalist Peggy Orenstein, have become her maternal "lines in the sand."[16] As Joan Peters has quipped, getting a mother to relinquish management of her children's daily lives is "roughly equivalent to the former Soviet Union converting to capitalism."[17] It follows that the efforts of fathers who attempt to facilitate such a conversion may be met with a veritable Berlin Wall of resistance, to the surprise and dismay, generally, of both parties. Granted, in many cases such attempts are fledgling, halfhearted, and tentative. But is there any doubt that women's gatekeeping behavior is helping to guarantee that they will remain so?

Our collective horror of the Incredible Sulk, which we observe our men predictably becoming, is yet another stumbling block to genuine structural change within our families. And, like gatekeeping behavior, it is an impediment of our own devising. The expectation that our mates will cheerfully perform much more work in partnership than they observed their own fathers doing may be morally unproblematic but in it remains a big behavioral "ask." Getting men to do their fair share is difficult enough. Insisting that they do so happily and without resentment may be not only unrealistic but downright counterproductive. When you end up fighting not only about what he does but about how he feels, he's got you right back where he (and the entire culture) wants you: in the familiar feminine role of emotional fixer. If he wants to go off into his cave and sulk for a while every Saturday morning, that's his business. (As long as he does the work first, of course!)

Rhona Mahoney relates her aunt's favorite story: the night the Prince of Wales came to dinner and stayed to wash the dishes. Not surprisingly, whenever the aunt starts to tell it, a hush falls over the dining room. Well, who wouldn't be impressed? As it happens, the story has been fabricated by Mahoney herself to dramatize women's unwitting complicity in their own domestic oppression. "In male-female couples in which the woman feels deep down that the man really is the Prince of Wales, the man has an extra dollop of bargaining power."[18] It's an interesting way to frame the problem. We joke that men expect to be treated like royalty, yet we never joke about the fact that we are still organizing a good deal of our lives as families around the task of protecting that illusion.

We do this implicitly whenever we brag that our husband does half the cooking, when we consider ourselves "lucky" that he changes soiled diapers or helps with bathtime. I am continually amazed at the number of women who use words like "babysitting" and "minding" to describe the time their partners spend in child care. The language we use betrays the assumptions we still accept: that men who "help out" with the kids or the housework are doing women a favor. One does not "help out" with one's own life. One lives it. Evidently, this is a conceptual leap precious few families have succeeded in making.

The structure of pseudo-egalitarian family life may in fact be as oppressive to men as it is to women, although in an entirely different way. Canadian sociologist Amy Rossiter argues that the continuing inequities in the gendered division of labor within contemporary family life have disempowered fathers to the same extent that they have overburdened mothers. We are by now familiar with the figure of Superwoman, the all-competent, all-knowing, ceaselessly achieving and inwardly seething masked mother. But behind every Superwoman, Rossiter argues, is an increasingly ineffectual man. She calls this figure "Nothingman" (although I prefer to think of him as "Stuporman") and argues that he too is firmly caught within a domestic Catch-22. For reasons to do both with the still-powerful imperatives of breadwinning and with his wife's conscious or unconscious gatekeeping, Stuporman is denied any real opportunity for amassing the skills needed to perform competently as a parent or a homemaker. Increasingly constructed by his Superwoman partner as unneeded and unable, Stuporman "can only continue to do nothing right or to find ways of withdrawing."[19]

The fallout of all this is inevitable. It is difficult for most women to tolerate Stuporman, let alone to desire sexual and emotional trust and intimacy with him. He becomes a kind of domestic deadweight, an obstacle around which to maneuver rather than an object of desire. Fathers trapped within a Superwoman-Stuporman arrangement typically report feeling irrelevant to family life. They complain that they have been reduced to the status of a "walking wallet"—economically indispensable but emotionally exiled and peripheral. Yet neither partner seems able to discern their own responsibility for this crisis.

Perhaps understandably, women are particularly prone to take the moral high ground. As Rossiter observed of one couple she studied, "it is Tina who tells Ernie how to manage the baby; it is Ernie who is free to ride his bike."[20] Women who feel there is something inherently unjust about such a partnership are not wrong. Yet self-righteousness is a poor substitute for self-examination. Women have not created the cultural contradictions that increasingly plague family life. But by refusing to examine our own behavior, to acknowledge our own ambivalence and mixed messages, we cannot fail to perpetuate them.

The issue of the domestic division of labor dominates the literature on the transition from partnership to parenthood. As the Cowans explain, it is clearly the source from which all other marital discord springs. "From the reports of men and women in both one-job and two-job families," they found, "the division of the workload in the family wins, hands down, as the issue most likely to cause conflict in the first two years of family making."[21] It is important to recognize that the perceived quality of gender-related work and the differential quantity of that work are at least equally crucial. Hours spent in child care, as we have already observed, often constitute "invisible" labor. The work of child care is continuous, cyclical, and maintenance-driven. The emotional gratifications it affords are intense, but they are also diffuse and incremental over long periods of time.

Many women have confided to me that they feel most "motherly," and most rewarded as mothers, while gazing at their children asleep. Most seem to feel rather sheepish about this. Yet it is easy to understand these feelings. The intensity of continuous "in your face" interaction often makes it virtually impossible to get enough perspective, enough distance, to behold the fruits of one's labors. During my youngest child's first year—when my three children were all under five years old—the opportunities for observing them at a distance were particularly rare. In those odd moments when I was able to step back, to observe them at play with their father or another adult, I was rendered almost weak with happiness, almost limp with adoration. To say that I felt "rewarded" at such moments of genuine transcendence would be a pathetic understatement. Yet adults require more mundane types of gratification, too (not to mention more regular ones).

One that is consistently denied to primary caregivers of young children is the satisfaction of seeing a task through from beginning to end. Childless adults and most fathers take for granted the continuity of their endeavor and the expectation of achieving closure on tasks undertaken. For most mothers of young children, however, these are unimaginable luxuries. When my second child was still an infant, I recall one instance in which my husband and I fought bitterly about who was going to clean the oven. We both wanted to do it! We both wanted to be left alone, braving noxious fumes and slimy gunk, to complete a task that would not only yield decisive and visible results but that had recognized status as a "big job." Looking after the kids, by contrast—while much more onerous—was perceived by both of us (but especially me) as a "non-job" with no start, no finish, and no particular credit earned. A few weeks later, when my husband agreed to let me clean out the shed, I felt I had achieved an important victory. Looking back, I can only shake my head with wonder at the quicksand of unexamined assumptions in which both of us, as parents and as partners, were sunk. Yet I know, too, that our predicament is as common in today's marriages as it is absurd.

At the same time, I know such conflicts would not have arisen in my own parents' marriage or, heaven knows, in that of their parents. For contemporary women, the desire for what psychologists call "instrumentality" (and what the rest of us call "getting important things done") has far exceeded the capacity permitted them by traditional gender-driven roles. And, even in situations where both partners are working equally "hard" at domestic tasks, the quality of that labor remains stubbornly inequitable. In the pseudo-egalitarian family, women with young children are grateful to obtain their husband's "permission" to engage in uninterrupted housework. When mopping the floor, cleaning the oven, or finishing a garment are seen as privileges for women, yet freedom to pursue paid work or "big jobs" around the house are deemed necessities for men, we have fallen demonstrably and tragically short of our egalitarian ideals.

Another issue related to the quality of workload division within families is the fact that the "psychological labor" of family functioning continues to be borne almost exclusively by women. As psychologist Diane Ehrensaft points out, a mother is far more likely to function "as the psychological task-manager, carrying the daily burden of the child's day-to-day needs in her head and wishing the father did it more."[22] Even in those rare families in which shared parenting is an authentic reality, Ehrensaft found, it is the women who "carry around in their head knowledge of diapers needing to be laundered, fingernails needing to be cut, new clothes to be bought."[23] Rhona Mahoney confirmed this pattern among the professional American couples she studied, where the "mental work" of child care—"arranging doctor's appointments and babysitters; worrying about whether she's teething, has an ear infection, or is simply fussy; reading the baby book to see what developmental stage comes next; asking around about preschools and waiting lists"—fell consistently to the woman.[24]

As we have already seen, women frequently conspire—whether consciously or unconsciously—to maintain this inequity. But regardless of who is to blame (or praise, depending on your point of view), the resulting fatigue cannot help taking a toll on the marriage itself, and in particular on the sexual relationship between partners. There is no doubt that the "fatigue gap" has enormous and often disastrous consequences for intimacy in marriages after children. Although most relevant research has focused on the short-term impact of children on a couple's sex life, there is every indication that the consequences are depressingly far-reaching. The Cowans found that both husbands and wives reported a decisively negative change in their sexual relationship after the birth of a first child. "The frequency of lovemaking declines for almost all couples in the early months of parenthood, after having declined for about half of them during the last stages of the pregnancy," they report. One informant, "Sharon," is quoted as speaking for "all new mothers": "It's all I can do to keep my eyes open until nine o'clock. As soon as the baby is down I race for the bed, and I'm asleep most nights before my head hits the pillow."[25]

As we have seen, for mothers of children even as old as four or five, the prospects for an uninterrupted night's sleep once the head does hit the pillow may remain bleak. In the early weeks and months there will inevitably be demands for feeding and changing and pacifier retrieval. Later it will be teething or rolling off the bed or out from under the covers. Later still, drinks of water, nightmares, or toileting needs. When there is more than one young child in a family, the demands of nighttime parenting may be doubled or trebled. These are the realities of mothering young children. Yet they are such frightful realities that we conspire with success to keep them secret (which is why many fathers, and virtually all childless adults, can remain blissfully and outrageously unaware of their extent). Adrienne Rich speaks the unspeakable when she recalls what it was like returning to bed "starkly awake, brittle with anger, knowing that my broken sleep would make next day a hell . . . I remember thinking I would never dream again (the unconscious of the young mother—where does it entrust its messages, when dream-sleep is denied her for years?)"[26]

While the struggle for sleep consumes the lives of mothers, for fathers the battleground becomes the struggle for sex with those mothers. This remains one of the least discussed, and for many couples one of the most distressing, consequences of the transition to parenthood. I recently read a chirpy article in a women's magazine titled something like "Sex After Baby" which, it seemed to me, typified our collective coyness on the subject. It was full of useful advice about timing (do it while the baby is napping) and technology (stock up on K-Y Jelly), yet it failed to address any of the real sources of difficulty which, for many couples, render "sex after baby" a virtual contradiction in terms.

The first of these is the unsavory fact that a woman's libido typically plummets after the birth of her first child and may not regain its former cruising altitude for years thereafter. Not weeks. Years. The traditional six-week postnatal celibacy period for new parents allows enough time, in most cases, for the biological mechanisms of female sexuality to normalize. By that time, all the bits have more or less fallen back into place. The episiotomy has "healed" (although in many cases it will remain painful for months afterwards). Hormone levels have begun to stabilize (although in breast-feeding women the composition of that stasis will be markedly different from that of non-breast feeders). By this time, in other words, a woman's biological equipment for sex is theoretically functional. Sexual intercourse is unlikely to cause women "damage" from this point on. The problem is it may not cause them much pleasure either—and the reasons have little to do with the technical details of vaginal lubricity.

The most obvious cause of diminished libido in new mothers is fatigue. The question "What do women want?" which vexed Freud, and countless millions of males before and since Freud, can be answered very simply in the case of postpartum females. What they want is *sleep*, and if not sleep then at least undisturbed rest. And in a nuclear family structure in which a woman is solely responsible for infant care both day and night, she is not likely to get either of these for a long, long time. Few women expect that sleep deprivation will be a significant factor in their postnatal adjustment; even fewer ever contemplate the direct consequences of that deprivation for their sexuality and the quality of partnership they can expect as new parents. It is a subject on which our prenatal education, our child-care manuals, and our self-help parenting guides have kept the most chaste of silences. Exactly whom, one wonders, do we imagine we are protecting? The question is a disturbing one, but there is at least one sure answer: we as a society are not protecting women by keeping silent, nor are women protecting themselves.

The problem of sexuality in early parenthood becomes, if anything, even more complex the further we travel from the six-week baby shock period. In our society, research indicates, the average infant "sleeps through" by three months of age (the norms of infant sleep behavior vary astonishingly across cultures). Yet to suggest that the fatigue gap between parents will end at this point is as mindless as proposing that a "dirty weekend" away will put paid to the problem of family sexual politics. For one thing, women lie and lie freely about how much and how well their babies sleep. For some bizarre reason, it is taken as a point of honor among parents (but especially mothers) to be seen as having produced a particularly soporific infant. We need to remember, too, that researchers typically define "sleeping through" to mean sleeping continuously from midnight to daybreak. This is good going for an infant; yet for most mothers it still means at least one feeding interruption per night's sleep.

I know of no systematic study of sleeping patterns among new parents, yet anecdotal evidence suggests that mothers can expect to fall asleep anywhere between one to three hours earlier than their partners do, or than they themselves did before the baby's arrival. Many, many women continue to regard nine-thirty as a "late night" up to and beyond that baby's matriculation to preschool. The bedtimes of their male partners, by contrast, appear little altered by the presence of the first child. Indeed, if anything, women report that their partners appear to be staying up later than ever (possibly in order to savor the suddenly rare commodity of silence in the house). This pattern of divergent bedtimes first appears in the stress-filled early days of new parenting; yet it persists far beyond them, with obvious consequences for the couple's sexual relating.

Beyond sleep deprivation, or, as is more usually the case, in tandem with it, virtually every mother of young children faces the additional problem of sheer tactile overload. Women who assume primary care of young children necessarily spend a good part of each day, and often of the night as well, in direct skin-to-skin contact with live and demanding bodies—feeding, changing, cuddling, playing, lifting, soothing. Many women who resist "stressing out" under the weight of these demands nevertheless report becoming "touched out" by them. The result is a kind of tactile satiation or overfullness. In these women, the "hungers of the flesh," which are typically but quite illogically imagined as synonymous with sexual lust, are satisfied (if not glutted) by physical interaction with their children. Under the circumstances, the prospect of even great sex is a bit like sitting down to a gourmet meal after a day of being force-fed Happy Meals. One just loses one's appetite. Again, the research is silent on this issue, yet the whispered voices of mothers momentarily unmasked suggest a factor of enormous depth and extent, with direct consequences for women's sexual receptivity.

There is no doubt that family life entails a greatly accelerated struggle for women's bodies, and that demands for "privileged access" by men and children will clash inevitably and in many cases painfully. The silence we collectively conspire to keep on this dynamic of family life is an indication of how profoundly our society privileges the heterosexual tie relative to the maternal one. (For an extended discussion of this concept, I recommend Martha Albertson Fineman's book *The Neutered Mother and the Sexual Family*.) I suspect that the notion that a child's right to nurturing—let alone a woman's responsibility for self-nurture—might legitimately outweigh a man's "conjugal rights," remains almost unthinkably subversive.

The arena of sexuality provides yet another site—and a particularly sacred site, as we have seen—in which couples will tend to revert to traditional gender type after the birth of their children. Basically, women will tend to want much less sex (rather as they suspected their mothers did) and men will continue to want as much and more. For partners who came of age in the wake of the so-called sexual revolution of the 1960s and 1970s, the divergence of sexual energies and desires will be experienced as shocking and profoundly disappointing. Formerly childless Generation X feminists for whom the vibrator under the bed was standard equipment will be almost as ill-prepared for the shock of their libido loss as their unsuspecting male partners.

Sexually speaking, we were all supposed to be created equal. More to the point, we were supposed to stay that way. When we find that we aren't and don't, we are less likely to question the adequacy of our assumptions than we are to question the adequacy of our experience. The conviction grows that one has somehow gotten it all wrong (and everyone else has gotten it right) or that one is not "cut out" after all for family life (and everyone else is). In this way, the simple frustrations of marital life with children can become complicated beyond endurance. We are doubly disabled—first, by our lack of knowledge about the changes parenthood entails, and second, by our lack of nerve about revealing what we do discover.

Remember the study from the 1980s concluding that a single woman past the age of forty had as much chance of finding a marriageable mate as she did of being hit by a terrorist bullet? On the evidence given, the odds that any of us is going to achieve a truly egalitarian marriage may be even slimmer (roughly the same as being hit by a meteor, maybe). Couples who do succeed in sustaining such relationships are a bit like exotic birds who have been induced to take up residence in a suburban backyard. They are not only elusive, but the care and feeding they require is downright exorbitant.

As Rhona Mahoney points out, partnerships that come closest to genuine, fifty-fifty sharing in both instrumental terms (paid and unpaid labor) and relational ones (responsibilities for nurture and care of others) are more cumbersome to maintain, and in many ways less efficient, than relationships in which partners "specialize." Safeguarding democracy at home, it turns out, is much like safeguarding democracy at large: the price is eternal vigilance, and an enormous expenditure of energy on negotiation and renegotiation of tasks and privileges. The point is, genuinely shared parenting is a high-maintenance enterprise. As a result, those couples who do manage to walk the egalitarian tightrope are (and will continue to be) "oddballs."

One potential drawback of dividing tasks down the middle instead of following traditional gender lines is the danger that depth will be sacrificed for breadth: competence for all, Mahoney argues, may mean excellence for none. Things will get done, in other words, but perhaps none of them will get done particularly brilliantly. Where men and women specialize, by contrast, just as one partner can excel at the office, "high levels of performance in unpaid family work can create a special, warm atmosphere at home."

Couples who genuinely share the paid and unpaid workload may have to forgo both the job promotion and those "extra domestic touches." "They may pay the price willingly," Mahoney concedes, "Still, they pay it."[27] She concludes that the losses that result from the failure to specialize will continue to ensure that the egalitarian ideal of family life will remain just that—an ideal.

A more realistic and more satisfying arrangement, Mahoney argues, would be to support specialization and diversity in the division of a family's paid and unpaid labor, but to sever the gendered imperatives that have traditionally determined our assumptions regarding who ought to be doing what. The primary parent, she suggests, probably should be home much of the time, and probably should assume an "unequal" share of the family's unpaid labor. Life is simply more efficient that way—and often more rewarding for all its members. Having said that, Mahoney argues that there is no reason whatever that this primary parent/homemaker be the female of the pair. To this end, she advocates an affirmative action policy for men that would provide specific rewards and bonuses (including tax breaks) for "Mr. Moms" at home. A woman's place is no longer necessarily in the kitchen. But a society full of empty kitchens can't possibly be a workable alternative either. Somebody's got to be in there, Mahoney suggests. Why not men?

While I appreciate the logic of Mahoney's argument, I am slightly more optimistic about the possibility of forging alternative family structures. In particular, it seems to me that the option of part-time paid work for both parents—leaving both free, at least theoretically, for truly shared participation at home—presents an obvious way forward. It would preserve possibilities for that much-needed domestic specialization that often makes the difference between a pit stop and a home. I see no reason why a special interest in or aptitude for, say, orchestrating grand family meals should necessarily be linked with full-time parenting. Or why parents who are particularly good at engaging in creative or active play with their children (often fathers) should therefore also be skilled at interior decoration or gardening. Generally, it seems to me, the real obstacle to specialization among dual-earner couples is not the division of paid and unpaid labor per se, but simply the amount of time that two full-time jobs inevitably eat up. At the same time, of course, I am aware that implementing such an "obvious" solution under the prevailing conditions of American work culture would be about as practical for most couples as starting up a neighborhood commune. In fact, part-time work is subversive not only of our prevailing economic ideology, but of a whole host of entrenched values in the wider culture—complexities that cannot begin to be tackled adequately in the present discussion.

Even those few couples who manage to buck the greatly stacked odds in favor of gendered tradition—and who do succeed in forging a more-or-less equal partnership in parenting—may find themselves precariously placed. Their heads have been educated in the 1970s or 1980s, but their hearts, it seems, belong to the 1950s or 1960s. Quite often, such "success story" families look good but feel bad. Contemporary couples who feel like they can't do anything right now have an impressive research base to prove the point. The point is not that social change is impossible—as (to cite one recent source) the impressive case histories in Joan Peters's *When Mothers Work* attest. Rather, it is that substantive change unfolds so much slower than most of us would prefer or even admit, and in directions often entirely unanticipated.

At the moment, as the Cowans have observed, most modern couples are penalized whichever way forward they choose: "When one parent brings home the bacon while the other stays home to look after the child, both can feel underappreciated and strapped economically, which burdens the marriage and the children. When both parents work outside the family, they tend to feel better about themselves and about their contributions to the family economy, but parents and children are breathless, often missing the opportunity for intimate moments."[28] Thus, the more different we become as parents, the greater the tension we experience as partners. Yet the project of minimizing those differences, whether it proves, in the final analysis, worth our collective while to pursue, remains for the current generation of new parents a risky venture.

There is something seriously absurd about the notion that children are bad for marriages, yet—absurd or not—it is part of the social reality in which we are mired. What we expect of ourselves as partners and what we require of ourselves as parents tallies poorly, if at all. The result is a deal in which everyone feels short-changed without ever quite understanding how they got that way.

Conclusion

The words are being spoken now, are being written down; the ta-boos are being broken, the masks of motherhood are cracking through.

—Adrienne Rich

TWO DECADES HAVE PASSED since Adrienne Rich observed the fissures in what she was the first to call "the masks of motherhood." Her own book, *Of Woman Born*, a brave and eloquent account of mother-hood as experience and institution, constituted one of the earliest and deepest of these cracks. Yet Rich remained acutely aware of the riskiness of the enterprise she had un-dertaken. Unmasking motherhood, she grasped, was a greater challenge to the feminist imagination than all the other "women's issues" put together.

The centuries-old conspiracy of silence surrounding the experience of motherhood lay embedded in the patri-archy—but it was first and foremost women's business. The familiar gender politics of "us" versus "them" simply didn't apply. Whereas the remainder of the feminist agenda—centered largely around the pursuit of educational, eco-nomic, and sexual equality—could legitimately be seen as "their problem," motherhood was something different. Motherhood was *our* problem. The silences we chose to maintain about our feelings, the taboos we chose to observe, the lies we consented wordlessly to circulate were a snare that women had constructed all by themselves. The legacy that Rich called the masks of motherhood may have been jointly protected by the fathers, but the line of descent was distinctively matrilineal, passing directly from mother to daughter.

Rich prefaced her book with a quotation from Dante's *Inferno*: ". . . but to treat of the good that I found there, I will tell of other things I there discerned." The poignancy of this plea, a plea for permission to name the shadows in order to know the light, reflects tellingly the extent to which the Motherland was still regarded as hallowed cultural ground. By the late 1970s, as critic Neil Postman has observed, virtually the entire culture was coming out of the closet, asserting long-denied rights to speak and to be heard. Yet the great tidal wave of civil rights protest—which included of course the "women's movement" in its first, post-Friedan wave—managed to wash over the core experience of motherhood, leaving its contours remarkably intact. To the extent that motherhood made it onto the agenda at all, its terms of reference were strictly operational. "Free and universal day care" was a standard entry on every feminist wish list, as was "abortion on demand." The best we were capable of doing about motherhood, it seemed, was asserting our right to evade it. It was as if the shadows—the ones that Rich and a handful of others had begun so courageously to inspect—had proven too ominous even for feminists to face.

This was a generation sick to death of empty romanticizing about "the good to be found" in the experience of mothering, yet overwhelmed by the sheer emotional complexity of "the other things there" to be discerned. As a result, the masks of motherhood that women wear today, while somewhat altered in expression, have retained a startling tenacity. Twenty years on, we are still afraid to speak too loudly or too clearly on the subject of our own experiences as mothers; still at pains to prove a point that should have been obvious long ago: that in the constellation of most women's experience, our children are no mere satellites; they are the very sun around which life revolves. And that this fact, however inconvenient, bespeaks no character flaw of gender, but rather the very greatest of human gifts. And also, as it happens, the very greatest of human challenges. It follows that those who attempt to deny or subvert the centrality of motherhood to the human project—including feminists who have conspired to throw out the baby with the ideological bath water—are acting in a way fundamentally hostile to women's interests.

The taboos surrounding motherhood remain potent. And the fear that they continue to inspire remains a peculiarly female fear. It is as if we believed motherhood to be a privilege we might lose, might be deemed unworthy of, rather than our birthright as females of the species.

Our cultural discourse increasingly frames motherhood as a "lifestyle option." At one level this is of course true. Yet at another, motherhood lies—today, as it has always done—at the very core of the experience of being female. The bearing and raising of children is no longer our inevitable biosocial destiny. Yet it remains the single most potent tie that binds the diversity of our experiences as women. Whatever else it may or may not be, motherhood is nonnegotiably "ours" to construct—or to deconstruct.

At the same time, and to an extent that it has become politically incorrect to concede, motherhood is an experience of the body as much as it is of the mind. As a biological reality, motherhood is supremely indifferent to ideology, to historical or technological "progress," to culturally imposed norms and values. The experiences of pregnancy, childbirth, and lactation are physiological events with indisputably physiological consequences. So, too, is child care itself, in which the dialogue between skin and skin, the rhythms of sleep and wakefulness, the interplay of touch and tickle are as eloquent as any of the more elaborated forms of communication in which humans engage. The experience of motherhood is mediated through the body to an extent unparalleled by any other form of relationship. Women who speak of being altered by motherhood from the inside out are not engaging in metaphorical flights of fancy; they are expressing a literal truth.

I believe that the mask of motherhood has prevented women from recognizing the power they possess, and from acknowledging the necessities to which they must bow as mothers. The issue of control is central to both of these tasks—which perhaps explains why we are so obsessed with maintaining control over our mothering lives and so inefficient at achieving it. Why we have grasped that the balance is off, that for all that we do (which feels way too much), there seems so much more that remains undone, or done too halfheartedly to count. It has become commonplace to observe the enormity of the "gains," the rich multiciplicity of options, that contemporary women enjoy. There is no doubt that, compared with our own mothers and grandmothers, we are onto a good thing. Yet too much of a good thing— and the present reckoning suggests that's exactly what we're up against—can be almost as disheartening as not enough.

Almost, but not quite. Even if we could turn back the tide to the certainties of an earlier age, there are few women who would seriously take up the option. There is, after all, no "golden age" to return to. The vanished certainties of traditional gender roles had the advantage of coherence for women, yet at a price that was oppressively high for individuals and for society as a whole. The "problem that had no name" for our mothers' and grandmothers' generations, while not precisely "solved," is nevertheless an historical artifact today. Women can and do compete on a roughly equal footing with men in most of the arenas that legislation and social policy can touch. But there remain other places that they cannot touch, shadowy places in our minds and hearts and—perhaps most important of all—in our bellies. To put it bluntly, the feminist agenda has succeeded up to a point, and that point is motherhood. Beyond motherhood, our sexual politics remain more fraught and tense than ever, with both women and men staggering under a new weight of contradictory and extravagant expectations.

And it is mothers who stagger worse. It is mothers who struggle to reconcile the urge for primary parenting with an equally insistent longing to retain the full range of adult (formerly "male") entitlements. Sociologist Ann Oakley argues that postfeminist motherhood poses one of the greatest dilemmas of our time: "Can women be both people and mothers; can mothers be people?" The question, she admits, is oversimplified, yet real.[2] The struggle of fathers, by contrast, while also real, is primarily reactive. Parenthood will not precipitate a crisis of the same order, and it will introduce far fewer behavioral or emotional changes in the life of the average man. Indeed, arguably the biggest impact of parenting for most males will be coping with the changes that their female partners undergo.

Our collective denial that the motherhood versus personhood question exists at all, that it is worthy of notice or attention, is what I have been calling the mask of motherhood. Motherhood remains a "motherhood and apple-pie issue" for women themselves, "off the point, irrelevant to the main purpose," writes sociologist Judith Lumley.[3] Lumley and her colleagues were surprised as well as dismayed to find that "women had very low expectations of anyone being interested in their experiences as mothers, or that anyone would think that these experiences were important."[4] Other research confirms these dispiriting findings.

Yet the evidence also suggests that, for individual women, the private experience of motherhood unmasked is quite another matter—infinitely more profound and meaningful, more joyous and transcendent, yet more vexed and ambivalent, more downright dangerous, than we have yet dared to voice. "Being a mother means having radical surgery," writes Melissa West.[5] Yet it remains for most of us a back-street operation. Like other "women's problems," public revelation of its indelicate, murky depths is a clear breech of cultural protocol. And we would rather die, many of us, than reveal its scars. We are expected instead—and we expect of ourselves—to "take it like a woman": stoically, singly, silently. There is undeniable gallantry in the brave faces we put on. But most of all, there is fear.

Researchers have noted a marked reluctance among women to discuss the emotional impact of motherhood, as well as the related conviction that it is "unnatural" for mothers to feel stress or anger, frustration, or tedium. Research also suggests that while virtually every mother does experience such emotions, most consider that they have no right to do so, that such feelings are aberrant and shameful. "Such a disclosure can feel like an expression of personal failure as a woman and as a mother, which reinforces the view that if other people knew about these unmothering, unfeminine feelings, they would react with disapproval and rejection. Anticipating a reaction of this kind is a potent incentive for remaining silent."[6]

Perhaps paradoxically, today's women—who have consciously determined to redefine "femininity" in nontraditional terms—seem to experience even more performance anxiety, and are even less inclined to expose the chinks in their maternal armor, than previous generations. More and more, we approach motherhood in a spirit of oddly misplaced professionalism, as if it were a project on which our promotion depended. We do our research, we purchase our infrastructure, we develop plans, and forecast outcomes. And when all that gets blown to bits—as inevitably it does—we scramble to cover our flanks. "Saving face" is what masks are all about. Yet for whom, or from whom, do we seek protection?

Increasingly, women come to motherhood as mature, achieving, independent adults with fully formed expectations of entitlement. Unlike our mothers and grandmothers, for whom the onset of motherhood marked the conferral of adult status, we haved forged alternative paths to female adulthood. Today, the average woman will have experienced at least a decade of more or less autonomous adult life by the time the first child arrives. To expect to keep that life intact is not unreasonable. It is simply unrealistic.

The fact is, the presence of children does not simply "add" to the lives of adult caregivers; it transforms those lives utterly—for better, for worse, and in all manner of subtle and tricky ways too complex to inventory. The momentousness of this transformation is no longer muted by the fusion of motherhood and female adulthood into a monolithic sociobiological necessity. In the course of a mere generation or two, technology and social change have turned the imperative into an interrogative. Motherhood is no longer what women must do, virtually by definition. It is now an open question: something we can do, might do—

perhaps even ought to do—but above all something we decide to do.

Yet "decide" is perhaps not quite the right word after all. The term implies a rational process, a sifting of argument and counterargument, a dispassionate audit of pros and cons. At the very core of decision making lies information. Where information is partial or unreliable, so too will be the performance of the decision maker and the efficacy of her choices. Where a decision is largely uninformed, the power of the decision maker is largely illusory. This is precisely the dilemma we now face in regard to our destinies as mothers: we have the power to decide, all right. We have the power to define our own terms. What we lack is the wherewithal on which to base those decisions and to formulate definitions that will work. The "knowledge base," such as it is, continues to lie where we can't get at it: on the far side of the great divide which our own silences have erected. The ancient channels of succession which saw the secrets pass from grandmother to mother to daughter have been disrupted, if not severed outright. As people, we may be flying high. Yet as mothers, most of us are flying blind. Is it any wonder we land with such a devastating crash?

What human beings need to know about mothering is perhaps the greatest story never written. The journey to motherhood is an odyssey of epic proportions, and every woman who undertakes it a hero. Celebrating our role at the very core of humanity means learning to sing every line of that epic freely, the lamentations along with the hymns. When the masks of motherhood do crack through, they will have been eroded by tears that have been shed and shared, by the tremor of secrets unclasped, by the booming laughter of relief. What lies beneath the brave and brittle face of motherhood is a countenance of infinite expressiveness, a body of deepest knowing.

It's been more than a half century since Dr. Benjamin Spock assured young mothers, "You know more than you think you do." So we do. And so, too, do our mothers and grandmothers, our daughters and aunts and nieces, and the woman who lives next door. We do know more than we think we do. We know more than Spock thinks we do, too. We always have. When we stop being so brave, we might even find the courage to say so.

Notes

INTRODUCTION

1. Friedan, p. 7.
2. Hochschild 1997, p. 138.

CHAPTER 1. FAKING MOTHERHOOD

1. Lerner, p. 14.
2. Ibid.
3. Barrett, p. 142.
4. Rossiter, p. 177.
5. Kitzinger 1992, p. 7.
6. Ibid, p. 8.
7. Friedan, p. 59.
8. *The West Australian*, May 17, 1996.
9. Cited in Knowles and Cole, pp. 4–5.
10. Gibson, p. 30.
11. Knowles and Cole, p. 3.
12. Oakley 1979, p. 263.
13. Rossiter, p. 168.
14. Rich, p. 36.
15. Leach 1994, p. 241.
16. Chesler, p. 133.
17. Rabuzzi, p. 63.
18. "Connections around Childbirth," in Adelaide, p. 120.
19. Adelaide, pp. 2–3.
20. "Apocalypse Now," in Adelaide, p. 44.
21. "Connections around Childbirth," in Adelaide, p. 120.
22. Caplan, 1989.
23. Dally, p. 20.
24. Cited in O'Barr et al.
25. Chodorow, 1987.

26. Dinnerstein 1976.
27. Chesler, p. 92.
28. Caplan 1981, p. 99.
29. Ibid., p. 16.
30. Brown et al., p. 162.
31. Caplan 1981, p. 30.
32. Rabuzzi, p. 188.
33. Chesler, 1981.
34. West, p. 28.
35. Ibid.
36. Oakley 1992, p. 188.
37. Dally, p. 245.
38. Ibid., p. 122.
39. Bernard, p. 79.
40. Apter, p. 154.
41. Dally, p. 245.
42. Hrdy, p. 7.

CHAPTER 2. "FALLING"

1. Jeffery et al., p. 91.
2. Richardson, p. 108.
3. Bourne, p. 7.

CHAPTER 3. LABORING UNDER DELUSIONS

1. Estimate supplied via e-mail by the American Society for Psychoprophylaxis in Obstetrics in March 1998.
2. Quoted in Gottleib and Pancer, p. 270.
3. Quoted in Davis-Floyd, p. 307.
4. Crouch and Manderson, 1993, p. 65.
5. Ibid.
6. Gibson, p. 61.
7. Crouch and Manderson, p. 112.
8. Davis-Floyd, p. 38.
9. "Apocalypse Now," in Adelaide, p. 61.
10. "Desiring the Unknown," in Adelaide, p. 213.
11. Lamott 1993, p. 18.
12. Introduction in Adelaide.
13. "Apocalypse Now," in Adelaide, p. 61.
14. "All points of the compass," in Adelaide, p. 36.
15. Brown et al., p. 98.

16. Mackey 1990.
17. Ibid., p. 148.
18. Davis Floyd, p. 115.
19. Ibid.
20. Davis-Floyd, p. 195.
21. Ibid.
22. Ibid., p. 281.
23. Ibid., p. 283.
24. Crouch and Manderson 1993, p. 66.
25. Ibid., p. 96.
26. Ibid., p. 123.
27. Kitzinger 1987, p. 19.
28. Nice, p. 168.
29. Mackey, p. 134.
30. "Apocalypse now" in Adelaide, p. 66.
31. Quoted in Barrett, p. 3.
32. "Harvest day" in Adelaide, p. 285.
33. Mackey, p. 153.

CHAPTER 4 · PENELOPE LEACH MEETS GODZILLA

1. "Desiring the Unknown," in Adelaide, p. 216.
2. Ibid.
3. Rabuzzi, p. 71.
4. Cited in Davis-Floyd, p. 42.
5. Iovine 1997.
6. Barrett, pp. xi–xii.
7. Price, p. 126.
8. Davis-Floyd, p. 43.
9. Rabuzzi, p. 217.
10. Brown et al., p. 162.
11. Dix, p. 19.
12. Ibid.
13. Mercer, p. 132.
14. Ibid.
15. Barrett, pp. 52–3.
16. Caplan 1981, p. 110.
17. Dix, p. 77.
18. Ibid.
19. Price, p. 134.
20. Cowan and Cowan 1992, p. 29.
21. Cited in Kitzinger, p. 13.

22. Dix, p. 16.
23. The phrase is Ann Oakley's.
24. Dix, p. 16.
25. Brown et al., p. 176.
26. Bernard, p. x.
27. Brown et al., p. 202.
28. Ibid.
29. Price, p. 130.
30. Leach 1989, p. 94.
31. Brazelton, p. 63.
32. The West Australian, 30 August 1996, p. 7.
33. Boulton, p. 62.
34. Oakley 1979, p. 263.
35. Ibid., p. 261.
36. Brown et al., p. 164.
37. Walker and Best, p. 71.
38. Barris, p. 62.
39. Kitzinger, p. 12.
40. Ibid.
41. Crouch and Manderson 1993, p. 27.
42. Ibid., p. 28.
43. Oakley 1979, p. 67.
44. Ibid., p. 69.
45. Gibson, p. 60.
46. Barris, p. 62.
47. Ibid.
48. Rich, p. 12.
49. Rossiter, p. 179.
50. Price, p. 126.
51. La Leche League International, p. 88.
52. Ibid, p. 89.
53. Eisenberg et al., p. 293.
54. Spock, p. 3.
55. Leach 1994, p. 79 (emphasis retained).
56. "Normal parents: institutions and the transition to parenthood" in Palkovitz and Sussman, pp. 305–6.
57. eg. Abernethy (1973), cited in Gottleib and Pancer, p. 256.
58. Price, p. 129.
59. Welburn (1980), cited in Brown et al., p. 249.
60. Caplan 1981, p. 70.
61. Leach 1994, p. 54.

CHAPTER 5. LACTATION INTOLERANT

1. Figures compiled by Ross Laboratories, supplied to the author courtesy of the Center for Breastfeeding Information.
2. Price, p. 55.
3. Brown et al., p. 107.
4. St. James-Roberts, et al., p. 107.
5. Ibid., p. 111.
6. Elias, et al. (1986), cited in St. James-Roberts, et al., p. 168.
7. Carey (1975), cited in St. James-Roberts et al., p. 165.
8. St. James-Roberts et al., p. 112.
9. Price, p. 63.
10. St. James-Roberts et al., p. 113.

CHAPTER 6. THE JUGGLED LIFE

1. Peters, p. xiii.
2. Bail, p. 15.
3. Ibid., p. 14.
4. Henderson and Roitman, "Corporate Warriors," in Bail.
5. Ibid., p. 116.
6. Ibid., p. 117.
7. Glendon, pp. 11–15.
8. Ibid., p. 14.
9. Hayghe, p. 41.
10. Cited in Perle McKenna, p. 266.
11. Barnett 1996, cited in Perle McKenna, p. 220.
12. Cited in Perle McKenna, p. 262.
13. Cited in Hochschild 1997, p. 27.
14. Ibid., p. 34.
15. Ibid, p. 28.
16. National Center for Health Statistics, cited in Perle McKenna, p. 82.
17. Cited in Wolcott and Glezer, p. 6.
18. Major 1993.
19. Cited in Starrels 1994.
20. Cited in Waldrop 1990.
21. Cited in Starrels 1994.
22. *USA Today*.
23. Starrels 1994.
24. Cited in Hochschild 1989.
25. Mitchell 1996.
26. Hochschild 1996, p. 8.

27. Cited in Crispell 1997.
28. Bittman 1991.
29. Starrels 1994.
30. Bittman., pp. 47–48.
31. Ibid.
32. Cowan and Cowan, p. 12.
33. Ibid., p. 97.
34. Ibid., p. 98.
35. Mahoney, p. 3.
36. Woolf, p. 69.
37. Mahoney, p. 3.
38. Peters, xiii..
39. Pollitt, p. 13.
40. Cited in Mahoney, p. 12.
41. Cited in Mahoney, p. 139.
42. Cited in Mahoney, p. 219.
43. Betcher and Pollack (1993), cited in Mahoney.
44. See Hrdy.
45. Moir and Jessel, p. 144.
46. Brown et al., p. 221.
47. Mahoney, p. 99.
48. In Adelaide, p. 171.
49. Hochschild 1997, p. 135.
50. Ibid., pp. 228–232.
51. Figures cited in Hayghe 1997, Hochschild 1997.
52. Cited in Wolcott and Glezer, pp. 81–3.
53. 1991 Virginia Slims Poll cited in Perle McKenna, p. 157.
54. Cited in Perle McKenna, p. 147.
55. Ibid., p. 59.
56. Brown et al, p. 221.
57. "The secret circle," in Adelaide, p. 173.
58. Hochschild 1997, pp. 39–40.
59. Bittman, p. 3.
60. Hochschild 1989, p. 9.
61. Hay, p. 133.
62. Cited in Boulton, p. 200.
63. Cited in Oakley (1974), p. 215.
64. Weisner and Gallimore.
65. Johnson, p. 26.
66. Perle McKenna, p. 220.
67. Ibid., p. 268.

CHAPTER 7. SUPERWOMAN AND STUPORMAN

1. Miller, p. 82.
2. Ibid., pp. 3–4.
3. Hobbs (1965), cited in Cowan and Cowan, p. 117.
4. Cowan and Cowan, p. 29.
5. Belsky et al.
6. Cherlin (1977), cited in Emery and Tuer.
7. Cited in Cherlin (1998), p. 39.
8. Jacoby (1969), cited in Emery and Tuer, p. 127.
9. Cited in Cowan and Cowan, 1992.
10. Russel (1974) cited in Emery and Tuer, p. 127.
11. Cowan and Cowan, p. 112.
12. Peters, p. 10.
13. Dowrick 1991, p. 110.
14. Hochschild 1989, p. 20.
15. "Sex and Harassment," in Bail, p. 141.
16. Orenstein, pp. 42–48.
17. Peters, p. 82.
18. Mahoney, p. 57.
19. Rossiter, p. 146.
20. Ibid., pp. 146–47.
21. Cowan and Cowan, p. 108.
22. Ehrensaft, p. 450.
23. Ibid.
24. Mahoney, p. 109.
25. Cowan and Cowan, p. 106.
26. Rich, p. 32.
27. Mahoney, p. 80.
28. Cowan and Cowan, p. 203.

CONCLUSION

1. Oakley (1992), p. 248.
2. Brown et al., p. 263.
3. Brown et al., p. 260.
4. West, p. 29.
5. Brown et al., p. 161.

Bibliography

Adelaide, Debra, ed. (1996). *Mother Love*. Milsons Point, NSW: Random House Australia.

Apter, Terri. (1985). *Why Women Don't Have Wives: Professional Success and Motherhood*. London: Macmillan.

Badinter, Elisabeth. (1981). *Mother Love: Myth and Reality*. New York: Macmillan.

Bail, Kathy, ed. (1996). *DIY Feminism*. St. Leonards, NSW: Allen & Unwin.

Barnett, Rosalind C. and Caryl Rivers (1996). *She Works/He Works: How Two-Income Families Are Happier, Healthier, and Better Off*. San Francisco: HarperCollins.

Barrett, Nina. (1990). *I Wish Someone Had Told Me*. New York: Simon and Schuster.

Barris, Beverly H. (1991). "Employed mothers: The Impact of Class and Marital Status on the Prioritizing of Family and Work." *Social science quarterly*. Mar Vol 72 (1), 50–66.

Baxter, Janeen (1993). *Work at Home: The Domestic Division of Labor*. St Lucia, Qld: University of Queensland Press.

Belenky, Mary Field, Blythe McVicker Clinchy, Nancy Rule Goldberger, Jill Mattuck Tarule. (1986). *Women's Ways of Knowing*. New York: Basic Books.

Belsky, J., Lang, M., & Rovine, M. (1985). "Stability and change across the transition to parenthood: a second study." *Journal of Personality and Social Psychology*, 50, 517–522.

Bergum, Vangie. (1989). *Woman to Mother: A Transformation*. Granby, Mass: Bergin & Garvey.

Bernard, Jesse. (1974). *The Future of Motherhood*. New York: Penguin.

Bernard, Jesse. (1975). *Women, Wives, Mothers: Values and Options*. Chicago: Aldine.

Berryman, Julia C. "Perspectives on Later Motherhood," in Phoenix, et al. (1991).

Bittman, Michael. (1991). *Juggling Time: How Australian Families Use Time*. A Report on the Secondary Analysis of the 1987 Pilot Survey of Time Use.

Prepared for the Office of the Satus of Women, Department of the Prime Minister and Cabinet. Canberra: Commonwealth of Australia.

Boulton, Mary Georgina. (1983). *On Being a Mother: A Study of Women with Pre-School Children.* New York: Tavistock Publications.

Bourne, Gordon. (1989). *Pregnancy.* London: Pan Books.

Brannen, J. & Moss, P. (1990). *Managing Mothers: Dual Earner Households after Maternity Leave.* London: Unwin Hyman.

Brazelton, T. Berry (1992). *Touchpoints: Your Child's Emotional and Behavioral Development.* Reading, MA: Addison-Wesley.

Brown, Stephanie, Lumley Judith, Small Rhonda, Astbury Jill. (1994). *Missing Voices: The Experience of Motherhood.* Melbourne: Oxford University Press.

Bryson, Lois. (1993). Equality, Parenting and Policy Making, *Australian Journal of Marriage and Family.* Vol. 14, No. 2, 66–75.

Caplan, Paula J. (1981). *Barriers Between Women.* Lancaster: MTP Press Limited.

Caplan, Paula J. (1989). *Don't Blame Mother: Mending the Mother-Daughter Relationship.* New York: Harper & Row.

Cardozo, Arlene Rossen. (1986). *Sequencing.* New York: Athenum Publishing.

Carroll, Lewis. (n.d.). *Alice in Wonderland and Through the Looking Glass.* New York: Grosset & Dunlop.

Cherlin, Andrew J. (1998). By the Numbers. *The New York Times Magazine.* April 5, 1998, p. 39.

Chesler, Phyllis. (1981). *With Child: A Diary of Motherhood.* New York: Berkeley.

Chodorow, Nancy. (1978). *The Reproduction of Mothering: Psychoanalysis and the Sociology of Gender.* Berkeley and L.A.: University of California Press.

Cobb, John. (1980). *Babyshock: A Mother's First Five Years.* London: Hutchinson & Co.

Comer, L. (1974). *Wedlocked Women.* Leeds: Feminist Books.

Cowan, C. P. & Cowan P. A. (1992). *When Partners Become Parents: The Big Life Change for Couples.* New York: Basic Books.

Coward, Rosalind. (1983). *Patriarchal Precedents: Sexuality and Social Relations.* London: Routledge & Kegan Paul.

Crispell, Diane (1997). Why men take out the garbage. *American Demographics.* Nov. 1997 v19 n11 p35(1).

Crouch, Mira & Manderson, Lenore. (1987b) Keeping afloat: post-partum experience among Australian women, paper presented at the Public Health Association of Australia and NZ, Sydney.

Crouch, Mira & Manderson, Lenore. (1993). *New Motherhood: Cultural and Personal Transitions in the 1980s.* Sth. Australia: Gordon & Breach.

Dally, Ann. (1982). *Inventing Motherhood: The Consequences of an Ideal.* London: Burnett Books.

Davis-Floyd, R.E. (1992). *Birth as an American Rite of Passage.* Berkeley & Los Angeles: University of California Press.

Dinnerstein, Dorothy. (1987. this ed. orig. published 1976). *The Rocking of the Cradle and the Ruling of the World.* London: The Women's Press.

Dix, C. (1986). *The New Mother Syndrome.* Sydney: Allen & Unwin.

Dowrick, Stephanie (1991). *Intimacy and Solitude.* Auckland, NZ: Reed Books.

Ehrensaft, Diane (1994). "Dual Parenting and the Duel of Intimacy," in Handel & Whitchurch, (1994).

Eisenberg, Arlene, Heidi Eisenberg Murkoff and Sandee Eisenberg Hathaway. (1990). *What to Expect When You're Expecting.* North Ryde, NSW: Collins/Angus & Robertson.

Emery, Robert E. and Michele Tuer. (1993). "Parenting and the marital relationship," in Luster and Okagaki, (1993).

Entwistle, D.R. & Doering, S.G. (1981). *The First Birth: A Family Turning Point.* Baltimore, MD: Johns Hopkins University Press.

Everingham, Christine. (1994). *Motherhood and Modernity.* St. Leonards, NSW: Allen & Unwin.

Fineman, Martha Albertson. (1995). *The Neutered Mother and the Sexual Family.* New York: Routledge.

Firestone, Shulamith. (1972). *The Dialectic of Sex: The Case for Feminist Revolution.* London: Paladin.

Friedan, Betty. (1963). *The Feminine Mystique.* New York: Dell Publishing Co.

Gavron, Hannah. (1968). *The Captive Wife.* Harmondsworth: Penguin Books.

Genevie, Louize, & Margolies, Eva. (1987). *The Motherhood Report: How Women Feel about Being Mothers.* New York: Macmillan.

Gerson, Mary-Joan, Alpert, Judith L. & Mary Sue Richardson. (1986). "Mothering: The View from Psychological Research," in Jean F. O'Barr, Deborah Pope, Mary Wyer, eds. *Ties That Bind: Essays on Mothering and Patriarchy.* (1990). Chicago and London: The University of Chicago Press.

Gibson, Margaret. (1986). *Becoming a Mother: A Book for Australian Women.* Sydney: Hale and Iremonger.

Glendon, Mary Ann. (1997). Feminism and the Family. *Commonweal,* Vol CXXIV, No. 3, pp. 11–15.

Glenn, Evelyn Kanao, Grace Change and Linda Rennie Forcey, eds. (1994). *Mothering: Ideology, Experience, and Agency.* New York: Routledge.

Gottlieb, Benjamin H. and S. Mark Pancer. (1988). "Social Networks and the Transition to Parenthood," in Michaels and Goldberg, (1988).

Hafner, Julian. (1993). *The End of Marriage.* London: Random House.

Hayghe, Howard V. (1997). Developments in Women's Labor Force Participation. *Monthly Labor Review*, Sep 1997 v120 n9 p41(6).

Hays, Sharon. (1996). *The Cultural Contradictions of Motherhood*. New Haven: Yale University Press.

Hochschild, Arlie Russell. (1997). *The Time Bind: When work becomes home and home becomes work*. New York: Henry Holt and Company, Inc.

Hochschild, Arlie Russell and Anne Machung. (1989). *The Second Shift: Working Parents and the Revolution at Home*. New York: Viking Penguin.

Hrdy, Sarah Blaffer. (1981). *The Woman that Never Evolved*. Cambridge: Harvard University Press.

Iovine, Vicky. (1997). *The Girlfriends' Guide to Surviving the First Year of Motherhood*. New York: The Berkley Publishing Group.

Jeffery, Patricia, Roger Jeffery & Andrew Lyon. (1989). *Labor Pains and Labor Power*. London: Zed Books.

Johnson, Miriam H. (1988). *Strong Mothers, Weak Wives: The Search for Gender Equality*. Berkeley: University of California Press.

Kitzinger, Sheila. (1992). *Ourselves as Mothers*. London: Transworld Publishers.

Kitzinger, Sheila. (1987). *The Experience of Childbirth*. Harmondsworth: Penguin Books.

Knowles, Jane Price and Ellen Cole, eds. (1990). *Motherhood: A Feminist Perspective*. Binghampton, NY: Haworth Press.

La Leche League International. (1988). *The Womanly Art of Breastfeeding*. North Ryde, NSW: Angus & Robertson.

Lamott, Anne (1993). *Operating Instructions: A Journal of My Son's First Year*. New York: Fawcett Columbine.

Leach, Penelope. (1989). *Who Cares: A New Deal for Mothers and Their Small Children*. Harmondsworth: Penguin Books.

Leach, Penelope. (1989). *Baby and Child*. Harmondsworth: Penguin Books.

Leach, Penelope. (1994). *Children First*. London: Penguin.

Lerner, Harriet. (1993). *The Dance of Deception: Pretending and Truth-Telling in Women's Lives*. New York: HarperCollins.

Lette, Kathy. (1996). *Mad Cows*. Sydney: Pan Macmillan Australia.

Luster, Tom and Okagaki, Lynn, eds. (1993). *Parenting: An Ecological Perspective*. Hillsdale, NJ: Lawrence Erlbaum Associaties, Inc.

McDonald, Peter. (1995). *Families in Australia: a Socio-demographic Perspective*. Melbourne: Australian Institute of Family Studies.

Mackey, Marlene C. (1990). "Women's Preparation for the Childbirth Experience." *Maternal Child Nursing Journal*. Vol. 19, no. 2. 143–173.

Mahoney, Rhona. (1995). *Kidding Ourselves: Breadwinning, Babies, and Bargaining Power*. New York: Basic Books.

Major, Brenda (1993). Gender, Entitlement, and the Distribution of Family Labor. *Journal of Social Issues,* Fall 1993 v49 n3 p141(19).

Marshall, Helen. (1993). *Not Having Children.* Melbourne: Oxford University Press Australia.

Martin, E. (1987). *The Woman in the Body: A Cultural Analysis of Reproduction.* Boston: Beacon Press.

Mercer, Ramona T. (1986). *First-Time Motherhood. Experiences from Teens to Forties.* New York: Springer Publishing Co.

Michaels, Gerald Y. and Goldberg, Wendy A., eds. (1988). *The Transition to Parenthood: Current Theory and Research.* Cambridge: Cambridge University Press.

Miller, Naomi. 1992. Single Parents by Choice: A growing trend in family life. New York: Plenum Books.

Minturn, L. & Lambert, W.L. (1964). *Mothers of Six Cultures: Antecedents of Child Rearing.* New York: Wiley.

Mitchell, Susan. (1996). Who Does the Shopping? *American Demographics.* Aug 1996 v18 n8 p56(1).

Moir, Anne & Jessel, David. (1989). *Brainsex.* London: Mandarin Paperbacks.

Nice, Vivien E. (1992). *Mothers and Daughters: the Distortion of a Relationship.* London: Macmillan.

Oakley, Ann. (1979). *Becoming a Mother.* Oxford: Martin Robertson & Company.

Oakley, Ann. (1980). *Towards a Sociology of Childbirth, Women Confined.* Oxford: Martin Robinson & Company.

Oakley, Ann. (1984). *The Captured Womb: a History of Medical Care of the Pregnant Woman.* New York: Basil Blackwell.

Oakley, Ann. (1984). *Taking it Like a Woman.* New York: Random House.

Oakley, Ann. (1990). *Housewife.* London: Penguin. (First published by Allen Lane 1974).

Oakley, Ann. (1992). *Social Support and Motherhood.* Oxford and Cambridge: Blackwell.

O'Barr, Jean F., Pope, Deborah, Wyer, Mary, eds. (1990). *Ties that Bind: Essays on Mothering and Patriarchy.* Chicago and London: The University of Chicago Press.

Ochiltree G. & Greenblat, E. (1991). Sick Children: How Working Mothers Cope. AIFS Early Childhood Study Paper No. 2, Australian Institute of Family Studies, Melbourne, 1991.

Orenstein, Peggy. (1998). Almost Equal. *The New York Times Magazine,* April 5 1998, pp. 42–8.

Palkovitz, Rob & Sussman, Marvin B. eds. (1988). *Transitions to Parenthood.* New York: Haworth Press.

Perle McKenna, Elizabeth. (1997). *When Work Doesn't Work Anymore*. New York: Delacorte Press.

Peters, Joan K. (1997). *When Mothers Work: Loving Our Children without Sacrificing Ourselves*. Reading, MA: Addison-Wesley.

Phoenix, Ann, Woollett, Ann & Lloyd, Eva, eds. (1991). *Motherhood: Meanings, Practices and Ideologies*. London: SAGE Publications Ltd.

Pollitt, Katha. (1996). *Babymania*. London Review of Books, 21 March 12–14.

Price, Jane. (1988). *Motherhood: What It Does to Your Mind*. London: Pandora Press, Unwin Hyman Limited.

Rabuzzi, Kathryn Allen. (1988). *Motherself: A Mythic Analysis of Motherhood*. Bloomington: Indiana University Press.

Rich, Adrienne. 1977. *Of Woman Born*. London: Virago.

Richardson, Peggy. (1990). Women's Experiences of Body Change During Normal Pregnancy. *Maternal Child Nursing Journal*. V. 19 (2), 93–111.

Rossiter, Amy. (1988). *From Private to Public: A Feminist Exploration of Early Mothering*. Toronto: The Women's Press.

Rothman, B.K. (1989). *Recreating Motherhood: Ideology and Technology in a Patriarchal Society*. New York: W.W. Norton.

Ruddick, S. (1989). "Maternal Thinking" in Trebilcot, J., ed. (1984).

Ruddick, S. (1989). *Maternal Thinking: Towards a Politics of Peace*. Boston: Beacon Press.

Schaef, Anne Wilson. (1990). *Meditations for Women Who Do Too Much*. New York: HarperCollins.

Sherekeshefsy P. & Yarrow, L. (1973). *Psychological Aspects of a First Pregnancy and Early Postnatal Adaptation*. New York: Raven Press.

Spock, Benjamin. (1957). *Baby and Child Care*. New York: Pocket Books, Inc.

Starrels, Marjorie. (1994). *Husbands' Involvement in Female Gender-typed Household Chores*. Sex Roles: A Journal of Research. Oct. 1994 v31 n7/8 p473(19).

St. James-Roberts, Ian, Harris, Gilland & Messer, David. (1993). *Infant Crying, Feeding and Sleeping: Development, Problems and Treatments*. Hempstead: Harvester Wheatsheaf.

Thurer, Shari. (1995). *The Myths of Motherhood: How Culture Reinvents the Good Mother*. Harmondsworth: Penguin.

Trebilcot, Joyce, ed. (1984). *Mothering: Essays in Feminist Theory*. Totowa, NJ: Rowman & Allanheld.

USA Today (magazine) (1994). Women Still Chained to Housework. Jan 1994 v122 n2584 p10(1).

Waldrop, Judith (1990). Dirty Laundry and Clean Dishes. *American Demographics*, Dec. 1990 v12 n12 p15(1).

Walker, Lorraine and Mary Ann Best. (1991). *Well-being of mothers with Infant*

Children: A Preliminary Comparison of Employed Women and Home-makers. Women and Health. Vol 17 (1), 71–89.

Walkerdine, V. & Lucey, H. (1989). *Democracy in the Kitchen: Regulating Mothers and Socialising Daughters.* London: Virago.

Wearing, Betsy. (1984). *The Ideology of Motherhood.* Sydney: Allen & Unwin.

West, Melissa Gayle. (1992). *If Only I were a Better Mother.* Walpole, N.H.: Stillpoint Publishing.

Wolcott, Ilene & Glezer, Helen. (1995). *Work and Family Life: Achieving Integration.* Melbourne: Australian Institute of Family Studies.

Woolf, Virginia. (1995). *A Room of One's Own and Three Guineas.* Harmondsworth: Penguin Books Ltd.

Index